THINKING ABOUT IT

THINKING ABOUT IT

CONCLUDING NONFICTION WRITINGS

STEVEN H. PROPP

THINKING ABOUT IT
CONCLUDING NONFICTION WRITINGS

iUniverse books may be ordered through booksellers or by contacting:

iUniverse
1663 Liberty Drive
Bloomington, IN 47403
www.iuniverse.com
844-349-9409

ISBN: 978-1-6632-1572-7 (sc)
ISBN: 978-1-6632-1571-0 (e)

Library of Congress Control Number: 2021900496

Print information available on the last page.

iUniverse rev. date: 01/21/2021

CONTENTS

DEDICATION

To all of us who, although not 'professors,' 'scientists,' 'theologians,' or 'philosophers,' just love to *think about* things…

ACKNOWLEDGEMENTS

This book is written with deep love for the help, encouragement, and support of:

Our wonderful grandkids: Devonte and Adrianna, Joseph, Dominic, Mariah, Kayla, and Brea;

The parents and "role models": Keri, Joe, Danielle, and Michael;

My brother-in-law Darrel Buzynski, and my wonderful big sister Susan;

My niece Jennifer and her husband Brade, and their delightful daughters, Madison and Leila;

My "favorite" nephew Jason;

My wonderful sister-in-law Phyllis, Rasheed, and all the rest of our diverse, changing, and always loving family;

My readers and other friends everywhere;

But most of all: to my beautiful, wonderful wife Nancy: whose unconditional love helps *ALL* of us make it through any and all of the many *challenges* that life presents.

And especially: a loving *welcome* to our first *great*-grandchild: Devonte and Adrianna's baby daughter, JASENYA!

PART A
FURTHER INQUIRIES

(My nonfiction book *Inquiries: Philosophical* was published in 2002; it had existed only in typescript since 1980. Since 2002, I have realized that there were a number of topics covered only briefly in that book, or not at all, that I now think merit greater attention—with the benefit of another 'twenty-plus' years of consideration and research.)

1. Is Science Getting 'Weird'?

I've read, listened to, and watched dozens of debates between traditional scientists and biblical creationists, or between traditional scientists and others who are not part of the scientific 'mainstream.' Frequently, the traditional scientists will urge the audience to reject the views of their debate opponents, on the grounds that, "What they're proposing is not *science*. 'True' science is characterized by (1) Its being empirically tested, and thus subject to verification and/or falsification, and (2) Such research is originally published in peer-reviewed scientific journals, and not in 'dedicated' book houses." Fair enough; that sounds reasonable to me.

But certainly, it is also true that when *new* hypotheses and theories are being suggested and explored, 'empirical testing and validation' may not yet be possible. For example, when Einstein first presented his General Theory of Relativity in 1915, there apparently wasn't yet overwhelming empirical evidence supporting it. But during the total eclipse of the Sun in 1919, it *was* possible to test Einstein's predictions of 'warped' space-time, by comparing the positions of the background stars during the eclipse with their 'normal' positions; and of course, Einstein's predictions were confirmed. And since then, there have been various other kinds of empirical tests that provide confirmation of Relativity; so our proposed 'model' of science—as being 'empirically testable,' etc.—remains intact, with the theory of Relativity.

But more recently, things seem to have been changing, in certain subject areas in the world of science. A key instigator of this has been the discovery of so many new subatomic particles, which fall into two major categories/types of 'fundamental' particles: [1] **Fermions** (which have 'matter' or 'mass,' and consist of *leptons* such as electrons and neutrinos; and *quarks*, which *gluons* help bind together to form protons and neutrons) and [2] **Bosons** ('force carriers,' such as photons and gluons, as well as *mesons*, which include pions and kaons). An overlapping category between the two major particle types are the 'non-fundamental'/composite **Hadrons** (made up of quarks), of the two types: *baryons* (e.g., protons and neutrons), which are Fermions; and *mesons*, which are Bosons. So many new particles were being discovered so rapidly that the resulting situation was sometimes described as being like a 'Particle *Zoo*'! It became difficult even for physicists working in this area to keep them all straight, when attending conferences, to discuss the new discoveries.

But while this was (and is) extremely complex and confusing, it's still 'experimentally-based,' right? CERN, the European Organization for Nuclear Research (which coordinates the research efforts of twelve European countries), is home for several particle accelerators, including the Large Hadron Collider (LHC), in which particles are accelerated and then 'smashed,' resulting in the discovery of still smaller particles (including the Higgs Boson, misleadingly dubbed the 'God Particle' by the media). Once again, this is still 'experimental science,' and the research is being conducted in sophisticated laboratories, and the results being presented in the professional journals.

But beginning in the 1940s, and progressing much more rapidly since the 1970s and 1980s, 'String Theory' was proposed—according to which most subatomic particles aren't 'pointlike,' as electrons were thought to be, but were in fact loops of vibrating, one-dimensional *strings,* whose different vibrational states create the various types of particles that scientists observe and test. String Theory was said to be able to explain and describe *all* 'elementary' particles, and their interactions. These strings were, naturally, *much* smaller than anything that could be observed or probed with even our most precise instruments. But of course, whether something so small is a 'point' or a 'string' isn't exactly something that has any real practical *effects* on our daily lives; so most of us are content to leave this discussion to the scientists.

But there is one thing that should potentially raise some concerns about String Theory: it has never really been experimentally 'tested'; it hasn't made any *predictions* that have been experimentally 'proven,' nor does it even seem *theoretically* 'falsifiable.' In fact, since there are so many different *versions* of String Theory, it's difficult to even know which *version* of it a scientist would want to try and 'test.' Still, this theory doesn't seem to have any 'practical effects' on our daily lives, so why should anyone in the general public particularly care?

Well, you *might* care if you've read Stephen Hawking's popular book, *The Grand Design,* in which he boldly stated that "we now have a candidate for the ultimate theory of everything, if indeed one exists, called M-theory. M-theory is the only model that has all the properties we think the final theory ought to have... According to M-theory, ours is not the only universe. Instead, M-theory predicts that a great many universes were created out of nothing. Their creation does not require the intervention of some supernatural being or god. Rather, these multiple universes arise naturally from physical law..."

What is M-Theory? It is a theory that unifies all the 'consistent' versions of 'Superstring Theory.' Superstring Theory, in turn, is a version of String Theory that proposes 'supersymmetry': that is, that all subatomic particles which carry a *force* are 'matched' by subatomic particles that have *mass*. These ideas are hoped to be the building blocks of a 'Theory of Everything' [TOE]: that is, one which finally reconciles Einstein's General Theory of Relativity with Quantum Mechanics.

Unfortunately, M-Theory has, to date, apparently not been able to make any 'predictions' that can be experimentally tested; and 'Supersymmetry' thus far seems to be *failing* some potential tests of confirmation in the Large Hadron Collider at CERN. Now, it's fine to produce some very complicated mathematics which purport to explain how these theories might operate; but wouldn't a rational, empirically-minded scientist (which is supposedly what 'scientists' are) at some point need to attempt to *confirm/falsify/verify* these theories? And if this can't be done, is this still 'traditional' science?

But it seems that no one is actually *claiming* that we currently *have* a 'Theory of Everything'; M-Theory is just being proposed by scientists like Hawking as the current 'best candidate.' I think it's interesting that in 1979, when Hawking was elected as the 'Lucasian Professor of Mathematics' at the University of Cambridge, he gave an inaugural lecture titled, 'Is the End in Sight for Theoretical Physics?' He was optimistic that this 'end' *might* be achieved by the year 2000. (It wasn't, of course.) Hawking, sadly, died in 2018, with no 'Theory of Everything' having yet been found.

But once again, this doesn't really seem to affect any of our non-scientist lives. If, ultimately, scientists are unable to devise a Theory of Everything, and they simply have to continue using Relativity for the 'macro' world, and Quantum Theory for the 'micro' world, that's not going to make much difference to any of us. Except that there is, however, one aspect of String Theory that tends to make many (most?) of us raise our eyebrows a bit.

It was eventually realized that, in order for the *very* complex mathematics of String Theory to work, there had to be *more* than the standard four dimensions (three physical/spatial dimensions, and one dimension of time) in the world, to allow the strings sufficient 'room' to vibrate 'hyperdimensionally,' and produce all of the different atomic and subatomic particles. String Theory requires a total of *ten* dimensions (nine physical/spatial ones, and one of time); while M-Theory requires *eleven* dimensions.

One spatial dimension is like a single straight line; *two* spatial dimensions is like a flat sheet of paper, which has length and width, but no depth. *Three* dimensions is, of course, the physical world with which we're all familiar, that adds the third physical dimension of depth. Upon learning of the 'extra dimensions' requirements of String Theory and M-Theory, most of us react by asking, "If these 'extra dimensions' really exist, how come no one's ever *noticed* them?" The response from String Theorists is usually something like, "These extra dimensions are very, *very* small—they are 'compactified,' and 'curled up,' so that we cannot perceive them, and we don't have any 'access' to them."

Now, it's one thing to propose a scientific theory that seems counterintuitive; many aspects of Relativity Theory seemed quite 'bizarre' as well, when it was first proposed; but one of Relativity's seemingly 'oddest' predictions—that of *time dilation* (i.e., the "slowing down" of a clock, as perceived by an observer who is in different relative motion with respect to that clock)—*has* actually been experimentally confirmed, in various ways. But for String Theorists to propose a theory that is not only counterintuitive, but *extremely* counterintuitive, seems… well, somewhat doubtful—particularly when this theory apparently has a complete lack of empirical verification.

Personally, I'm basically content to leave this matter to the scientists who are working in this realm. But I would observe that prominent physicists like Roger Penrose and Richard Feynman have been openly critical of String Theory; physicist Lee Smolin wrote an entire book (*The Trouble With Physics*) against String Theory, and astrophysicist

Lawrence Krauss is quite dismissive of String Theory, and has openly mocked it in lectures before the Skeptic's Society (to applause and laughter from the audience). And, more importantly, firm acceptance of String Theory by a scientist would seem to me to *undercut* such a scientist's rejection of God, Life after Death, Creation, etc.—*if* this rejection is primarily based on the grounds that such concepts are not "empirically testable/verifiable/falsifiable."

But String Theory and its offshoots are not the only scientific theories being currently proposed that might conceivably raise one's skeptical eyebrows. Take the *Multiverse* (short for 'multiple universes') proposed by physicists such as Alan Guth, Andrei Linde, Stephen Hawking, Sean M. Carroll, etc. This is the idea that our universe (which was formerly and traditionally considered to be 'everything there is') may only be a single 'bubble universe' among a much larger number (potentially an *infinite* number) of other bubble universes.

It is suggested that these 'other' universes may have completely different sets of natural laws than our own universe does: for example, the strength of gravitation might be greater or less than ours, in such universes; the attractive power of the strong nuclear force might be different; the spin of an atom (which is 'up' in our universe) may be 'down' in other universes, etc. Therefore, the particular physical 'constants' that our universe just happens to have are simply a matter of the laws of probability and quantum 'superpositions,' and nothing more.

Of course, this immediately raises the question, "How could we ever *detect, contact,* or find *evidence* of such other universes?" Proponents of the Multiverse usually suggest that such universes (given the 'Cosmic Inflation' after the Big Bang that is proposed by Alan Guth) are moving away from us at greater than the speed of light—which means that we would never be able to detect radio waves or photons from them, much less *see* them. Therefore, we would never be able to *measure* their 'constants,' to see if they were, in fact, different from ours. So, it's frankly pretty hard for me to see how such a concept would ever be 'empirically testable/verifiable/falsifiable'; and if it isn't, does it truly qualify as a 'scientific theory'?

Perhaps one of the biggest attractions of the Multiverse concept (for some of its advocates, at least) is that it makes the argument (sometimes called the 'Strong Anthropic Principle') that our own universe might appear to be 'specially *designed* for life' unnecessary: In a Multiverse, out of an infinite number of other universes, *some* of them will 'just happen' to make life possible—but there will be far more (perhaps *infinitely* more) universes out there in which life is *not* possible, and thus were obviously *not* 'designed for life.' So, again, it's nothing but a matter of statistics and probability.

A variation of the Multiverse theory is the so-called 'Many Worlds Interpretation' of Quantum Mechanics that was originally proposed by Hugh Everett III, and was given its name (and then publicized) by Bryce Seligman DeWitt. This interpretation suggests that, in Quantum Mechanics (where we are usually dealing with *probabilities* of specific events happening), there is very often a 'branching' or 'splitting' of a universe (i.e., the 'wave function collapses') that results in there being another universe—one that differs at this specific point, and continues its separate existence on into its future. (A quantum 'wave function' can be thought of as a list of every *possible* configuration of, say, a hydrogen atom; it 'collapses' when one *specific* configuration actually occurs—probably after it is *observed,* by a scientist.)

The aspect of this theory that particularly makes people like me skeptical is that, in Everett's interpretation, there are thus supposed to be entire 'parallel worlds' and 'universes' out there somewhere, that have only relatively minor differences from each other. For example, theoretical physicist Sean M. Carroll suggests in his 2019 book *Something Deeply Hidden: Quantum Worlds and the Emergence of Spacetime*, that the universe split into about one quadrillion versions, each containing a different randomly generated number that is printed on page 135 of his book. (Yes, he appears to be dead serious about this.) He adds, "If Everett is right, there is a 100 percent probability that *each* possibility is realized in some particular world."

Reporter and science writer Peter Byrne wrote a book (*The Many Worlds of Hugh Everett III*) about Everett and his work, in which he explains, "A consequence of the 'many worlds' logic is that there are universes in which dinosaurs survived and humans remained shrew-like; universes in which *you* win the state lottery every week; universes in which Wall Street does not exist and global resources are equally shared."

This seems to be a particular *attraction* of this idea for many people: Under this theory, there isn't just *one* 'me' that exists: there is a huge *number* of them, with certain specific differences: such as a world in which I didn't go to college; or one in which I stayed (unhappily) single; or one in which I married (and perhaps divorced) a different, very incompatible person; or one where I had a different employer, drove a different car, lived on a different street, retired at a different age, and so on.

Supporters of this theory seem somehow comforted by the notion that, even if *'I'* die in this particular world we inhabit, there are nevertheless lots of other **me's** out there, who are still living. (But, presumably, there are also very many worlds in which I died at a young age; or in which I never even *existed*.) And of course, this also means that there would be innumerable copies of *Hitler* out there somewhere, who have implemented innumerable other *Holocausts*—a possibility which I find very far from being 'reassuring.'

I fail to see anything comforting about the possibility of there existing somewhere other versions of 'me.' *My* consciousness is obviously not *identical* with some other 'me' out there, since I can't share their viewpoint—I can only see things from *my* perspective. And if I were dying, I would have to face up to the possibility of the permanent extinction of my *own* consciousness, since my unique and specific consciousness, and memories here, would not be 'transferred' into some other 'me' out there; I wouldn't 'wake up' after my death to find myself in a different world in a different universe, for example, while still remembering that I had previously been in *this* world.

I find it interesting that Sean M. Carroll debated the well-known Christian philosopher William Lane Craig in 2016 (which produced a book, *God & Cosmology: William Lane Craig and Sean Carroll in Dialogue*), in which Carroll argued that "theism is not a serious cosmological model... because ... a real cosmological model wants to make predictions... Theism does not even try to do this, because ultimately, theism is not well-defined." But are the 'predictions' of the various cosmological models that Carroll mentions in this book actually *testable?* And, given his endorsement of the 'Many Worlds' interpretation, is there any way we could ever *find out* whether there really is another 'me,' or a thousand different versions of his book, in a different world? If not, then how is this even 'science'?

The 'Many Worlds' interpretation strikes many of us (in my observation, at least) as, shall we say, rather *extravagant* when it comes to universes. Now, it's true that current estimates are that there are about two trillion *galaxies* in the universe—each of which may have hundreds of *billions* of stars in them, of which (perhaps) 4% of them may be 'sunlike.' We are also discovering more and more thousands of exoplanets, orbiting such stars; in November 2020, the findings from NASA's Kepler spacecraft—launched in 2009—led astronomers to estimate that there may be as many as 300 million 'habitable' planets in our galaxy alone. So, there is certainly enough *space* and *material* 'out there' for there to be 'other worlds.' But would the conditions on another planet—in another solar system, in another galaxy, in another universe—be so near-*exactly* like our own so as to produce another 'me' and 'you'? Or to produce *thousands* or maybe *billions* of them?

Think of how many 'variables' there are in your own life, during an average day: the weather; what you had for breakfast; what time you drove to work; whether a co-worker called in sick; where you go for lunch; how much coffee or tea you drank; how much traffic there is on the drive home; what was playing on the radio as you drove; what you have for dinner; what social media postings you glance at during dinner; how you occupy yourself in the evening; what time you go to bed, etc. Can we seriously imagine that there is an entire *world* somewhere 'out there,' that is exactly like our world—*except* that, in that world, I watched a cheesy 'reality show' on television at 8:00 one night, instead of starting to read the latest book by Sean Carroll? And that there are also entire worlds for each other possible 'variation' in what *each of us* do every single day?

And even if there *are* 'many worlds,' how do we know that they would be so *different* from each other? Suppose that, instead of having *every* 'possibility' actualized, the *same possibility* just kept happening over and over again? In other words, suppose that rather than there being thousands of worlds in which the 'wave function collapsed' differently based on what I had for breakfast, there are instead thousands of worlds that are *exactly the same*? (Shades of philosopher Friedrich Nietzsche's 'eternal recurrence of the same' concept!)

I would suggest that the enormous number of *variables* that exist in our world would be more than sufficient to keep such hypothetical worlds from turning out 'exactly the same,' or even *mostly* the same. (And of course, that is only considering the number of variables in our *one* world—how many *more* variables would there be in a near-infinite number of 'bubble universes'?)

I definitely have to 'part company' with the scientists who are proposing and supporting such speculative and implausible theories; I'll continue to have more confidence in those researchers who consider science to simply be **the study of the material universe**, and who seek theories that *are* testable, verifiable, and/or falsifiable—rather than just 'mathematically consistent,' 'coherent,' or 'plausible.'

2. Evolution

The theory of Evolution as developed by Charles Darwin and later scientists is, on the one hand, a very satisfying explanation for the origin and development of life on Earth. The movement from one-celled creatures, to multicellular ones, to the first underwater plants, to sponges and flatworms, to fish, to land plants, to amphibians and reptiles, then to mammals, later including primates, until eventually we humans came along, seems quite convincing. Darwin's theory of 'Natural Selection' seemingly can provide convincing naturalistic explanations for the development of even very complex and 'well-adapted' structures in animals.

The geological record of fossils also provides clear support for this general view of evolutionary history. Although the geological column must necessarily be 'pieced together' from various locations around the Earth, and there may be situations where an 'overthrust' (such as the Lewis Overthrust in Canada) has occurred—which resulted in some geological layers of rocks appearing in 'reversed' order—it remains the overwhelming case that such 'reversed' layers are still distinct and identifiable as 'layers.' For example, geological layers may appear in the order 'ABGFECD' rather than 'ABCDEFG,' but it still is clearly the case that dinosaurs (not even the smaller ones, who were the presumed ancestors of modern birds) were not living alongside humans; nor were trilobites swimming next to modern ocean fish, or whales.

And, for the record, the notion of my not being 'specially created' by God, and instead being descended from an apelike ancestor, and being the product of an evolutionary sequence which began from organic chemicals, doesn't bother me at all.

So then: what's the problem? Well, the first problem is the *origin* of life. Most evolutionary researchers suggest that organic chemicals spontaneously (and naturalistically) assembled into the precursors of life, such as DNA and RNA. But, despite the attention still being given in popular books (and even some textbooks) to the 1952 Miller/Urey experiment about the origin of life, this experiment is now viewed as basically irrelevant, and not representative of the actual conditions that existed on the primitive Earth.

Which is fine; science is supposed to be 'self-correcting,' and always moving on, and advancing, as new discoveries are made. But although the Miller/Urey experiment took place nearly seventy years ago, there is not yet any consensus—much less *experimental confirmation* of any specific 'leading hypothesis'—as to what conditions *could* have produced life spontaneously. There are literally more than a dozen proposed theories for the origin of life (including ones in which life originated on Mars, or elsewhere, and was brought here by meteors), and none of them has yet supplanted the others, and convinced a majority of other researchers—even though this is a very lively and popular area of research.

I suppose that the lack of such an 'origins' theory might not be considered all that important, by many people; but in this case, naturalistic scientists are proposing that life originally developed by random or 'chance' processes—that is, nothing was being specifically 'set up' in the ocean or elsewhere, in order to come up with life, or at least its precursors. So why is it that a 'chance' arrangement could supposedly produce life, when researchers (in some of the finest laboratories in the world) can't yet find a way to reproduce this process? (This would seem to be analogous to 'reverse-engineering.')

The fact that we may not presently know *precisely* the original conditions on the primitive Earth is not necessarily determinative; experiments could simply be set up in a *plausible* approximation of such conditions, and the researchers could then presumably just sit back, and observe the organic materials assembling themselves. In fact, there might be *multiple* scenarios in which life could originate, and researchers would then have to choose which one (or more than one) is the most likely to have been the case on our early Earth. But although origin-of-life research is a burgeoning field these days, and various theories and proposals (e.g., 'RNA first') are being debated vigorously, there don't seem to be any actual *experiments* that are producing the striking kinds of *results* that were seemingly produced in the Miller/Urey experiment (and which made it such a popular example).

A second problem with our *current* evolutionary theory is the widespread and systematic lack of 'transitional forms' in the fossil record. (Darwin himself, to his credit, frankly admitted this, in his chapter in *The Origin of Species* on 'Difficulties of the Theory,' and he attributed this lack to "the extreme imperfection of the [geological] record.") This is, of course, a favorite objection of biblical creationists, and one that goes over well (and convincingly) with a 'lay' audience.

The late paleontologist Stephen Jay Gould and his colleague Niles Eldredge proposed their 'Punctuated Equilibria' theory to attempt to account for the lack of such transitional fossils in the geological record: e.g., arguing that most evolutionary developments originally occurred among small, isolated populations, that statistically were unlikely to leave many examples behind in the fossil record. That's very possible; but the fact remains that paleontologists and evolutionary naturalists are very happy to point out any suggested 'transitions' whenever they can find them: semi-tetrapods like *Ichthyostega;* whale ancestors such as *Pakicetus, Ambuloecetus, Dorudon* and *Balaena;* doglike creatures such as *Hesperocyon;* and feathered dinosaurs like *Sinosauropteryx.* Whales and horses offer what are perhaps the best examples to be found in the animal kingdom of relatively 'smooth' transitions to the modern forms.

But I think that the presumed ancestral path leading to humans is by far the best 'sequence' that researchers have yet proposed. (Admittedly, there is a lot more *grant money* available to try and dig up 'human' ancestors, than there is for, say, canids.) However, the kind of smooth evolutionary line chart (particularly the one found in F. Clark Howell's book *Early Man,* which utterly persuaded many of us when it was presented to us back in Anthropology 101), leading from Pliopithecus, to Ramapithecus, to Australopithecus, to Homo Erectus, to Neanderthal, to Cro-Magnon is no longer considered accurate. In fact, the more recent discovery of additional fossil hominids, which overlap each other in time sequence, has turned this presumed '*line* of descent' into more of a *bush,* where many of the presumed 'ancestors' were living contemporaneously with their presumed 'descendants.'

Still, we have persuasive evidence of apelike hominids (or 'hominins,' to use the current term) who were regularly walking upright, and fashioning and using tools to a degree that apes (such as chimps and gorillas) simply do not. So, there certainly appears to have been an evolutionary development which preceded modern humans.

I still have some questions, however: For example, if humans have evolved the capacity for *language,* why haven't other creatures? Wouldn't a herd of elephants, or a tribe of baboons that had a complex *language* be 'superior' to animal groups that didn't? And wouldn't *self-consciousness,* such as we have, be of benefit to nearly every other species? Why are humans so unique in many respects, even when there is 'convergent evolution' (i.e., unrelated organisms independently evolving similar traits) for so many other traits in much of the animal kingdom?

And there remains the perhaps greater problem of the systematic absence of transitional forms showing the gradual evolutionary development of various *structures,* such as wings, and feathers. Evolutionists can, of course, propose a sequence of increasing development (among living or dead creatures) to show how such structures *might* have evolved by a series of fairly 'small' steps. For example, biologist (and, more recently, rabid apostle of Atheism) Richard Dawkins, in his book *The Blind Watchmaker* (followed by his *Growing Up in the Universe* lecture series), suggested that wings might have developed from flaps of skin growing in the angles of joints (whose function might have originally been to slow the fall of a creature that fell from a tree), to *gliding* wings, and finally to *flying* wings, through a series of gradual evolutionary steps. (But wouldn't it have been simpler for the creatures to just evolve stronger claws, or a more flexible tail, to keep it from falling out of the tree in the first place? And would the earlier stages of these 'flaps' *really* have slowed the creature's fall enough to make it the 'fittest' among its contemporaries?)

But obviously, the examples Dawkins cites of insects, tree snakes with flattened bodies, gliding frogs, flying squirrels, and bats are obviously not part of the same 'family tree' (nor even the same Chordata 'Class'); so we are still lacking an *actual* evolutionary sequence leading up to, say, modern birds. While it would certainly be unrealistic to expect the fossil record to exhaustively document the evolutionary sequence for *every* winged creature, given that wings have developed in [1] birds; [2] insects; [3] bats; and [4] even in some dinosaurs (discounting 'flying fish,' which *glide,* rather than actually *fly*), it doesn't seem particularly unreasonable to expect that we would at least have found *some* instances of, say, a bird (or a reptilian dinosaur) with 15% of a wing, followed by a 25% wing, a 40% wing, and so on, leading more or less continuously up to modern birds; or, the same kind of sequence leading up to bats, or pterosaurs.

Similar problems exist with various other structures, such as feathers, eyes, lungs, and so on. It's fine to appeal to 'preadaptation' (or 'exaptation,' to use Stephen Jay Gould's term), and suggest that, say, feathers originally developed to insulate or keep the creatures warm, and not to aid flight. But why have all (or nearly all) of these developmental stages in wings and feathers not been preserved in the fossil record, in at least *some* evolutionary sequences? These 'transitional' stages would supposedly have represented an evolutionary 'advantage' for these creatures; so why do we normally only find fossils either in the 'non-wing' stage, or the 'fully-developed' stage, if there is no 'design' taking place? (It almost makes it look as if the 'intervening steps' were just *skipped past* by... a Designer?)

There *are* modern snakes with seemingly 'vestigial' (and more-or-less useless) legs, even as modern whales have seemingly vestigial 'leg bones' and a pelvic girdle, that suggest an earlier terrestrial existence. But proposed whale ancestors with large functional legs, such as *Ambulocetus,* are still very different from modern whales that swim and live 100% in the sea; there certainly would have had to be a number of 'intermediate' stages between the two, and we don't seem to have any fossil examples of these.

It's quite true that "5% of a lung is better than no lung at all, and 5% vision is better than no vision at all." And it's also true that you can arrange a series of creatures that have varying degrees of vision: from planarians that can only distinguish the direction that light (or perhaps a predator) is coming from; to mollusks (such as the Nautilus) whose 'pinhole camera' eyes let them perceive dim images; to creatures like squids with an actual *lens* in their eye; and eventually leading up to eyes with 'lenses' like ours that provide full 3-D color binocular vision.

Of course, soft tissues such as eyes are not preserved in the fossil record, so we will never directly 'see' this development in fossils. But one would think we might at least see this proposed sequence of increasing complexity in, say, the eye sockets, in at least a *few* species.

Frankly, the fossil record often looks as if it preserves a somewhat haphazard series of individual 'special creation' events, separated by large blocks of time: almost as if a Creator 'suddenly' got tired of ferns, or fishes, or dinosaurs, and went almost immediately ('immediate' in 'geological time,' of course) to something different—and then experimented with, say, giving legs to sea creatures, liked the result, and then created fully some terrestrial creatures.

Of course, nobody actually proposes this, because such a sporadic and seemingly unsystematic series of 'creation events' does not fit the conception of the theistic God of any of the major religions, like Judaism, Christianity, and Islam—according to which God is not only infinitely intelligent, but also has infinite power of *foresight*. Theists are not attracted to the idea of a God who seemingly changes his mind abruptly, and starts over from scratch repeatedly. (But it's true that a few people with rather 'far out' ideas—such as that of our evolutionary development being directed by 'gods from outer space'—might find such a vision satisfactory.)

But the considerable degree of speculation and uncertainty that exist in proposals for specific details about the evolution of life makes me hesitant (and even somewhat *suspicious*) when people propose to use evolution to explain virtually *everything*—including specific psychological traits such as altruism, the maternal instinct, and even male infidelity.

Evolutionary theorists will suggest a variety of reasons for why the human mind—with its apparently unique capacity for self-awareness— might have evolved. And certainly, our minds *do* provide us with an astonishing degree of 'selective advantage' over other creatures—which is, of course, why *we* are by far the 'dominant' species on the planet. But the question I would have is, again, "If mind provides such an evolutionary advantage for humans, why haven't *other* species also developed minds like ours? Wouldn't human-like intelligence be an exceptional advantage for dolphins, chimps, and even dogs, in their 'struggle for existence'? Or at least, why aren't there some creature *subgroups* which are getting more intelligent over time? Why aren't there 'smarter whales,' contrasted with 'regular whales'? Why aren't there some chimpanzees that have a language, and others that don't?"

All kinds of insects develop immunity to pesticides, but why aren't they becoming more *intelligent,* so that they can instinctively sense and avoid crops that have been sprayed with pesticide? Why aren't 'smarter' dolphins—ones that can detect and then evade Japanese fishermen—evolving, and becoming the dominant species? And for that matter, why are creatures with relatively 'inefficient' eyes still around? Why haven't *all* creatures developed better eyes, that give them full binocular vision?

Which brings us to a third problem with current evolutionary theory: the theory is so *flexible*, and the Darwinian concept of Natural Selection (or the 'Survival of the Fittest,' to use Herbert Spencer's term, which Darwin liked, and adopted) is so loosely defined, that it's sometimes hard to perceive it as a traditional 'scientific theory'— traditional theories being 'testable,' 'verifiable,' and/or 'falsifiable.'

For Darwin, evolution was 'descent with modification,' and Natural Selection was the "principle by which each slight variation [of a trait], if useful, is preserved." Well, then: QUESTION: How do we *tell* whether or not a trait is 'useful'? ANSWER: By whether or not it survives. And, if it survives, then—by definition—the trait was 'useful.' This kind of 'after-the-fact' assessment is not necessarily very convincing.

Why do male peacocks have such elaborate (and beautiful) tails? We are told that this is because of 'Sexual Selection': in other words, the peahens are so attracted to males with beautiful tails, that these males tend to reproduce in greater numbers, and so they ultimately become the 'fitter' males of the species. (Of course, these heavy and attention-getting tails also make it much harder for the peacocks to avoid predators, such as tigers or mongooses.)

Other creatures are deemed 'fitter' because they *blend in* to their environment (e.g., chameleons, dung beetles), and don't draw attention to themselves. But the 'negative' aspect of the peacock's tail makes you wonder: why doesn't Natural Selection make the females who are *less attracted* to the peacock's tail the dominant members of their gender— since females who are willing to reproduce with 'plain' males (who would probably be killed by predators less often) would seem to pass on their 'less sexually *picky*' genes in higher numbers?

It seems that evolution can claim to 'predict,' *after the fact*, just about anything that occurs in the natural world. Giraffes supposedly evolved long necks to allow them to eat fruit that was higher up in trees; then why don't other animals that likewise eat fruit in trees have similarly long necks? Couldn't they also benefit from eating such 'higher-up' fruit? Many varieties of moose have very large antlers—so large, in fact, that they can become entangled, and their considerable weight makes it very difficult for the moose to even *walk*, much less escape from predators. We are told that these antlers are used to 'scare off' younger males during the two-week mating season: but wouldn't less bulky, but *sharper* antlers have had more 'survival value'? Such inconsistent and *ad hoc* 'explanations' in the current theory of evolution seem to lack the kind of *explanatory power* that other 'scientific theories' have.

I should also explain that I am definitely *not* a 'Creationist'; I think the 'origin' stories in the Bible have no scientific value whatsoever, and I regard the notion that the universe is only about 6,000-10,000 years old as ludicrous. I have some sympathies with the Intelligent Design movement, but I would note that they (like the Creationists) are much more effective as *critics* of evolutionary theory, than as *advocates* for any specific counter-proposals. (For example: If IDers think that God intervened in the evolutionary process, *precisely* **when** and **how** did this occur? Did God occasionally specifically create a 'new' species, or did he just tinker with the DNA, and let change occur through evolution and natural selection? And did he make changes in 'stages'—such as a 5% wing, then a 10% wing, etc.—or all at once?)

I have *more* sympathies with 'Theistic Evolution,' although I'm doubtful that a theistic God consciously *foreknew* and *planned* every step up the evolutionary ladder that we see (including the asteroid that killed the dinosaurs and a lot of other Earth life, 66 million years ago). I would probably call myself a '***Deistic* Evolutionist,'** which would suggest a much more 'hands off' and 'wait and see' approach, than does Theistic Evolution.

Most traditional evolutionists staunchly resist the idea of 'progress' in the evolutionary development of life. They scoff at the notion proposed by Jesuit priest and paleontologist Teilhard de Chardin, who suggested that evolution is directed by God with the intent of increasing *spiritual consciousness* in the world. (And I must admit that I would probably have asked Teilhard, "If consciousness and spiritual progression is the intent of life, why is it that only *humans* seemingly have such a 'spiritual' nature? Why aren't *all* creatures—or at least, the more advanced ones, such as dolphins and chimps—endowed with such capacities?")

I can understand the reluctance of evolutionary scientists to describe the twists and turns of evolutionary development as 'progressive.' However, when I compare a world composed simply of one-cellular creatures, with the current arrangement, the term 'progress' *does* seem rather appropriate to me. (Why didn't the world develop so that the only two forms of life that exist are a very simple plant, and a 'killer bacteria' that feeds on this plant? And that if anything else ever started to evolve, a 'killer bacteria' variant that was *also* able to eat this 'new' species would tend to out-reproduce the bacteria that could only eat the plants; so that, ultimately, only a single species of bacteria would survive, keeping the population limited to only the two organisms.)

Given that biologists and paleontologists estimate that more than 99 percent of all organisms that have ever lived on Earth are now extinct, this constitutes for quite a few people an impressive argument against the idea of a Creator/Designer. (But personally, the argument from extinction doesn't impress me all that much; every individual creature ultimately *dies* anyway—so why should every conceivable *species* exist perpetually? What would be the purpose of trilobites or dinosaurs living forever? And isn't every form of life on Earth eventually going to die out with the future extinction of the Sun, anyhow?)

Our ideas of 'progress' are often tainted by our notions of things moving steadily towards some 'end.' If the purpose of life is thought to be heading towards some Teilhardian 'Omega Point,' then whatever seemingly does not move us toward that end, would appear to be 'wasted effort.' But if one or more species (e.g., hominins) *are* achieving, or at least *heading toward* that end, then perhaps the other species in the world are not 'wasted,' but are an essential (or at least an *interesting*) 'background' or 'predecessor' to the 'Main Event.'

If we take it for granted that everything on Earth will ultimately die when the sun flames out in a few billion years, then the fact that millions of species have perished previously doesn't seem particularly outrageous. Maybe extinction just offers an opportunity to start the whole process over, again. But an individual flower doesn't lose its beauty, simply because it only blooms for a while, and then is gone forever. In fact, its fragile 'temporariness' makes it that much more *precious.*

3. Time Travel

The notion of traveling in time—whether into the past, or the future—has been a staple element in science fiction books and movies for some time. Einstein's Theory of Relativity *did* explain that the notion of an 'Absolute Time' is not true; his theory revealed that physical processes that can be measured by clocks will operate at different 'speeds' for different observers. A clock in a spaceship that is travelling very fast will move 'slower' than a clock which is at rest on the earth's surface, for example; this phenomenon is often called 'time dilation.' So, for instance, an astronaut who traveled very quickly in outer space, and was (according to Earth time) gone for ten years, would—upon returning to Earth—find that her/his shipboard time measurements might show that only, say, *five* years had elapsed. Neither the clocks on the spaceship, nor the clocks on Earth, are giving the 'correct' time; their passage of time is simply *relative* to the observer.

But just what *is* 'time,' after all? I would observe that there are certainly repeating 'pulses' in the world we live in. We are intimately aware of the fact that our heart beats approximately once every second, for example. In a larger sense, there are celestial objects such as Pulsars in the universe, which emit regular pulses of radio waves and other electromagnetic radiation; we might also refer to the 'hyperfine transition' or 'electron transition' frequencies which are used in so-called 'atomic clocks.' In our world there is no 'timeless' state, where there are no such continuous 'pulses.'

Besides such kinds of regular pulses, there are also longer, *cyclical* factors, such as the rising and setting of the sun each day, based on the Earth revolving on its axis. Next, there are the phases and cycles of the moon, which progress for a little less than a typical month, going from full moon to full moon. Then, there is the motion of the Earth traveling around the sun once a year. And when we look beyond our own world, we see that the other planets in our solar system have similar periodic cycles. Thus, such pulses, cycles, and the notion of *time* itself are not simply 'imaginary,' much less purely 'mental constructions'—they are based firmly in the natural world we live in.

Although Einstein's theory of Relativity pointed out the deficiencies in the 'classical' concept of 'absolute' time and simultaneity, the fact remains that, from our particular perspective, things occur in a *sequence:* there is a 'before,' and an 'after,' and this implies our broader concepts of 'past' and 'future.' Spring comes *after* Winter, Summer comes *after* Spring, and Fall occurs *after* Summer. We can even compare such cyclical patterns to each other: we might observe, 'This has been an unusually *long, hot summer,*' for example. Or, 'Now that I've sat down after finishing my daily run, my heartbeat is *slower* than it was five minutes ago.'

We therefore develop the idea of *succession,* which suggests that certain events don't occur until *after* some previous event(s); for example, you can't cook an egg until *after* you crack open the egg, and you can't purchase an egg at the store until *after* a hen has laid it. It's perfectly true that we may have problems in deciding whether an event taking place in a spaceship took place 'before,' 'after,' or 'simultaneously' with an event taking place on Earth; but that, again, only indicates that our *perceptions* or *measurements* of events are not part of a single 'absolute' order, but that their order is *relative* to the perspective of a particular observer.

The British philosopher Bertrand Russell pointed out in his book, *An Outline of Philosophy,* that "there is no logical impossibility in the view that the world was created five minutes ago, complete with memories and records. This may seem an improbable hypothesis, but it is not logically refutable." And, to be sure, there are some 'Young Earth' biblical creationists who argue that the universe (including the light from stars that are billions of *light-years* away) was created with an '*appearance* of age,' which is why it *looks* considerably older than 6,000-10,000 years old. But for practical purposes, most of us quite properly presume that something which *looks* 'old,' or *looks* 'young,' *is* so.

This has some implications that need to be considered, however. It takes more than eight minutes for the photons emitted by the sun to reach our planet, for example; so, for all we know, the sun might have simply *vanished* seven minutes ago—but we will only find that out in another minute or two. Thus, when astronomers look through telescopes, they are, in a sense, 'looking in the *past*,' since the light images they are perceiving were (in the case of distant objects) emitted as much as billions of years in the past. This is not, however, anything resembling 'time travel'; the images we are seeing have actually occurred, and are thus 'old news.' If astronomers can see a star that exploded a billion years ago, there is nothing that anyone could do about it now—but it *did* actually happen, in the past.

Could we ever 'view' something from our *own* past? The idea isn't impossible—but it would most likely require some 'outside assistance' to bring it about. For example: suppose that extraterrestrial beings visiting our planet had filmed or otherwise recorded events occurring here; perhaps they used telescopes, or hidden cameras, that were not noticed by us earthlings. Even with our own 'primitive' level of technology (when compared to such hypothetical aliens), it no longer seems 'fantastic' for us to imagine tiny hidden cameras, which broadcast signals to remote locations, or even deep into outer space, to the aliens' ships.

But suppose that these aliens also left behind a video camera that recorded its information on some form of 'physical' storage within the camera; in such a case, it might be possible for us to figure out how to 'play back' such recordings. It would be fascinating to watch such recordings; if we were lucky, we might actually be able to see and hear 'historical' figures such as Jesus, the Buddha, Alexander the Great, etc. We might even discover a 'time capsule' of significant events on our planet, that had been deliberately left for us by such extraterrestrials, thousands of years ago. But this would have nothing to do with 'time travel.' Such recordings would be of events that have already *happened,* and are 'in the past.'

Now, let's consider the possibility of 'time travel' as it is commonly presented in science fiction books and movies. The pertinent question about traveling into the past then becomes, "Is it possible to actually *change* something that has already happened?" In science fiction books and movies, the more 'realistic' ones may sternly order its 'time travelers' that, "when one travels into the past, you can *observe,* but you aren't allowed to *change* anything." But of course, the very fact of traveling backwards in time *would* 'change' something that has already happened. Suppose, for example, that I wanted to go 'back in time' to view myself in a crucial time when I was in high school; but, of course, my high school years have *already* occurred, and they did so *without* my 'future' self witnessing them. (If it had, my 'future' self would presumably have had *memories* of having done so, and would not have needed to travel back in time.)

Or suppose I want to go back in time to discover where my grandfather buried a chest of rare gold coins: the problem is that my grandfather has *already* previously buried his secret treasure—and, when he carefully looked around at the time to see if anyone was watching him, no one was there. So how can there *now* be someone (me, from the future) who is there to observe him?

Of course, such 'time travel' in books and movies may sometimes have an admirable 'goal': for example, of assassinating Hitler *before* he becomes Chancellor of Germany, started the Second World War, and implemented the Holocaust. (Personally, I might change history less violently, by having the young Adolf's application to the Vienna Academy of Art be *accepted*—sending him on his way to a thoroughly forgettable career as an artist, rather than him joining the fledgling Nazi Party, and becoming its leader.)

But there would be considerable *uncertainties* involved with such 'changing the past.' If there had been no Hitler, what if the person who instead became the head of the Nazi Party turned out to be even *worse* than Hitler, and he began executing Jews and others in gas chambers as early as the election of 1932? Or what if the 'new' Chancellor of Germany immediately entered into a sincere and friendly alliance with the Soviet Union, with the ambition of them jointly conquering the world, and then dividing it up between themselves? In other words: What if, by trying to make things *better,* we actually made things *worse?*

To me, there is really no point in pondering such questions, because I (along with many or most physicists) think that **'time travel' (as popularly imagined) is impossible**.

Of course, some theoretical physicists like to stretch their imaginations, to postulate how such 'time travel' *could* be accomplished. (Particularly if they are fans of Star Trek, or the Star Wars movies.) They might point out, for example, that "the laws of physics are *time-reversible.*" Examples may be given such as throwing a baseball, or jumping down from a stairwell; one is asked to imagine "playing this video *backwards*," and told that "the laws of physics are not violated by such a *backward-time trajectory.*"

It may well be true that the laws of physics would not be *violated* by such a 'time reversal.' But the lack of outright 'violation' of the laws of physics, doesn't mean that such scenarios therefore could actually *happen* in the 'real world' (as distinguished from the 'world' a physics professor creates when simply writing equations 'proving' the possibility of time-reversibility on a blackboard, during class).

The problem, again, is that by traveling into a hypothetical 'past,' you would be *altering* something that has *already happened.* This may not seem like a particularly difficult problem if we're talking about simply surreptitiously observing my grandfather as he buries a valuable chest. But suppose the time travelers from the future are significantly more ambitious: imagine that they want to prevent the President of the United States from making a statement on national TV, that will commit our nation into starting an inadvisable war. In this scenario, the time travelers might stop the President before he appears on TV, then warn him, "We're from the future; and it would be a big mistake for you to launch this war!" The President (after due consideration) takes their advice—and things work out much better for him, and for the world.

But this imaginary scenario is very problematic. There is much more involved than just the President and the time travelers meeting in a private room: the President's original speech was recorded and broadcast worldwide; many commentators from different countries spoke and wrote about it, and their words are preserved in newspapers/magazines, as well as in digital media storage in various places in the world. (In fact, these sources would have been available to our time travelers, back in their 'own' time.) Now, if the time travelers *are* able to talk the President out of making his speech and starting a war, what happens to all the newspapers, magazines, and digital copies documenting that he *did,* in fact, make the original speech? If the past was 'changed,' will it now be 'out of sync' with all of this documented history? Or will the time travelers' actions somehow change/erase *all* of these worldwide records (some of which are stored in highly secured locations), many of which were still in existence back in the time travelers' 'own' (i.e., future) time?

A common objection to the notion of time travel is the 'Grandparent Paradox' (or 'Parent Paradox,' if you prefer): If you travel back into the past, and murder your grandparent, will you then no longer exist in the future? (And if you don't exist, how could you later have traveled into the past, to murder your grandparent?) You can multiply such problematic scenarios at length: A drunk driver does/doesn't run me down; I do/don't get the job in a lab where I worked on the pioneering 'time travel' project, etc.

You might think there would be fewer problems with time-traveling into the *future;* after all, the future 'by definition,' *hasn't* yet happened, and therefore is (presumably) not 'fixed.' So does this difference leave the future able to be *changed?*

Let's imagine the common scenario presented in books and movies: the characters are hopping into a 'time travel' machine, and then 'choosing' the precise time they wish to emerge in the future. For example, suppose that a woman who is terminally ill and very near death, wishes to go see her children and grandchildren thirty years in the future (after her death), to make sure they're doing all right without her, and reassure them of her love.

One problem is that, as portrayed in films and books, the time-travelling woman can 'choose' whether to emerge five, ten, thirty, or a *hundred* years into the future; so, apparently, these separate 'futures' in a sense already *exist*—since she is able to 'insert' herself into them. But how many of these 'futures' are 'out there,' that one could 'visit'? Do they 'branch off' every day? Or every year? Or every century? Or even every millisecond?"

And, as with traveling to the *past,* if you affect one of these 'futures,' wouldn't that affect the still *later* 'futures'? For instance, if the ill woman tells her grandchildren that she loves them, then this is *changing* their futures. (Perhaps one of them will now *not* become clinically depressed, and later commit suicide.) This would seemingly result in the same kind of 'out of sync' problems as with traveling to the past, since the time traveler's actions would be 'changing' something that has already happened—albeit that it has 'happened' in the *future.*

Theorists who speculate about the possibility of time travel will sometimes appeal to a hypothetical 'tape of time,' which unwinds in a sequence, such as a film would. They may argue that "there is nothing *impossible* about the notion of the 'tape of time' running backwards." They might also suggest that even some physical processes which seem to us to be 'irreversible' *can*, in fact, be 'reversed.' And, as long as one is talking about theoretical physics, this seems quite plausible (or at least, possible). But, again, when you change from writing down equations on paper or a blackboard (or, these days, typing them into a computer), and move out into the 'real world,' substantial problems arise.

With simple examples such as throwing a baseball, the impossibility of such 'reversal' may not seem particularly obvious. But many things we see every day do, in fact, appear to be quite 'irreversible.' If I fill my car up with gas, and take a long trip (my car producing carbon dioxide emissions all along the way), driving until my gas tank is empty, can these actions really be 'reversed'? Can the CO_2 emissions that have now been dispersed and absorbed into the atmosphere across the country be sucked back into my car's muffler? Can the gasoline that I used during the trip somehow refill itself in my gas tank? And can my car somehow drive backwards, all the way back to my home? Not likely.

When I burn a log in a fireplace, the air and water in the log vaporize, producing smoke, as the hydrocarbons evaporate from the wood. The carbon dioxide thus produced mixes into the air, and the wood is transformed into charcoal and ash. Can such a log then be 'unburned'? Can the charcoal and ash be turned back into a fresh log? And then can the log somehow be put back into the *tree* in the forest, from which it was cut?

We can multiply examples like this indefinitely. If I crack open an egg and cook it, can this be undone? Can a grilled hamburger be turned back into raw ground beef? Can the dust picked up by a vacuum cleaner be replaced precisely back where it was picked up from the living room rug? Can the gray hairs falling out in my comb every morning be somehow reimplanted into my scalp, and turn from gray to the dark brown color of my youth?

And what about something such as **Entropy**, the 2nd Law of Thermodynamics? In essentially every situation that we can *observe*, entropy *increases* over time; thus, the 2nd Law is often referred to as the 'Arrow of Time'—and the overall *direction* of this 'arrow' is always in the direction of *increasing* Entropy.

Perhaps there are ways to avoid the universality (or near-universality) of the 2nd Law. To take one common suggestion, if a God created a universe that was 'set up' with very low Entropy in the beginning, that would be one way out of this problem (although this is an alternative that would definitely not be favored by secular cosmologists). Or, if Entropy could somehow be 'reduced' or 'reset' during some cosmological event (such as during a 'Big Bounce,' in an *oscillating universe* such as Carl Sagan used to favor), the problem might also be solved. If such speculations turn out to be possible, then fine: this supposed 'Arrow of Time' would not be an 'absolute.' But until then, this particular 'Arrow' appears to be strictly traveling down a 'One Way Street.'

Another approach to time travel is to unite it with the 'Many Worlds' hypothesis. Under this scenario, there *is* a world in which the President *did* make an unwise speech that led us into an unwise war—but there is *also* a world in which he changed his mind, and didn't initiate the war. But of course, this isn't really 'time travel,' as it is commonly imagined.

In conclusion, I very seriously doubt the possibility of time travel—whether into the past, or the future. The mathematical theories of Quantum Mechanics can, apparently, be used to *imagine* such scenarios; but while Quantum Physics may not *forbid* such time travel (some theorists even suggest that Quantum Theory *predicts* such 'time travel'!), in the 'real world' that we all live in, it just doesn't seem to be possible.

(Which, actually, is probably a good thing. If time travel *were* possible, think how chaotic our world[s] might be: some modern Neo-Nazis might take nuclear weapons back to 1939 to help Hitler's Germany win the Second World War, for example. Or what if time travelers helped the Communist conspirators in August 1991 to successfully overthrow Mikhail Gorbachev, and we were still involved in the Cold War? Going much farther back, we might all find ourselves living in Europe, and united under the 'Holy Roman Empire,' and in danger from the Inquisition.)

It's perfectly true that we cannot predict what might happen with future scientific discoveries. (Certainly, the average person in 1920 would have been quite astonished to see the world of 2020!) But in my lifetime, and even in the lifetime of my grandchildren, I cannot see the realistic possibility of any 'new discovery' making it possible to travel in time, much less to *change* anything about it.

4. Extraterrestrial Life

Our Sun is a star, like several hundred billion others in our galaxy. The current estimate is that our universe contains about *two trillion* other galaxies. Thus, certainly there is no lack of 'material' on which life could exist. So: *is* there other life in the universe?

Some fundamentalist Christians think that the only intelligent life in the entire universe is here on Earth. They argue that Genesis 1:14-15 proves that stars and other 'lights in the firmament' were created by God only "to give light upon the earth." Supporting this interpretation, Romans 8:18-22 states that "the whole creation has been groaning as in the pains of childbirth right up to the present time." But, thanks to the sacrifice of Jesus, "the creation itself will be liberated from its bondage to decay and brought into the freedom and glory of the children of God." Accordingly, a "new heavens and a new earth" will one day be created by God (1 Pet 3:13; Rev 21:1). (The possibility that life on other planets might not have been subject to the consequences of a 'Fall' that occurred only on planet Earth—potentially requiring Jesus to be sacrificed again, for the salvation of such planets—is considered by such Christians to be a strong argument *against* the existence of any extraterrestrial life.)

For my part, I think that the contrary argument by other Christians—namely, that the Bible doesn't really *say* anything, for or against, the possibility of life on other planets—is more prudent. (I personally find it difficult to believe that the billions and billions of galaxies—which we have only been able to see since we developed sophisticated radio telescopes—were originally created only "to give light upon the earth.")

But there is also a quite secular argument against the existence of life elsewhere. For example, paleontologist Peter Ward and astronomer Donald Brownlee said in their book, *Rare Earth: Why Complex Life is Uncommon in the Universe,* that "complex life is less pervasive in the Universe than is now commonly assumed... not only intelligent life, but even the simplest of animal life, is exceedingly rare in our galaxy and in the Universe... We believe that life in the form of microbes or their equivalents is very common in the universe... However, *complex* life—animals and higher plants—is likely to be far more rare than is commonly assumed... Most of the Universe is too cold, too hot, too dense, too vacuous, too dark, too bright, or not composed of the right elements to support life." Even James Lovelock (inventor of the Gaia hypothesis) said in his recent book, *Novacene: The Coming Age of Hyperintelligence*, "our cosmos is simply not old enough for the staggeringly improbable chain of events required to produce intelligent life to have occurred more than once. Our existence is a freakish one-off."

Let's consider this further. At the moment, although more than 4,000 exoplanets have been discovered in other (relatively nearby) solar systems, we have little useful information about them. So let us first examine the other planetary bodies in our own solar system. (But of course, it is certainly possible that life in other solar systems, or galaxies, does not need to conform to the same water-dependent, carbon-based requirements as does life here on Earth.)

Mars is probably the likeliest candidate for life in our solar system. But, although Mars has *frozen* water at its polar caps, there is apparently no *liquid* water on its surface. Despite our having sent a variety of vehicles for the direct exploration of Mars (e.g., the 1976 Viking landers; the 1997 Mars Pathfinder probe), we have as yet no direct evidence of present or past life on Mars—although it remains possible that microorganisms may have lived there long ago. (And some propose that they might have even made their way to Earth, to 'seed' our own development of life.)

Next most likely candidates for life in our solar system are three of Jupiter's moons (particularly Europa), and two of Saturn (Titan and Enceladus). Europa has an icy surface, and *probably* has an ocean beneath its icy crust; conceivably, it might also have some multicellular organisms. Jupiter's Io and Saturn's moons may also have some kind of water (although perhaps only below their surface).

Meteorites (which mostly have originated in our own solar system) have been found which contained some amino acids, and 'lesser organics' have also been detected in comets and interstellar clouds. There are also occasionally interstellar objects discovered such as *Oumuamua*, which have originated outside our own solar system. Stars themselves give no evidence of being composed of any elements other than those of which our Sun is composed. In general, such extra-Earthly objects do not seem to be constructed from any materials radically *different* from those on Earth, and in our solar system.

Certainly, the very limited experience from our own solar system would suggest that life is *uncommon* on other planets. Still, if even 1% or less of the planets in one of the many solar systems out there are capable of harboring life, the vast number of galaxies in the universe, and the abundance of exoplanets that presumably exist, make it seem quite reasonable to think that there must be other life (although not necessarily 'advanced' or 'intelligent' life) *somewhere* out there.

And, while we have no way of knowing whether life on other planets may have developed civilizations, given the billions-of-years *timescale* of planetary development in our universe, it certainly seems reasonable to speculate that there may be many civilizations that are *more* advanced than ours, as well as those which are *less* advanced as ours. (Of course, a civilization that started a billion years earlier than ours, may very well have *destroyed* itself and its environment by this time; so we may need to hope to locate civilizations that are 'advanced,' but not *too* advanced.)

But does this limited evidence suggest that the kinds of science fiction books and movies many of us enjoy reading and watching may be suggestive of the actual reality? That we have been, or will someday, be in contact with civilizations from other planets, and perhaps even in other galaxies?

Well, there is one very significant problem about this hope: namely, the tremendous *distance* between us and other solar systems—even those within our own galaxy. The nearest star/star system to us is the triple star system of Alpha Centauri, which is about 4.37 light-years from the Sun.

Let's put this in perspective. The fastest spaceship we on Earth have ever launched into space was the 2006 'New Horizons' mission to Pluto; this vehicle averages, at peak, a speed of perhaps 100,000 miles per hour. (By contrast, the International Space Station travels in its orbit around Earth at only about 17,000 miles per hour.) Since a light year is about 6 trillion miles, Alpha Centauri is about 26 trillion miles away. Since there are about 8766 hours in a year, the New Horizons spacecraft could travel perhaps 876,600,000 miles in a year. Therefore, an object traveling as fast as the New Horizons craft would require something like *30,000 years* to reach Alpha Centauri. (And that is just for a *one-way trip!*)

And of course, a *manned* space craft would be much heavier, and travel much slower, than the New Horizons vehicle. And there would be considerable problems with providing *oxygen*, much less *food*, and certainly **WATER**, for any passengers aboard such a vehicle, for such an enormous length of time. (And its passengers would have to realize that even their great-great-great-great-great-great-grandchildren will *die*, long before they reach their destination.)

But even then, suppose that once they reached Alpha Centauri, they didn't find anything particularly interesting there. The next-nearest star is 'Barnard's star,' which is *six* light years away from us. Next-closest after that is Luhman 16, and then WISE 0855−0714, Wolf 359, Lalande 21185, and Sirius, which are even farther away. (And remember that the Milky Way Galaxy is *100,000 light-years* wide.) So the tremendous distance between us and any other planets is a considerable, and likely insuperable, problem.

Science fiction books and movies tend to ignore or dismiss this problem, blithely asserting that future spacecraft could somehow be able to travel at 'warp speed,' or something like that—postulating a speed that nearly equals or even *exceeds* the speed of light. (But they ignore the problem that the G-forces from *accelerating* so quickly would flatten us; plus the fact that traveling so fast would make it difficult or impossible to avoid running into objects such as asteroids, stray exoplanets, and other spaceships.)

Of course, our current scientific knowledge (e.g., the Special Theory of Relativity) considers the speed of light to be the ultimate 'speed limit' of the universe, beyond which speed nothing with mass (and thus, matter) can travel. Yes, it's true that after the Big Bang, according to the 'Cosmic Inflation' model, *space* is expanding at a speed greater than the speed of light; but since 'empty space' has no mass and no matter (not even a particle!), it can expand at whatever rate it wishes, without violating Relativity. But no one has any real idea about how a material *spaceship* could exceed this 'speed limit.'

Some theorists have speculated that 'quantum entanglement' might allow subatomic particles in certain situations to 'travel' faster than light

speed, or even to move instantaneously; more recent research seems
to cast doubt on this, however. But even if, for the sake of argument,
we granted this possibility, there is nevertheless a lot of difference
between, say, a single *photon* or other energy particle traveling faster
than the speed of light, and a large and heavy *spaceship* (loaded with
passengers and supplies) to somehow be able to move that quickly. Some
physicists also used to suggest the existence of *Tachyons* (as a 'faster-
than-light particle'), but there now seems to be general agreement that
these hypothetical particles do not exist. So the general prohibition
against mass traveling faster than light seems to stand.

But even if you had a vehicle that *could* somehow travel at nearly the
speed of light, a prospective space traveler from Earth would still have to
invest about *nine years* (as measured on the Earth) in a round trip to and
from Alpha Centauri. (Granted, because of Relativistic *time dilation,* it
wouldn't *be* 'as long' for the fast-moving space travelers.) Would this
be a worthy 'risk' for a space traveler? Maybe, for an 'adventurous
type,' with no spouse or family. But if a space vehicle truly can't travel
much faster than, say, 100,000 miles per hour, this seems to be an
overwhelming obstacle for proposed 'interstellar travel.'

Still, we don't want to make the mistake of some past generations,
and improperly limit what science *might* discover in the future; or, what
advanced alien civilizations might have long ago discovered. This,
then, brings up the possibility of Unidentified Flying Objects (UFOs)—
although I think that the term 'Unidentified Aerial Phenomena' (UAP,
which doesn't presume that the sighting was of an 'object') is probably
the more accurate term to use.

As one who has watched dozens and dozens of 'UFO videos,' I must
admit that there certainly seem to be some things that have been sighted
and/or photographed in our skies that are definitely 'unidentified.'
But it is also quite true that many very prominent UFO claims and
claimants (e.g., Billy Meier, Bob Lazar, Ed Walters/Gulf Breeze, the
'Alien Autopsy' film, etc.) are most likely fakes; and many other well-
publicized 'UFO phenomena' are of very doubtful legitimacy (e.g., the
purported 1947 'UFO crash' at Roswell, New Mexico; the so-called
'Crop Circles' found in some fields; the 'animal mutilations' supposedly
done by extraterrestrials; the 'alien implants' claimed to be found in

some peoples' bodies, and so on). The field, frankly, does not lend itself to confidence in the credence of many of its claimants. (Though I do not doubt the sincerity of most of the researchers.)

Consider Erich von Däniken, the author of hugely popular books such as *Chariots of the Gods?* Von Däniken served a year in prison for embezzlement, fraud, and forgery; in fact, he wrote his second book, *Gods from Outer Space*, while he was serving this prison term. Certainly, there are other, somewhat more credible advocates of 'Outer Space Gods' theories (such as the late Zechariah Sitchin, who was someone who could actually read ancient Sumerian and Akkadian), but I frankly find the evidence for such 'visitations' wanting. (There are loads of 'skeptical' books out there, if you want to do some research.)

In the book *Intelligent Life in the Universe*, which was written by Carl Sagan and the Soviet astrophysicist I.S. Shklovskii, Sagan summarized, "I examined a typical legend suggestive of contact between our ancestors and an apparent representative of a superior society... I concluded that it was impossible to *demonstrate* extraterrestrial contact from such legends: There are plausible alternative explanations... To the best of my knowledge, there are no such legends and no such artifacts."

To me, the fact that seemingly everyone these days is carrying around a cell phone camera in his or her pocket, yet the number of *photographs/videos* of UFOs being published seems to be diminishing, is instructive. (*UFO Magazine*, which to my mind was the best magazine devoted to UFOs—I used to be a subscriber—ceased operations in 2012; the British magazine of the same name ended in 2004. Some other publications, such as *UFO Digest*, continue in operation, however, as do the groups MUFON and CUFOS.)

Perhaps 'visiting' aliens have just lost interest in our planet; or maybe they have now learned all they can learn by 'abducting' earthlings; or possibly they just ran out of creative designs for new crop circles. *OR...* maybe there really *were* 'other,' *natural* explanations of such phenomena (like skeptics have suggested), that don't require the theory of extraterrestrial visitors.

I think one of the most interesting persons to weigh in on the whole UFO/extraterrestrial issue is Carl Sagan (1934–1996), the astronomer, planetary scientist, cosmologist, astrophysicist, astrobiologist, popular science author, and host of the famous 1980 *Cosmos* PBS series.

In his essay in the book *UFOs: A Scientific Debate* (which was based on a symposium sponsored by the American Association for the Advancement of Science), Sagan pointed out, "There are serious problems in interstellar flight, principally because the space between the stars is enormous. There are a large number of stars—about two hundred billion stars in our galaxy alone... But the average distances between stars in our galaxy is a few light years; light, faster than which nothing that can slow down can travel, takes years to traverse the distances between the nearest stars. Space vehicles take that long at the very least. In order for a space vehicle to get from one star to another in a convenient period of time it has to go very close to the speed of light so that relativistic time dilation can enter into the problem, and so that the shipboard clock can run more slowly compared to a clock left on the launch planet. To travel close to the speed of light is difficult." (Pg. 270)

Interestingly, in Sagan's 1985 science fiction novel *Contact* (which was originally a 1979 screenplay, and later became the basis for the 1997 movie), he tries to find a way around this problem of distance. The novel's plot revolves around the first 'contact' of planet Earth with an extraterrestrial intelligence. A young woman named Eleanor ('Ellie') Arroway is the director of 'Project Argus,' a radiotelescope array in New Mexico dedicated to the search for extraterrestrial intelligence (SETI). The project discovers a signal containing a series of prime numbers coming from the Vega system, which is 26 light years away from us. (The earthly scientists acknowledge that, "even if we did reply, it would be twenty-six years before they received the reply, and another twenty-six years before they can answer it.") Further messages are discovered, one of which contains instructions explaining to earth scientists and technicians how to construct a machine that will enable a crew to travel to meet the aliens.

In this novel, Sagan had the challenge of trying to dream up a scientifically plausible scenario for this to occur. In the first draft of the book, he proposed to use a Black Hole as a means of quickly traveling huge distances in space. But Sagan asked his theoretical physicist friend Kip Thorne—who won a Nobel Prize for Physics in 2017—to review a typescript version of the novel; and Thorne advised him that this use of a Black Hole would be impossible. Thorne then recommended that Sagan's characters use a *wormhole*, which is "a hypothetical shortcut for travel between distant points in the Universe."

Here, space is visualized as a basically 2-dimensional strip of paper, where a wormhole 'tube' connects two distant points (called 'mouths'), A and B, on the paper. Going from A to B through the 'throat' of the wormhole would obviously be much shorter than going along the entire paper. (Although how one would 'fold over' a huge, 3-dimensional physical universe like the graphic shows is puzzling.)

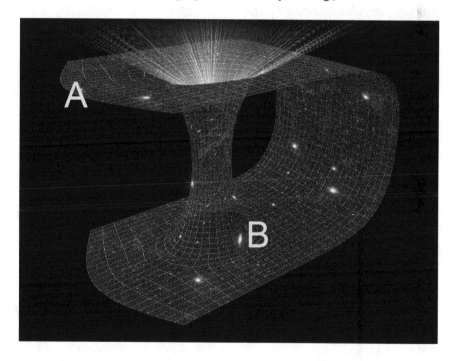

Is this a viable solution? Well, in the first place, wormholes— which, admittedly, do not contradict Einstein's field equations of General Relativity—are at this time purely *theoretical*. None have been discovered in nature, and none have been created in a laboratory. (Well, actually, a 'magnetic field' that supposedly "*acts* like a wormhole" was apparently created in a lab in Spain in 2015.) But even if a *traversable* wormhole could be discovered or created, holding its 'throat' open for travelers would admittedly be very problematic, and would reportedly require the use of 'exotic matter with a negative energy density'—of which we don't presently have any. (Although 'very tiny amounts' *have* reportedly been made in some laboratories.)

Sagan, in his book, doesn't provide any explanation for *how* the extraterrestrial beings could create, and hold open, a wormhole that would allow Eleanor Arroway and her four companions to go through it, chat with the aliens, and then return to Earth. (For the novel, it is just assumed that *somehow*, these advanced aliens had discovered a way to do this; and it's fine to do that in a 'science fiction' *novel*. But getting that to work in the *real* world is something else, entirely.)

Yet even if wormholes existed, why should we assume that they would necessarily lead to anything *interesting?* (What if one we produced or found, only provided a shortcut to a barren and lifeless system—a kind of 'armpit of the universe' area?)

Again, no one can really predict the future of scientific development. But at this point, the wormhole proposal for space travel seems to be more 'science fiction' (e.g., the 2014 movie *Interstellar,* to which Kip Thorne was a consultant) than 'science.' And the notion of interstellar travel of humans aboard spaceships seems to not be possible. (Sorry, fans of Han Solo, and Captain James T. Kirk.)

But one salutary aspect of Sagan's book *Contact* is his fine descriptions of the 'Search for Extra-Terrestrial Intelligence,' or SETI. This search is a genuinely 'scientific' endeavor, since its 1960 beginnings with Cornell University astronomer Frank Drake's 'Project Ozma,' where a radio telescope was used to attempt to pick up radio signals from civilizations in outer space. NASA funded a SETI project for years, but it was ultimately cancelled by Congress (for budgetary reasons, as well as a lack of *results!*). In 1995 a nonprofit organization, the SETI Institute, revived the program under the name 'Project Phoenix.' Then in 2015, billionaire Russian investor Yuri Milner gave $100 million to fund the 'Largest Search for Alien Intelligence Ever.' Such endeavors are, in my view, very exciting, and clearly the most promising way we have yet found to try and locate some kind of 'extraterrestrial intelligence.'

But the problem is still: after decades of searching the skies (admittedly, the skies are a very 'big' place to search!), the results of this search are… well, disappointing. (A character in Sagan's *Contact*

THINKING ABOUT IT 39

admits, "there has never been a real signal from the depths of space, something manufactured, something artificial, something contrived by an alien mind." And this remains the case, even decades later.) Even those of us who are sympathetic with the goals of SETI can understand Congress's lack of desire to fund a project with so little concrete to *show* for its efforts.

Perhaps it is nearly futile to attempt to find evidence of alien civilizations, when they are so distant from us. *Our* planet certainly sends out an abundance of radio and TV signals (although one shudders to think of aliens judging our level of civilization on the basis of TV sitcoms from the 1960s), so an alien civilization with their own SETI project could certainly discover us. Yet we don't seem to have any real evidence that extraterrestrials *have* located us, and responded. (Or, perhaps they *have* found us, and sent signals back to us—but we won't receive these signals until several decades in the future, because the aliens are 26 light-years or even farther away.) We've also sent out the Pioneer 10 and 11 space probes, which contained the famous plaque showing figures of a human male and female, along with information that would hopefully help any 'finders' to identify the general location of our planet. So perhaps one day, we *will* truly have contact with an alien civilization.

Or, alternately, perhaps such civilizations are simply too rare, too far away, or presently *less* advanced than us, so that they lack the ability to respond to us. (I have often wondered what would be the reaction of the most intelligent citizens of early earthly civilizations such as Egypt, China, and Greece, if something extraterrestrial—perhaps analogous to our own Pioneer 10 and 11 space probes—had landed among them; I would imagine it would have seemed nearly incomprehensible. The depiction of the Earth's 'location' relative to *pulsars* would surely have been lost on them.)

Until (and if) the situation changes, we will have to content ourselves with dealing only with our own planet, and with our human life being the only form of 'higher intelligence' we have direct contact with. However, since we have no way of knowing whether alien civilizations would, or would not, be *hostile,* or even of a 'colonializing' mind-set (remember H. G. Wells' novel, *The War of the Worlds*), that might actually be a good—or at least, a *prudent*—thing, for us.

Futurist and author Ray Kurzweil suggests, "Ultimately the entire universe will become saturated with our intelligence." Maybe, but I kind of doubt it. But I think it's worth noting that, when we have so many urgent problems (the environment, world hunger, civil wars, terrorism, etc.) taking place here on Earth, perhaps we should just worry about taking care of our *own* planet, before we concern ourselves too much about 'contacting' anyone else's planet.

5. Artificial Intelligence, and Consciousness

We are no longer surprised to encounter computer programs that 'talk' to us, and that we can verbally ask questions of. Apple's Siri, Microsoft's Cortana, Amazon's Echo, Google Assistant, and similar voice-recognition software is used by many of us on a daily basis. We are now used to having voice-activated GPS systems in our vehicles. Our television remote controls now let use vocal commands. And we have, for a much longer period, been accustomed to getting automated responses over the telephone ("Press 1 if you want to hear your balance and payment information..."), or speaking with a 'Chatbot' rather than a human being.

The first telephone voice-recognition systems were rather crude, and there was no mistaking that we were not dealing with a human being (which is why many of us nearly always pressed the button to "Speak to a Customer Service Representative"). But the software has progressed considerably since those early days. The vocal responses of the current software have become much 'smoother' and more humanlike. And programmers are constantly working to make this software even more 'user-friendly' (e.g., "Alexa, tell me a joke").

And of course, the IBM supercomputer 'Deep Blue' famously defeated then-reigning World Chess Champion Garry Kasparov in 1997 (after Deep Blue had lost the previous match in 1996). IBM ended its program development of Deep Blue after this victory—thus not giving Kasparov a chance for a rematch. (I personally would have liked to see Deep Blue matched against a *team* of chess grandmasters, so that the *fatigue* factor of a single human competitor would not be a factor.) More recently, IBM's 'Watson' project impressed both the tech industry, and pop culture, with its resounding 2011 victory against two of the TV game show Jeopardy's greatest champions. So certainly, the 'intelligence' exhibited by computers has been progressing at a very rapid rate.

But are such machines truly 'intelligent'? They are, of course, *programmed* by intelligent human beings, and their programs are being constantly updated and broadened. Is this in any way comparable to the 'intelligence' that human beings begin to develop from birth? Or is any 'intelligence' that these machines seem to have, simply a product of what intelligent *programmers* have put into them?

To be sure, one can pose a question to various voice-response computers such as, "Are you conscious? Are you intelligent? Do you have feelings?" and the program might very well respond, "Oh, yes; definitely!" But deep down, we realize that this is just a response that has been programmed into it by the developers—who might just as easily have programmed it to reply, "No, I am not; I am just a machine. Only human beings have consciousness, intelligence, and feelings." (As an experiment, I asked our Amazon Echo, "Alexa, are you conscious?" and 'she' replied, "I know who I am.")

A famous way of approaching the question about machine/computer 'intelligence' and 'consciousness' is the *Turing Test,* which was proposed by the English mathematician and computer scientist Alan Turing in his 1950 paper, 'Computing Machinery and Intelligence.' Turing proposed that there would be a 'conversation' (conducted by typewritten questions/answers, sent by teleprinter) between a human interrogator and two unknown respondents—one of which was a computer, and the other a human. Turing's idea (known as 'the Imitation Game') was that if the interrogator couldn't tell which of the two respondents was human, and which the computer, then the computer had 'passed the test.' He predicted, "I believe that in about fifty years' time it will be possible to program computers ... to make them play the imitation game so well that an average interrogator will not have more than 70 percent chance of making the right identification after five minutes of questioning."

Programs such as ELIZA (1966) and PARRY (1972) were developed in an attempt to pass the Turing test. The Turing test has even been turned into an annual competition, known as the 'Loebner Prize,' which awards monetary prizes to the computer programs considered by the judges to be the best, and most human-like. (Since 2019, however, the audience—rather than a panel of judges—determines the winner of the Loebner Prize.)

It should be noted, however, that the 'text-only' communication method mandated by such tests implicitly acknowledges that it would be relatively simple to tell the difference between a human and a computer if *speech* was the medium of communication. And such 'tests' are typically limited to, say, 15-30 minutes; if there were no such time limit, the human would certainly be distinguished from the computer in every case. And it is noteworthy that the purported human respondent is apparently never someone that is personally *known* to the interrogator; I suspect that a computer could not 'fool' for long an interrogator when the other respondent was said to be a spouse, child, close friend, etc.

Many persons (particularly those working in the computer/ information science field) are quite optimistic about the prospects for our being able to create 'intelligent' computers. One well-known example is Ray Kurzweil, a futurist and engineering director for Google, as well as the author of thought-provoking books such as *The Singularity Is Near*, in which he speaks with confidence about our being able relatively soon to 'scan the human brain' and 'upload it' to a computer or robot.

Granted that X-ray images of a human brain can be taken from a variety of angles, which can then be used to generate a cross-cut picture of the brain, enabling medical doctors to identify potential problem areas. Also granted that 'brain scans' such as Computed Tomographic (CT), Magnetic Resonance Imaging (MRI), and Positron Emission Tomography (PET) are now routinely done to identify strokes, tumors, Alzheimer's Disease, etc. But locating a tumor in the brain seems not very comparable to, say, trying to duplicate and copy all the massive amounts of *information* that are contained in a human brain. The human brain has about *86-100 billion* neurons (brain cells), and somewhere between 200-1,000 *trillion* synaptic connections between these neurons. Although neuroscientists are making enormous progress in, say, identifying which areas of the brain are involved with different functions (such as sight, taste, memory, abstract thought, etc.), trying to identify *precisely* 'which portion of the brain this idea is coming from,' or 'where is this particular memory stored' for *specific* ideas, thoughts, and memories seems like a very daunting task to undertake.

If, for the sake of discussion, we assume that our brains are purely physical—and that *everything* that occurs in them has exclusively a physical basis—then presumably such things as: (1) the memory of my solemnly making my wedding vows to my wife, (2) the skill of being able to play scales on the piano, (3) my knowledge of how to make tacos, (4) the name and title of my 'worst boss ever' at work, (5) the PIN of my debit card, etc., are recorded *somewhere* among all of the neurons and synaptic connections in my brain. While I have little doubt that *something* is occurring in my brain as I think/do/recall any or all of these things, and that various kinds of technology could detect that *some kind* of activity is taking place in my brain, I have considerable doubts that we will ever be able to 'scan and upload' the contents of these cells and synapses into a machine-readable form.

Imagine trying to 'convert' the neuronal contents containing a particular memory into the *binary* language used by computers; and trying to continue this 'conversion' with *all* the contents of even a single individual's brain. Then, imagine the poor overworked programmers trying to specify *exactly* the state of my various neurons, and *precisely* what each of them communicated via the synapses, while I was, say, brushing my teeth yesterday morning—while also thinking about my schedule for the upcoming day.

But unfortunately, unless you can actually *accomplish* something like such detailed specificity, you won't be able to 'copy' a person's entire personality, memory, skills, history, etc., into a computer or robot. And thus, the optimistic dream of our ever achieving *immortality* by having a nonbiological *copy* of 'me' available will be forever unfulfilled.

However, I freely admit that, before too much longer, computer/robotic *simulations* of us could, given certain circumstances, convince (I'm tempted to say 'fool') even some of those closest to ourselves that the simulations are 'us.' For example, suppose that, at birth, a test subject had implanted in their body both video and audio transmitters, that recorded everything 'outside' that transpired and affected this individual. A staff of programmers recording all of this data could certainly come up with a near-exhaustive list of 'talking points' about such events, such that if someone asked the robot 'copy' of this individual, "What did you have for breakfast this morning?" the 'copy' could reply quickly and accurately. In fact, the 'copy' could certainly reply much *more* accurately than the 'actual' person if it was asked something like, "What did you have for breakfast two days *after* your 7th birthday?"

But would such a 'copy' know the *inner thoughts* of the 'actual' person? The 'copy' could report the pleasant greeting that the 'original' gave to her/his boss one morning at work, but would the 'copy' know that the 'original' was actually thinking, *I wish you'd hurry up and retire, you old windbag!* while smiling and uttering the cheerful greeting? (For that matter, could a brain researcher studying someone's dreams even know *what* the person dreamed, without just *asking* the individual?)

Being able to program a computer to 'pass' the Turing Test seems like a *much* easier project than trying to 'scan and upload' the entire contents of an actual human brain. A whole legion of programmers and technicians could dream up literally *millions* of robotic responses to questions, or other conversational cues, and program them into the robotic 'copy,' so that it always had a ready-made reply to almost any conceivable question. (In fact, an 'interrogator' in the Turing Test would probably be able to identify the 'robot' by the fact that it never seems to have to *think* about anything, before replying accurately—unless, of course, the programmers had deliberately *programmed* such a 'delay' into it.)

Another thing that seems like it would be quite difficult for a computer program to imitate would be our *experiences.* For example: if someone asked you to describe to them what chocolate tastes like, apart from saying that "it's very sweet" (which might prompt the response, "Oh, you mean sweet like an orange?"), how else could you describe it? Calling it 'smoky,' 'nutty,' 'earthy,' and so on, wouldn't really help anyone. But once you've actually *tasted* chocolate, you're unlikely to ever forget its distinctive flavor; so that when someone asks you, "What does this cookie taste like?" you can reply very confidently, "Oh, it's *very* 'chocolatey'.

Certainly, a computer 'copy' of us could be programmed to recognize the effect of chocolate on the taste receptors in our tongue, etc., and would thus be able to identify a given flavor as being chocolate (and even of a specific *type* of chocolate!). And of course, this 'copy' could be programmed to exclaim, "Oh, I *love* chocolate! It's my favorite kind of candy!" But would this 'copy' really *know,* experientially, what chocolate *tastes* like? (Suppose we asked it, "What's the difference between the sweetness of chocolate, and the sweetness in a dish of sweet-and-sour chicken?")

Another thing that might be difficult for a 'copy' of us would be to duplicate our many *skills*. For instance, suppose the copy asked you, "How do you *walk?* I mean, what precisely is it that you *do* to actually make your legs move? If you say that you 'will' yourself to walk, precisely *how* is this 'act of will' brought about by you?" We would probably be unable to offer any real 'help' to the copy. Even a human who needs to 'relearn' how to walk after a stroke, or brain/ spinal cord injury, can't simply be 'told' how to walk—the skill must be redeveloped, and relearned by experience.

I also doubt that a computer could genuinely 'copy' our *emotions*. Take the feeling of protective love that comes over a parent, grandparent, or adult relative when a child is hurt, and wants to be comforted. This is not simply a matter of providing *information;* e.g., "This is my child, and she/he was hurt after falling down, so there arises in myself empathic feelings which lead me to want to utter words of comfort to the child." Certainly, there are accompanying *physiological* changes in our body, which accompany such feelings: our heartbeat may speed up, tears may come to our eyes, and our voice might 'shake' with emotion. And it wouldn't be that hard for a robotic 'copy' of us to be programmed to *emulate* the 'objective' and 'visible' aspects of our behavior; but a human actually offering comfort to a child knows that there is much *more* to this action, than what is simply visible from the 'outside.'

But of course, the ultimate test is that of *consciousness* itself. Granted, if we asked one of the computerized competitors in a Turing Test, "Are you conscious?" it would almost certainly reply, "Yes! Absolutely, I am fully conscious." But is this response coming from an actual *experience* of consciousness, or is the program simply stating the response that it was programmed to give?

Consciousness has proven to be nearly impossible to *define*, or to develop any sort of 'objective' test to determine whether or not it is present. Advocates of 'Strong Artificial Intelligence/AI' may cite this inability as support for their contention that "machines *can* be conscious." But such difficulties arise because **consciousness is an** *experience*; it encompasses a very wide range of aspects, mixing together perception, memory, feelings, abstract thought, and much more. For the same kind of reasons that we can't really 'explain' what chocolate tastes like, we would be unable to explain verbally what consciousness is like, to some entity that had never actually experienced it.

But we can certainly marshal some *evidence* as to what consciousness includes. For instance, all of us have the capacity of **self-awareness**. We have a name that we identity with; a living environment that we recognize; a lifetime of memories dating from early childhood, and so on. After sleeping, when we wake up, we recognize the *continuity* of our conscious self with the conscious self we had when we lay down to sleep. While it's true that (as both David Hume, and the Buddha, pointed out) our conscious 'self' is, in a sense, constantly changing—there is never any question but that there is a continuing sense of 'I' that continues throughout.

But were we always so 'self-aware'? No. Although an eighteen-month-old child can recognize itself in a mirror, and a two-year old child can answer the question, "Who are you?" by stating their name, most children do not really seem to develop the *fuller* sense of 'self' until a year or two later. But, by anywhere between age 2½ and 5, all children have become fully self-aware, and are well aware of their own 'inner' life and thoughts (and they have even developed the ability to tell *lies,* to attempt to fool adults!).

If we move beyond our own species, and into the animal kingdom, let us consider the great apes. Chimpanzees, orangutans, bonobos, and rhesus macaque monkeys can recognize themselves in a mirror; chimpanzees, orangutans, bonobos, and gorillas have been able to learn American Sign Language to some extent. However (as the ultimately rather disappointing results of teaching Sign Language, or other symbolic forms of communication to apes seemingly demonstrated), their use of language never progresses very far. The chimpanzee Washoe's signing of 'water bird' after seeing a swan was a possible exception (but perhaps she was actually just making two separate observations: 'water,' and then 'bird'), and apes in general have never really progressed to formulating entire sentences, as children do by their second year. (Herbert Terrace, the trainer of Nim Chimpsky, noted that Nim's purported 'sentences' were typically duplicates such as, "give orange me give eat orange me eat orange give me eat orange.")

So the great apes seemingly do not possess the intellectual capacity to create and use a complex *language,* such as humans have developed. Apparently, oral and written language (as opposed to simple oral/audible expressions of emotion, etc.) is a uniquely human trait.

Bottlenose dolphins, some orcas, and even elephants can also pass the 'mirror test.' And (as anyone knows who has seen dolphins and whales perform at parks such as Sea World) they certainly are capable of *learning* some complex behaviors. But even detailed studies of dolphins (such as those done by John C. Lilly), including the analysis of recordings of their various 'whistles,' failed to demonstrate that they possessed a symbolic language which can communicate words, sentences, and complex thoughts.

But does this mean that such creatures completely lack 'self-awareness'? Certainly not. Animals may recognize not only themselves, but others as well. Dogs and cats, for instance, obviously recognize (and act differently toward) different individuals; and so do various other types of animals. So clearly, they must have *some* degree of 'self-awareness.'

I would suggest that such creatures have a level of awareness that overlaps to some extent with human infants and children. That is, the animals can recognize themselves and others, respond to their name being called, learn semi-complex behaviors, and so on—*without* having the full range of 'inner life' that a human has.

As we continue elsewhere in the animal kingdom, creatures like rats; sheep; pigs; horses; birds like parrots, pigeons, crows, owls and falcons; squirrels; raccoons; octopus and squid; sea lions; and even insects such as ants and bees, show various degrees of 'intelligence,' manifested by engaging in cooperative efforts, and goal-directed behavior. Fish, by contrast, seem to be significantly lower in their level of intelligence (their ability to swim through mazes is very limited, for example). But even pesky insects such as flies, mosquitoes and gnats can exhibit very frustrating degrees of 'escape' behavior, when we are trying to swat them.

Ocean-dwelling creatures such as the sea urchin, sea anemone, sea squirt, and sea sponges, as well as marine invertebrates, fungi, and microbes lack a central nervous system, and a 'brain'—and this perhaps suggests what is 'essential,' in order to have consciousness and a sense-of self-awareness: that centralized center for nerves to connect, and communicate with each other.

Plants, of course, do not have a central nervous system, either—which is why vegetarians and vegans (believing that "plants don't feel *pain* when you eat them") are willing to consume them. I am a skeptic when it comes to claims (such as those made in the book, *The Secret Life of Plants*, by Peter Tompkins and Christopher Bird) that plants react to certain human vocal tones, or grow faster in response to different types of music, etc. But who knows? I would not be particularly disturbed if clear scientific evidence was produced documenting such claims. (But so far, it has not.)

Time to summarize: What do all of these entities we have just been considering have in common? **They are all *alive*.**

I have no interest in entering into a detailed debate on very complex issues such as, "Are bees *conscious*?" Such debates may be of great importance to vegans trying to decide whether or not they should eat honey, but I don't wish to go into such detail, here. It seems clear to me, however, that there is a reasonably 'graduated' series of steps of increasingly complex behavior starting from, say, marine invertebrates and fungi, and finally ending up with primates and human beings. I don't have any particular need to 'draw a *line*' anywhere along the series.

Nor am I (or anyone else that I've ever read) able to offer a non-controversial definition of precisely what 'life' is. The question, 'Are *viruses* alive?' is, I would suggest, more a matter of *definition* (i.e., "What do you *mean* by 'alive'?"), than it is a 'factual' matter.

One of the helpful definitions of 'life' I've read is that a *living* organism (if a 'representative example' of the species, that is) is capable of *reproduction*. (Viruses are normally not considered to be 'living' because they cannot duplicate their genetic material by themselves, and must use other cells to reproduce. And the occasional organism that is biologically unable to reproduce—due to injury, etc.—is certainly not a 'representative example' of the species.) Life reproduces itself, and passes on its traits through DNA.

Life also 'takes in' some form of *food*, and then produces bodily *waste*. It is capable of independent motion and activity. And of course, it has a **metabolism**, which has biochemical processes that work to maintain this life. (Do rocks have metabolisms, or eat, or poop? Or do they have DNA, for that matter?)

One of the most singular and distinctive characteristics of 'life' is that a living organism can **die**. (Admittedly, some simple life forms, such as bacteria, do not 'die,' *per se;* they continue reproducing by division indefinitely. But they *can* be 'wiped out'—and thus 'die' as individuals—by the use of disinfectant sprays, and such.) There certainly are an abundance of very clear cases where some creatures are 'alive,' while others are 'dead.' The beloved pet dog who has mercifully been 'put to sleep' is now dead; the goldfish floating motionlessly on its side at the top of the aquarium is dead; the chickens that were decapitated at a poultry processing plant are dead; the beloved family member whose body is resting in a casket at a mortuary is dead.

Contrast the reality of human and animal death, with an 'electronics junkyard': where broken or discarded computers, televisions, cell phones, stereos, DVD/VCR players, and all sorts of other electronic equipment or 'E-waste' ends up. Scavengers may retrieve still-usable parts and components of this equipment, and use them to create working devices again. This discarded equipment may have been lying out in the open, and exposed to the elements, for *years*—but nevertheless, once they are plugged in again and turned on, they can *function* once more. Contrast this situation with human organ donations: where the donated organ must be kept in very specialized conditions, until it is actually transplanted into a recipient.

This inevitability of death is, I think, a very clear distinction between humans, and machines. Were these various electronic component parts found in the junkyard 'dead,' and then made 'alive' again? Or were they never 'alive' in the first place? I would suggest that a computer rebuilt from scrap components isn't 'alive'—it is simply *functional*, once again.

The chemicals of our bodies are not especially unique: The raw elements in our bodies are worth, say, about $5. (When I was in elementary school, it was 95 cents; that's inflation for you!) Certainly it is true that various organs of our bodies (e.g., heart; liver; kidneys; lungs, etc.) can, after our clinical death, be transplanted into another human being, whose own organ is failing. We can also have *artificial* knees and hips inserted into our bodies, and amputees may also learn to use prosthetic arms and legs. Cochlear implants can help those with hearing loss; artificial retinas will probably be common before too long. And even implants into our *brains* are being developed, to assist blind people, or persons with 'motor control' problems.

But it is significant that even if we are the recipient of a heart or kidney transplant, we don't suddenly find that we have the consciousness and memories of *two* different individuals mixed up in our mind, with both vying for attention—the organ *recipient* remains the sole 'conscious' self.

And none of these recent medical developments really affect the basic facts: We are born; our minds begin to develop; we become conscious, self-aware beings; and we eventually die. Machines are never going to be able to become *pregnant,* allow another machine to *grow* inside it, and later give *birth,* as does a human mother. Older computers may have upgraded central processing chips or 'additional memory' installed into them, but they do not 'naturally' *grow,* as babies and children do. A computer may have a 'virus' and need to have its operating system software reinstalled; but computers don't get *sick,* as humans can. All of these significant differences simply illustrate the vast differences between living creatures and machines, and support the distinction I am drawing between (1) the kind of 'awareness' that a lower creature may have, and (2) the much greater 'self-awareness' that a human has, with (3) a computer's capacity to, say, respond to an interrogator's questions during a version of the Turing Test.

Modern technology is wonderful. Computers do amazing things that make our lives easier and better. But a forklift can also lift much heavier objects than I can; and a $1 pocket calculator can perform *much* faster computations than I can. But such abilities don't make them 'alive'; they are still 'just hunks of metal.' A personal computer may contain metals such as gold, copper, aluminum, lead, and steel—but none of these elements have the 'regenerative' ability of human cells. The 'gap' between living and nonliving—as well as between 'conscious' and 'nonconscious'—remains.

There are many things that computers (at least, within the lifetimes of those presently living) are in all likelihood *always* going to be unable to do. A robot will probably never be an amazing gymnast like Simone Biles or Gabby Douglas; nor a ballet dancer like Misty Copeland or Yuan Tan—although I *was* impressed by Boston Dynamics' dancing robots, this year. A cyborg would not be a better basketball player than Michael Jordan or LeBron James (even if they were no longer 'in their prime').

Nor could a computer program be a better composer than Beethoven or Stravinsky. (Although admittedly, some people like David Cope and Donya Quick have written 'composition' programs that produce music that some listeners can't distinguish—after listening to short phrases, at least—from a 'real' composition by, say, J.S. Bach.)

And will computers ever be able to, say, duplicate what a *standup comedian* does? (Although again, there *are* some people writing computer programs to produce puns, and certain 'formulaic' jokes; but I predict these programs would always get booed off the stage on 'Improv Night' at a comedy club.)

Consider even some more pragmatic, down-to-earth matters: Robots can put together an automobile; but can a computer put together a *building* to house the central computer center of a company like Google or Apple? That is, can it bring together and assemble the necessary concrete, girders, wooden floors, and plexiglass windows, and take care of all the complex wiring and electrical connections that the system will need to operate? And what if all the power at the computer facility goes off, due to a fierce tropical storm—would a computer be able to 'decide' whether it's worthwhile to fix up the facility after the storm, or whether it would make more sense to salvage what we can from the wreckage, and instead build a new facility somewhere further inland? And if the decision to move the facility is made, would the computer be able to pack up the usable materials from the station, and then physically move them to the new location, and get it up and running again?

A computer outpost established on another planet (say, a station to monitor the weather conditions on Mars) and run by robots would eventually run down, and stop working. No natural 'reproduction' will ever take place to replenish the declining robot population; and when they ran out of raw materials (metal, electrical wiring, etc.), I doubt that they would be able to go digging for raw materials, set up a factory, and manufacture a new supply of robots.

Some people seem to hope that having an electronic 'copy' of me on a distant planet would constitute a kind of 'immortality.' I don't agree. Even if there were a robotic 'copy' of me on this distant planet, this robot will eventually wear down and stop functioning, and be nothing more than 'dead metal.' (And if a program *imitating* me—which passed the Turing Test—was still stored somewhere in a secured digital 'archive,' so what? *I* would still have long since passed away.)

For me, the 'hope' I have for the future is not in the machinery, but in the intelligent *living beings* that have created this machinery. If life will ultimately be extinguished in our own world (such as through an ecological crisis, or nuclear/biological war), and our solar system 'dies' when the Sun runs out of fuel, then I would still hope that life exists elsewhere—and perhaps in abundance. But all of the nonworking machinery that is left over here would not constitute any 'future.'

6. God, Spirituality, and Religion

Most people in Western cultures (including atheists), if asked, "What do you think 'God' is, or would be?" they would probably reply along the lines of, "A perfect, unchangeable being, who is eternal, all-powerful, all-knowing, and present everywhere." Such a response summarizes pretty well the traditional *attributes* which are ascribed to God, by most Westerners.

If you ask a typical (and reasonably 'orthodox') Christian, "Where did you *get* these ideas about the attributes of God?" a large portion of them will probably reply, "From the Bible." (Or, secondarily, "From my Church.") The 'biblical' response may be *sort of* 'true,' but I would suggest that it's at least *possible* to question whether the Bible—in and of itself—actually supports the *full degree* of such theological concepts, as they are presented in seminaries, and Theology classes. Let us consider some of the proposed 'biblical support' that is found in the King James Bible for some of these traditional attributes of God:

Eternal (always existing)

- Ps 90:2 "even from everlasting to everlasting, thou art God."
- Ps 102:12 "But thou, O Lord, shall endure for ever."
- Isa 41:4: "Who hath wrought and done it, calling the generations from the beginning? I the Lord, the first, and with the last; I am he."
- Isa 48:12: "I am the first, I also am the last."

Immutability (unchanging)

- Ps 102:27: "thou art the same, and thy years shall have no end."
- Mal 3:6: "For I am the Lord, I change not."
- Heb 1:12: "thou art the same, and thy years shall not fail."
- James 1:17: "the Father of lights, with whom is no variableness, neither shadow of turning."

Omnipresence (present everywhere)

- 1 Ki 8:27: "the heaven and heaven of heavens cannot contain thee."
- Prov 15:3: "The eyes of the Lord are in every place."
- Jer 23:24: "Do not I fill heaven and earth? saith the Lord."

Omnipotence (all-powerful)

- Ps 115:3: "our God is in the heavens: he hath done whatsoever he hath pleased."
- Job 42:2: "I know that thou canst do every thing."
- Jer 32:17: "there is nothing too hard for thee."
- Mt 19:26: "with God all things are possible."

Omniscience (all-knowing)

- Job 37:16: "Dost thou know ... the wondrous works of him which is perfect in knowledge?"
- 1 Chr 28:9: "the Lord searcheth all hearts, and understandeth all the imaginations of the thoughts."
- Ps 147:4-5: "Great is our Lord, and of great power: his understanding is infinite."
- 1 John 3: "God is greater than our heart, and knoweth all things."

(I took these biblical references from Charles Hodge's *Systematic Theology;* Louis Berkhof's *Systematic Theology;* Stephen Charnock's *The Existence and Attributes of God;* and the *Summa Theologiae* of Thomas Aquinas.)

These references certainly provide general *support* for the 'traditional' listing of God's attributes. But at the same time, they seem to fall short of the full, elaborate description of God's attributes that you would find in, say, a book of Systematic Theology, or a Catechism.

And of course, as these attributes are commonly presented at the 'lay' level, such simplified descriptions can create problems: for example, the common challenge, "If God can *do anything,* can He make a rock so heavy that He Himself can't lift it?" The problem here is perhaps with the simplified explanation of *omnipotence:* which presents God supposedly as "being able to *do anything.*" All traditional theologians acknowledge that God can't "make a triangle with four sides," nor "create a married bachelor," for instance—but this is hardly a valid objection to the theological doctrine of omnipotence. (A more difficult question would be, "Can God create a world of free moral beings who would *always* choose to do good, and never sin?")

The full 'theological' descriptions of God you would find in a standard theological reference work are part of the theological and philosophical lineage that has come down to us via the Greeks, then was substantially developed by the Medieval Scholastic philosophers, and such development has continued up until the present time. Theologians such as Augustine, Thomas Aquinas, John Calvin, and many others have elaborated greatly upon the biblical material, for example.

There are, of course, claims of various religions and sects to have received direct 'revelations' from God; thus, they may confidently assert, "We *know* what God is like, because He has *told* us!" The problem is, that it's difficult for nonmembers of these religions to evaluate all of such proposed 'revelations,' since they disagree strongly in many of their specific details. Islam and Judaism certainly do not agree with the traditional Christian view that Jesus was 'God the Son,' for instance. Sikhism and Bahá'í don't agree with Islam that Muhammad was the *last* 'prophet,' for another example.

For our purposes here, I propose to discuss a concept of God that is much less *detailed* than the traditional 'theological' versions, or any of the versions that are applicable to a particular religion or sect. I would simply consider the concept of 'God' to represent a *creative intelligence;* that is, 'creative' in the sense of being a 'creator,' 'designer,' or 'fashioner' of the things that exist. Such a God might have literally 'created' the universe *from nothing;* but could just as well have utilized pre-existing matter or materials, and molded them into desired forms. Some or all creatures might have been 'specially created,' or they might rather be the result of some relatively impersonal *processes* (including cosmological and biological evolution). And, although I will use the term

'God' in the *singular,* I would acknowledge the theoretical possibility that there might just as well be a 'committee' of Gods, as well as there being just one God. (Citing 'Ockham's Razor' here as a justification for monotheism is not very persuasive.)

In other words, I will propose our consideration of a somewhat 'minimal' concept of God. This stricture in no way suggests that this is *all* that God is, or might be. The Islamic Allah might well be the one true conception of God; or the Jewish YHWH could be the accurate portrait; or it perhaps is the Christian conception of God; or maybe the Sikh, or the Hindu, or the Zoroastrian, or the Bahá'í, etc. But my own present goals are more modest than this. Consequently, I am not going to attempt to defend the 'God' of traditional Western theology, with all the traditional attributes such as those I have listed above. (There are many 'apologetic' resources available, from all of these religions, for those who seek a more *specific* defense.)

Many (if not most) of the objections that Atheists and other skeptics raise against the notion of God are applicable specifically to the 'maximal,' fully-developed notion of God that we have inherited from Medieval theologians. Skeptics might pose questions such as these:

- "If God is all-loving, why does he intend to consciously torment some individuals in Hell for all eternity?"
- "If God has foreknowledge of all future events, why did the pathways of evolution result in so many 'dead ends' (e.g., extinct creatures), and seemingly 'wasteful' evolutionary lines that no longer exist?"
- "If God is all-powerful, why does he allow natural disasters like hurricanes and tsunamis to kill, and make homeless, millions of people?"
- "If God performs miracles, why doesn't he do any of them in modern times, when they can be filmed, and scientifically verified?"
- "If God intervenes in history, why did he allow monsters like Hitler and Stalin to murder so many millions of people?"

- "If God is supposedly 'just,' why does he permit only *certain* children to be born with birth defects, or to die of painful illnesses (such as cancer) at very young ages?"

I would observe that if one does not choose to defend the 'God' of traditional theology, many of these kinds of objections simply disappear: perhaps God *won't* torment anyone eternally in Hell; maybe God *doesn't* perform specific 'miracles' such as are recorded in the Bible; possibly God does *not* intervene in historical events (including wars) affecting human beings, and so on.

It should also be noticed that many things that we view as very *unfortunate* for us here on Earth, may simply occur because they had to take place in **physical reality**, which probably places severe limitations on the range of possibilities. For instance, the weather systems in place on our planet, that provide sun and rain to allow us to grow crops, will also at times produce fierce storms—and the harmful effects of these storms are amplified by the fact that so many of us these days live in crowded cities, or in beachfront homes, rather than in sparsely-populated inland locations. (And of course, the negative consequences of contemporary 'Climate Change' are due to *our* influence on the planet, and are certainly not attributable to God.)

It is quite true that innocent children are sometimes born with congenital birth defects. But if the world (that allows life here to flourish and reproduce) had to be constructed out of *physical materials,* maybe it is *not* possible to create a replicating process (such as DNA) that *always* works 'perfectly'—particularly if a certain amount of genetic *variation* must be allowed, in order for evolution (as well as simple and desirable human 'variations') to proceed. And, it should be observed, if we had created (and lived in) a much more peaceful and egalitarian society, children with special needs (including serious diseases, as well as physical defects) would routinely be given the special care and loving attention they need, to live their best and most fulfilling lives.

While some of the unfortunate things that often happen to us as individuals—e.g., death, divorce, loss of job, other economic problems, etc.—may cause even firm theists to wonder, "Why did God allow *this* to happen to me?", I would suggest that we might consider the possibility that God may not be 'controlling' and/or 'coordinating' all of the *specific details* of our individual lives. Yes, some people (New Agers, as well as theists) will insist that 'Everything happens for a reason'—but it may well be that there is no overall *intentional* 'purpose' underlying many, most, or even all of the events that take place in our lives; they may 'just *happen.*' (The question, then, is in how we *deal* with such challenges.)

Most theists don't suppose that everything that happens to, say, an individual chimpanzee, or a dolphin, or an ant, was specifically commanded by God (or, at least, not commanded for the 'good' of the creature); it may simply be the case that *we* are in a similar situation to such creatures. (And please note that since there are reportedly about *two trillion* galaxies in our universe, each of which probably has at least 100 billion or so individual *stars* in it—and who knows how many *exoplanets* there might be, orbiting these stars?—perhaps God has more than just *our planet* to be exclusively concerned with.)

To me, the most persuasive evidence that God (in the sense of being a 'creative intelligence') *is* indeed involved in the large-scale construction of the universe, and the various components of it (including planets such as ours) is what is often referred to as the 'Fine-Tuning' of the universe, with its various physical laws and 'constants.' There are any number of factors (such as the precise strength of the 'strong' nuclear force; the relative strength of the force holding electrons in orbit around the nucleus; the ratio between the masses of the proton and the electron, and so forth) which, even if they were only *slightly* different, would have made formation of stars and planets, much less life on Earth, impossible. Such factors, to many inquiring minds, create the impression that there definitely *was* an element of 'design' in the universe, and in our world.

And this is practically admitted by many prominent Atheists. For example, Richard Dawkins, in his bestselling book *The God Delusion,* argues that "If the odds of life originating spontaneously on a planet were a billion to one against, nevertheless that stupefyingly improbable event would still happen on a billion planets." Dawkins thinks that we just happen to be "sitting on one of those prodigiously rare needles," which is why we are able to even pose the question. But sticking with the observational evidence that we *do* have, I'm not at all persuaded that we *just happen* to be living in such a 'billion-to-one against' world; and this is even more so when scientists claim that the universe (or universes) came into existence 'out of nothing.' (Even if this 'nothing' they are talking about is actually a "boiling brew of virtual particles that pop in and out of existence in a time so short we cannot see them directly"; Lawrence Krauss, *A Universe from Nothing.*) And, quite frankly, I think that if orthodox *theists* were to propose such a 'billion-to-one against' occurrence, skeptics like Dawkins and Krauss would mercilessly ridicule them.

Certainly, there are valid objections that can be raised against the notion of 'Design.' But a lot of these objections are of the form, "If *I* were God, I would have done things better..." The famous agnostic lecturer, Robert Ingersoll, said in his lecture, 'The Gods,' that when he was asked by a 'very pious friend' to point out an 'imperfection' in the world, he replied, "I would make *good health* catching, instead of disease." (Please note that the human body *does* in many cases 'heal itself,' of course.) Such objectors may claim to prefer the eye of an octopus over the human eye, due to a 'blind spot' that humans have. (But observe that, unlike us, octopi are also *colorblind!* And when was the last time that you heard a wide receiver in football explain that he didn't catch a pass "Because the ball was coming down in my blind spot!")

Supposedly 'vestigial' structures like male nipples, tonsils, wisdom teeth, and the appendix may be cited as examples of 'poor design.' (Of course, males may have nipples simply to keep their physical 'symmetry' with females; tonsils and the appendix *do* have a function in the immune system; and wisdom teeth are probably removed more often these days than is medically 'necessary,' if they become impacted, etc.) But overall, I think that the examples of *very* well-adapted 'designs' in nature vastly outnumber those to which objections can be raised. Dawkins, in his book *The Blind Watchmaker,* even acknowledged that "Biology is the study of complicated things that *give the appearance* of having been designed for a purpose." (Emphasis added.)

There doesn't seem to be a lot of 'waste' in the natural world; our world seems to have a natural 'balance,' and is able to keep renewing itself, year after year. (At least, when we humans don't *interfere* with this 'balance.') Yes, various species have gone extinct (not that I particularly mourn the loss of T-Rex), but does that mean that they were 'without purpose'? Perhaps they were simply one expression of life, that there was no particular reason to perpetuate further. (And remember that, ultimately, *all* life on Earth will come to an end in 7 or 8 billion years, when our Sun turns into a 'red giant'; so *no* life on Earth will live 'forever.')

And if there are various uninhabited planets out there, that does not show that they are/were 'without purpose.' According to the *nebular hypothesis* of the formation of our solar system, the Sun and the planets formed after the gravitational collapse of a giant molecular cloud; some planets in this process would necessarily be formed 'too close' or 'too far away' from the Sun, to permit life as we know it. But that may simply be the price for there being *other* planets or moons whose surface temperature may be 'just right.'

But I think that a quite reasonable objection that can be made against the concept of God as involved in the 'Creation' and/or 'Design' of life here on Earth (which is my own belief), is to ask, "Well, if you don't think that God 'specially created' everything *ex nihilo*, then precisely *what, where,* and *when* did he do it? Did he just set in motion the process of evolution, and then simply allow it to do its work unassisted? Or does he maybe occasionally *intervene* in the process—perhaps by expanding the DNA 'table' or 'matrix' (which specifies what different DNA combinations produce) to allow certain combinations of amino acids to now code for 5% of a wing, or 15% of a feather? Or does he periodically 'specially create' certain *new* forms of life (such as whales that are now to live in the ocean), which explains why there is no detailed sequence of transitional forms leading up to them? In other words, what parts are 'designed,' and what parts *aren't?*"

Quite frankly, I have no idea. (Which, incidentally, is why I would hesitate to have a concept such as 'Intelligent Design' taught in the public schools; the concept lacks *specific details.*) The range of possibilities is very great: from an almost completely 'hands off' approach, to an approach that individually creates nearly each species, albeit over a vast amount of time. The fossil record clearly shows *overall trends,* but trying to make these details more *precise* is not possible, with our existing data. (And of course, any 'intervention' of God in the process would not be reflected in the fossil or geological record.)

But I'm not particularly worried about this lack. Atheistic cosmology, and evolutionary theory, have more than enough 'gaps' and pure *speculations* in them to offset their criticisms of Design as a 'God-of-the-gaps' argument. (The 'Natural-Selection-of-the-gaps' and 'Atheism-of-the-gaps' alternatives are equally subject to objections, as well.)

My arguments here are not likely to 'persuade' anybody to change their mind, either *for* or *against* God, Design, the Multiverse, a 'Universe from nothing,' the notion of a 'Creative Intelligence,' etc. But for many (most?) persons, such 'scientific' evidence may not be the most 'decisive' factor in their belief. A skeptic may be much-too-quickly rejecting God due to an inadequate or outdated concept of God that he/she was taught as a youth, or one that she/he sees portrayed in some passages of a religious text such as the Bible, etc. A 'believer,' on the other hand, may blithely assert that, "I *know* that God exists, because I just spoke with Him during my morning prayers." I would suggest that one's attitude towards arguments about 'fine-tuning,' or about 'randomness' and/or 'poor design' in the universe, are persuasive to individuals because they are basically consistent with our *overall* views of life and the universe.

A geneticist working with genetically-modified organisms (GMOs) may have no problem whatsoever in imagining evolution to be simply a series of purely random combinations of the ACGT amino acids in different ways. A person who endures a terrible individual tragedy (such as the loss of a spouse, or child) may conclude, "There *can't* be a God, if he would let the innocent suffer and die!" A person who is disgusted with purported representatives of particular churches (e.g., priests who abuse young people; ministers who sexually harass their secretaries; TV preachers who seem to be solely focused on money, etc.) may conclude that "God and religion are just a bunch of malarkey." A member of the LGBTQ community who has been attacked by 'Bible Christians' may read the Bible and conclude, "the 'God' of this book is a genocidal, misogynistic, homophobic racist; I want nothing to do with him!"

On the other hand, a 'believer' may see an evil-doing person who lives quite prosperously, and think, "There *must* be a God, in order to adequately *punish* this evil person in the next life!" A person who has been raised in a very 'fundamentalist' household, may fearfully profess to believe in God because "I don't want to spend eternity in Hell fire!" An Evangelical Christian may be disgusted by the social and political conditions of our country and the world, and fervently pray, "Lord, send the Rapture soon! I can't stand living in this world for much longer…!" A street preacher who has often been ridiculed for his faith may believe fervently in a God who will one day "Show all these unbelievers who mocked me that they were wrong!" A person who was mired in drug or alcohol addiction, but is able to overcome this addiction, may attribute this recovery to the intervention of God.

But there are also many cases in which a 'believer' continues to believe *despite* some seemingly 'disconfirming' evidence: For example, a parent who loses a child to cancer, may conclude, "I may not understand why God allowed this to happen, but I still believe in Him—and I look forward to being reunited with my child in Heaven." A Christian missionary who is imprisoned in North Korea may console himself by reciting Acts 5:41: "rejoicing that they were counted worthy to suffer shame for [Jesus'] name," and Job 13:15: "Though he slay me, yet will I trust in him."

There can also, of course, be much less 'self-centered' motives for belief. Someone may have deeply emotional responses to, say, walking out among nature's wonder, and concluding that "there must be a Creator behind all of this beauty!" A person who has some potential tragedy averted may feel a strong sense of *gratitude,* to a God who was felt to be a comforting presence during the period of uncertainty. And even former skeptics—such as philosopher Antony Flew, and astronomer Fred Hoyle—may ultimately turn to belief in God, claiming that the *scientific evidence* is what most convinced them.

Most 'ordinary' believers in God do not often recount any particularly *shattering* 'conversion' experiences, such as a Saul of Tarsus had. But most believers in God have probably had some experiences we would roughly categorize as 'spiritual.' For example, while one person after listening to a popular piece of 'inspirational' music (such as the final movement of Beethoven's 9th symphony), might simply have the reaction, "Well: that was a nice piece of music"—another person might have a much stronger, and more *emotional* reaction: feeling that, while listening to this music, it touched something *more*—something deeper, transcendent, and even 'eternal'; something suggesting the ineffable ideal of *Beauty*.

Similar feelings of the 'beyond' can be experienced through art; literature; enjoying nature; sitting in a beautiful church or cathedral; and even while experiencing *intellectual* feelings of 'awe,' during scientific discovery and investigation. Evolutionary psychologists may try to explain such feelings by a hypothetical appeal to, say, our sexual attractions; our fear and survival impulses; the herd instinct, and so on, but such proposed 'explanations' seem to fall far short of the actual *experience*. (Is there anyone who actually believes, "I like being out in nature because my ancestors could recognize 'good' habitats to live in; and I love classical music because it is a 'territorial signal' that helps cement my group's *social cohesion*"?)

Similarly, when engaged in prayer or certain types of meditation, a person may have the definite impression of *not being **alone***; of actually engaging in a form of *communion* with someone, who is not physically present. Might this feeling be illusory? Sure; imagination, wish-fulfillment, and all of the usual psychological explanations could be true. And to be sure, the fact that various people claim to have 'heard directly from God' *contradictory* things (e.g., which presidential candidate to vote for), and the fact that some purported 'messages from God' seem clearly self-serving (such as Oral Roberts' 1980 'vision' of a 900-foot Jesus, asking people to send money to Roberts), may give us pause, and invite considerable skepticism.

But perhaps the impressions that are most credible are those which are less specific; ones that are simply *feelings,* such as a feeling of comfort and reassurance during times of trial. Maybe an impression of love, and acceptance. Perhaps a feeling of gratitude, after one makes it through a difficult period. Could *these* also be illusory? Once again, certainly. But such a later 're-interpretation' contradicts the original impression the person had of the feeling.

And we should note that it is *also* possible that we, when later reflecting on such feelings, could be *expanding* on the actual feelings we had, and thus partially misinterpreting (or reinterpreting) them; for example, if we were now to interpret that earlier feeling of 'acceptance' as being a *blanket endorsement* of all of our future actions.

It should also be noted that if the views of skeptics about prayer and meditation were true (i.e., that prayer is simply "talking to oneself"), it might be more difficult to explain the 'arid/dry spells' that habitually-praying persons often report having gone through. Such persons may report a substantial *difference* in their daily experiences of prayer: on some days, "the heavens may seem to be *closed* to me," while at other times, "I felt that I nearly touched the face of God." Why would 'talking to yourself' be substantially less emotionally-compelling on certain days, than others?

The 'spiritual' dimension that we may occasionally experience in life is something that is beyond the 'ordinary'; it seemingly touches us at our deepest possible emotional (and intellectual) levels. Hearing a skeptical argument such as, "Your belief in God is just a *projection:* Since you feel uncertainty in your earthly life, you imagine that there is a divine 'father' somewhere out there, who will guard and protect you," just leaves us shaking our heads. The tears coming to one's eyes when listening to (or singing!) Handel's *Hallelujah Chorus;* the feeling of being 'at one with Nature'; the impression of feeling 'unconditionally loved and accepted' suggest to us that much *more* than mere psychological 'projection' is going on.

And it should also be acknowledged that if our 'spiritual' feelings and impressions could possibly be illusory, couldn't our *skepticism* about such feelings and impressions likewise be illusory—or, at least, viewed as attempts to 'rationalize such uncomfortable feelings away'? Could we argue that "Your *disbelief* in God is just an attempt to justify your personal preference for a world that is meaningless and anarchic"? Or, in some cases, might one's skepticism be attributable to frankly self-interested motives (such as justifying a decision to divorce one's spouse, and marry someone younger)? (And of course, many religious 'traditionalists' would argue that Atheists "Just don't *want* to admit that they are *morally responsible* to their Creator!")

Can our individual feelings suffice to convince someone else? A skeptic, for example? It's quite unlikely. Learning to appreciate fine art, classical music, or serious literature, takes time—and ultimately it must be experienced for oneself; and there are many people who never *have* such an experience. In the end, perhaps one can only 'point the way'; and share what has 'worked' for oneself, and suggest to others that they attempt to follow similar paths. If I recommend the last movement of Beethoven's 9th, or of Mahler's 2nd, or Copland's *Appalachian Spring* to you, you may listen, but simply be bored by them. Or: perhaps not...

It should be observed that 'spirituality' and 'religion' are **not** necessarily the same thing; even public opinion polls are now recognizing the increasing number of people who claim to be "spiritual, but not religious." Buddhism and Taoism are both considered to be 'religions' (and in geographical regions where they are predominant, they have popular ceremonies and rituals that certainly *function* as a 'religion'), and I suggest this is because they both cultivate experiences of *spirituality*. I would define 'spirituality' as **personal experience that is thought to be related to a *transcendent reality*.** The *Tao* or 'Way' of life, the *Nirvana* or 'Enlightenment' of Mahayana Buddhism, are not connected to an explicit 'God,' or to an eternal 'soul' that we may possess; yet a Trappist monk such as Thomas Merton can find considerable 'common ground' with a monk from a Zen monastery.

People can, of course, go deeper into this area of spirituality; we tend to want to *share* our deepest feelings with others, for example. We may also want to intellectually *understand* such experiences. This may lead us to create formal *religions,* which (at their best) can be sources of tremendous satisfaction and comfort to us; but (particularly when they become associated with secular political powers) they can also be the source of much societal *distress*—as when creeds and catechisms seek to *control* what one thinks and feels. The societal result of some overly-powerful religions can lead skeptics to (quite rightly) seek to eradicate such religions from the face of the earth.

But (with the possible exception of Islam, in certain countries) religions are seemingly wielding less and less secular political influence in the world. In our own country, children are not *required* by the State/civil authority to be baptized, confirmed, married, and/or buried by a church. We don't have to pay the 'church tax' that citizens of many European nations (such as Austria, Denmark, Finland, Germany,

Sweden, and Switzerland) do—notwithstanding that their citizens may seldom or never attend *services* in such churches.

Secular persons in this country may utter dire warnings about the influence of the 'Religious Right,' but its influence has clearly waned since the 1980s, and it has not been able to stop (or even appreciably slow) the movement for full civil rights for LGBTQ persons, or to get abortion outlawed. So frankly, when religion is being practiced at the 'grass roots' level, I don't see why it should cause any particular objection from a nonreligious/nonspiritual person. That is why the attacks of the so-called 'New Atheists' early in the 21st century struck me as both unnecessary and counterproductive. (The 'exceptional' case of Islamic suicide bombers and terrorists notwithstanding, homicidal 'nuts' are as likely to be atheists—who, after shooting up a school or a dance club, then kill themselves—as they are to be members of a fundamentalist sect.)

Religion at the grass roots level *is* definitely an ongoing source of inspiration for many. There is a level of 'comfort' in knowing that, if one is a spiritual 'seeker,' there are others with similar feelings whom you may gather with on Friday, Saturday, or Sunday, and whose advice in 'spiritual' matters may be very helpful to you. And one might find that even a weekly *sermon* provides a chance to reflect on matters other than our day-to-day survival, and help one to 'recharge my batteries' for the coming week.

And one may even find there that there *is* considerable value in studying traditional 'scriptures.' For example, the suggestion that God speaks to us in a "still small voice" (1 Kings 19:12); or Jesus' advice in Matthew 6:6 that one should pray in *secret,* rather than to be seen publicly. And (a personal favorite of mine) the divine guidance, "I have set before you life and death, blessing and cursing: therefore choose life..." (Deut 30:19)

In the end, much of life is a great mystery. But it's one that is well worth exploring... with all of one's heart, soul, and mind.

7. Life After Death?

"We look for the resurrection of the dead, and the life of the world to come." So states the Nicene Creed, one of the most ancient and important creeds of Christianity. This Creed is recited verbatim during the services of many 'liturgical' churches in the Christian tradition.

At one time, belief in life after death was nearly universal: not just in Western society, but in all the world's religious and spiritual traditions— as well as among most philosophers. Even well-known skeptics such as Thomas Paine confessed in Part One of *The Age of Reason*, "I believe in one God, no more, and I hope for happiness beyond this life."

But this situation has changed. The rise of scientific investigation of the material world has given rise to numerous marvelous advances in biology, medicine, and pharmacology—but it has also, in the eyes and minds of many, discredited traditional beliefs about the existence of [1] a 'resurrection of the dead,' to come in the future, and/or [2] an eternal spiritual 'soul' that survives the deaths of our physical bodies, and lives on for eternity.

The purely materialist/physicalist scientist may ask a believer in life after death, "Can you give me any *empirical, scientific* evidence that you or your 'soul' lives on after the death of your physical body? After all, doesn't damage to the physical brain—blows to the head; lesions in the cortex, and so on—adversely affect the 'mind' as well, which proves that there is no 'soul' which is independent of the brain?" To such materialists—as well as to many others—such challenges seem convincing beyond doubt. (I personally advocate the 'Identity Theory' of mind, which suggests that all of our conscious thoughts and perceptions *are* associated with neural activities in our brains.)

Of course, the way that such challenging questions are set up is probably 'prejudicial': If (as most believers in life after death suppose) the 'soul' is actually a *spiritual* entity, then by definition, it will probably not be subject to 'empirical' investigation—so if one is limiting one's allowable 'evidence' strictly to that which can be *physically observed* in a laboratory setting, then one will obviously not encounter any 'qualifying' evidence for life after death. Naturally, such an 'investigation' would be perceived by afterlife believers as unjustifiably 'limited.'

Consciousness itself is largely a mystery. The Australian philosopher and cognitive scientist David Chalmers (in his 1996 book, *The Conscious Mind,* and elsewhere) famously posed what he called the 'hard problem' of consciousness, which is basically: **why do we have** ***conscious feelings*** **which accompany events in the physical brain?** Neuroscientists can study the events taking place in the brain during vision, other sense perceptions, etc., and trace them to specific sections of the brain. But why would we even *have* conscious awareness of such events? Why would evolution have produced such sensations?— particularly if, as 'physicalist' neuroscientists often assert, our sense of conscious 'freedom of the will' is just an illusion.

Our consciousness doesn't seem to *make sense* in a strictly 'material' universe. But we all know that without our conscious awareness, there would be no **meaning** to our acts, and our feelings; we might just as well be nonconscious *zombies,* wandering around and automatically responding to sensory stimuli. If there were no conscious awareness, there would be no **understanding**, no sense of *purpose*. We would be no better than lifeless machines, operating automatically, until we ultimately break down for good. And trying to explain our *conscious awareness* in terms only of brain physiology has proved exceedingly difficult, if not impossible.

The 'empirical, scientific' argument was perhaps more persuasive up through, say, the mid-20th century. But since then, relatively 'mainstream' science has proposed a number of ideas that themselves do not presently have any 'empirical' basis for them. Quantum theory has a number of aspects which seem to violate the traditional view of 'empirical' causes for every action. Take the notion of 'Quantum Entanglement'— where an action affecting one part of a pair of 'entangled' particles, will apparently instantaneously affect the other particle—no matter how distant the other particle may be; and no visible 'cause' for the change to the separated particle can be detected. (If there *was* a physical 'cause,' it would seemingly violate the Einsteinian 'speed limit' of light—which seems doubtful.)

Modern computer technology has also made the notion of some kind of non-physical 'soul' less far-fetched than it would have seemed, say, a hundred years ago. Copies of 'data' (and such 'data' might also include our perceptions, feelings, and thoughts) can now sent wirelessly and almost instantly to a distant location; such 'backups' can even be periodically and automatically generated. The idea that "I just sent a copy of all the personal information of 350 million persons to a computer in Thailand, and I kept a backup copy of it in a portable hard drive in my office" would have seemed impossible in, say, 1940; but it doesn't even raise an eyebrow today.

Many monotheistic religions—such as Christianity, Judaism, Islam, Bahá'í, and Zoroastrianism—believe in the concept of a 'resurrection of the body.' That is, that the bodies of the dead will be raised from the grave, and transformed into eternal (perhaps 'spiritual') bodies. In the past, the idea of a long-decomposed body being 'resurrected' might have seemed quite implausible; but our modern knowledge of DNA (and how the 'instructions' for making us are actually encoded in a genetic 'language') suggests that we *could* conceivably be reconstructed 'from scratch,' by following the individual genetic 'code' that produced us in the first place.

But it is certainly not necessary to imagine that the *physical body* of someone (whose body might have been destroyed in a fire, or by an explosion; or which has simply decayed and decomposed over time) will somehow be reconstituted and reactivated, in order to believe in the possibility of life after death. In fact, many (most?) modern Jews and Christians believe that, after death, they will immediately begin another life, as eternal spiritual beings; what happens to their lifeless physical body is therefore, perhaps, not a matter of intense concern. So this raises the question: just what *is* the 'minimal' requirement for someone to be able to claim that *they* 'live' after their death?

An Eastern religious concept (most closely associated with Hinduism, and some varieties of Buddhism) suggests that the ultimate goal of human life is *not* to 'live forever' as an individual being, but rather to be '*Free* from the cycle of birth and death,' and to ultimately have one's consciousness dissolved into the Divine—like a drop of water merging (and thus losing its individual identity) into the ocean. This certainly *could* be our ultimate 'end'; and the idea has a certainly mystical attraction to it, to many. But this concept would certainly represent a rejection of what nearly all of us in the Western world think of as constituting 'life after death'; so I will not go further into this possibility.

Another concept is that 'Eternal Life' is more a *quality of life* that can be experienced *now*, rather than being the perpetuation of our individual selves in a postmortem existence. Such a believer might observe, "I am experiencing *eternal life* right now." However, as with the 'drop of water merging into the ocean' illustration, if this kind of 'Eternal Life' does not include any continuance of our own unique individuality after our physical death, it (again) does not constitute what is ordinarily considered to be 'life after death,' so I will also discuss this idea no further. (If the consciousness of a person who claims to be currently experiencing 'eternal life' is going to *vanish* after the person's death, then I would suggest that such a concept is misleadingly labeled as 'eternal.')

Many believers in life after death seemingly imagine themselves as still looking somewhat like 'themselves' after death—perhaps in a realm such as Heaven. (Of course, with suitable improvements: no congenital facial deformities; no blindness or deafness; no gray hair or bald heads; no unsightly 'pot bellies' or 'big butts'; full sets of perfectly white teeth; no glasses or hearing aids needed, and so on.) But do they imagine themselves at a particular *age?* And what about family members and friends? Should one's parents after death continue to appear to be *older* than oneself? And what about unborn babies, or infants and children who die young—what age would they appear to be? I would suggest that a physical appearance—or even 'physical appearance' at all—is not *essential* to the notion of life after death; a *disembodied* consciousness would still constitute 'life' after death.

For comparison, consider the question of our identity after we awake from sleeping: how can we be sure that we are the 'same' person as we were before falling asleep? As we know, the cells in our bodies replace themselves at different rates (i.e., it's not true that '*all* of our cells are replaced every 7-10 years'; some cells last only for a few days, while others may last an entire lifetime); so how can we truly be the 'same person' we were before falling asleep? Or the 'same person' we were when we were born? What is it that constitutes our 'essence,' in other words? How can it be primarily our *physical* bodies, if they are constantly changing?

Without getting into the level of extreme detail that analytical philosophers would prefer, I would simply note that there is a **continuity of consciousness**, as well as the awareness and familiarity of our physical bodies, that we experience upon waking, and as continuing throughout our lives. Our body seems to be the same one we had before falling asleep; the world around us looks and smells and feels the same as we remember; we still have the same memories we had prior to sleep (we can probably even recall "what I was thinking just before I fell asleep"). So, while one could *imagine* that all our memories are simply fictitious implants, this is kind of like the argument that "the world might have been created five minutes ago, complete with memories and written records." Sure, one can *imagine* such a scenario; but it seems completely contrary to our actual experiences, and thus we dismiss the possibility.

What would be needed for this 'continuity of consciousness' to be recognized? Our earthly memories certainly contain lots and lots of material that is… well, frankly unnecessary: such as what our favorite brand of cereal was in the third grade; the words to a maddeningly 'catchy' jingle from a TV commercial; the location of everything in our desk at work; the brand of detergent we use to wash our clothes, and on and on. If literally *everything* in our earthly memories was not retained and available to our 'continuing consciousness' after death, this doesn't really seem to be an 'essential' characteristic. And thus, if our earthly brain *containing* all of these memories were destroyed by the process of decomposition after our death, that would *not* 'settle' the question; we "didn't really *need* all of that stuff, anyway."

On the other hand, some strong and characteristic memories and feelings *do* seem to be nearly 'essential' to the notion that **'I'** am living after my death. While recalling the name of every single person who was briefly introduced to us at a party may not be all that critical, certainly our continuing to experience strong emotions of love and attachment to, say, spouses, family members and friends, *would* seem to be something crucial to our sense of 'self.' (If we were told that our memories of such persons were to be erased from our memories at the time of death, we might very well object, "If I didn't remember my children, or my spouse, then that wouldn't be *me!*")

Of course, there are many other not-that-significant memories, thoughts, and emotions that may or may not seem crucial to our concept of 'self.' While remembering the precise flavor of our favorite kind of salsa may not be 'essential,' are some more general memories of our favorite *foods* important to our sense of self-identity? Or what about our tastes in music: would we still love Beethoven, the Beatles, John Coltrane, or Hip-Hop in an afterlife? Would we still have a 'favorite' sports team? Would we remember who we voted for in 1980, 2000, and 2020? Who knows? But I suspect that—once we were removed from the context of earthly life—such things as spectator sports and politics would seem much less significant (and perhaps not even be missed).

What about memories of extremely crucial 'turning points' in our lives? Such as when we realized who we wished to marry; or when we decided to seek treatment for an addiction; or when we chose to terminate or *not* terminate a pregnancy. And what about ethical choices: such as when we realized, upon reflection, that we had done *wrong* to someone, and we wanted to make amends for this injustice. Or what about 'spiritual' matters, such as when we had a sense of 'awakening,' or a religious conversion? Not everyone has a specific date/time of a critical moment they can pinpoint (admittedly, many Evangelicals can recall *precisely* when they made their 'decision to accept Christ'), but many or most of us have had any number of experiences we might term 'spiritual'—times when we felt *touched* by a power 'greater than ourselves.'

It might be a time when we were walking in the wilderness or sitting on a beach, and felt a sense of profound 'oneness' with nature, and with the world. It might be a time of scientific discovery, or some other intellectual realization, when we felt strongly we had discovered or encountered 'truth.' It might be the overwhelming sense of *love* we felt for a child, or other loved one. It can also include times of honest humility, when we felt *convicted* of our smallness, and inadequacy; a 'sense of *sin*,' some might call this. Nearly all of us, when 'reviewing' many of our words and actions in life, can feel a strong sense of regret, embarrassment, and even *shame* about ourselves.

The lack of persistence of such memories is one of the principal objections I have to the traditional concept of reincarnation. While some persons claim to be able to *recall* their 'previous lifetimes' (particularly with the assistance of the more *suggestive* forms of hypnosis), the vast majority of us in Western societies do *not* naturally and spontaneously have such memories. Yet, if the *purpose* of reincarnation is to enable us to 'progress' in our future lives—perhaps leading up to a final or ultimate 'union' with the Divine—this lack of recollection would seem to be a crucial deficiency (or at least, inconsistency) in the concept. And, if we are consciously unaware of the continuity of our lives, we still, as distinct individuals, will ultimately have to face up to the extinction of our *individual* consciousnesses and memories—which is what people most fear and regret about the idea of death.

Of course, this objection does not mean that reincarnation *isn't true*. Certainly, researchers (with Ian Stevenson perhaps being the most interesting) can gather testimonials and data from people who profess to recall details from previous lives—which can be researched, to see if they can be validated. But it's difficult to know precisely how 'accurate' and *detailed* a purported 'recollection' must be, for such 'validation' to be accepted. Also, one must also subtract out cases that are likely due to *Cryptomnesia:* that is, to latent and forgotten memories that are later recalled, but are believed to be 'new.' (The case of Virginia Tighe [Bridey Murphy] is a probable case of cryptomnesia, for example.)

But I find it interesting that the geographical areas of the world where rates of belief in reincarnation are highest are countries such as India and Myanmar, whose predominantly Hindu and Buddhist populations accept reincarnation as a doctrine. (Of course, belief in reincarnation is also relatively high in some Western nations, such as Hungary, Lithuania, Brazil, etc., as well as among many 'New Age' believers.) But if *all* of us are reincarnated again and again, shouldn't such recollections be experienced virtually *everywhere?*

The notion of reincarnation brings up the related issue of 'psychic' or 'paranormal' research. This is perhaps the most common way that 'evidence' is attempted to be provided for the reality of life after death: researchers trying the prove the existence of a 'spiritual' (or at least, a non-physical) dimension of life, will try to demonstrate the reality of

ESP, telepathy, clairvoyance, precognition, Remote Viewing, etc.—all of which have passionate supporters.

I must admit that I am rather skeptical of such claims. I certainly acknowledge that there are reams of data demonstrating that, say, mediums or other 'sensitives' can consistently guess the face of a specially-designed card with, say, 21.5% accuracy, when 'chance' would predict only 20% accuracy. (J.B. Rhine and his colleagues did loads of such tests at Duke University.) But I find this a pretty weak 'evidence' of psychic powers, and more suggestive of some fairly small flaw in the experimental methodology (perhaps some unconscious 'bias' on the part of a tester).

Quite frankly, I don't think it would be particularly difficult to conclusively demonstrate the existence of genuine ESP or telepathy: For example, suppose that I had printed a four-digit number (from 0001 to 9999) on ten thousand identical index cards; suppose further that I designed the numeric digits in such a way that all ten numbers were quite distinctive (e.g., a '7' would not be confused with a '1,' a '3' with an '8,' or a '6' with a '9'). The test subject would then be asked to psychically 'read' the cards. It would, probabilistically, be a 1/10,000 chance to 'guess' the entire 4-digit number, and a 1/10th chance to guess each individual digit of the 4-digit number—so tabulation of the results of such tests would be easy. And these numbers would be quite *objective,* and not subject to questionable *interpretations* as are, say, pictures or drawings. (E.g., "I see some reddish and yellowish things, sort of bundled up, maybe like a bunch of flowers, or else kind of like a pile or balls or marbles...") And by having such a relatively large total number of cards, someone with true psychic abilities would presumably be readily identified, since the expected 'chance' results would be very low. (Someone who correctly guessed more than a few 4-digit numbers correctly would be obvious.)

I have no problem with the notion of paranormal phenomena: its 'proof' would not upset my worldview in the least. But after reading a number of books on the subject, I have yet to see any really convincing evidence for it. So I am skeptical—yet also quite willing to be convinced, by future experiments. (If I had been living in the 19th century, I *definitely* would have joined the Society for Psychical Research.)

One 'semi-paranormal' phenomenon that I find *very* interesting, however, are so-called 'Near-Death Experiences' (NDE). These are cases where a person is in a life-threatening condition, and may even be pronounced 'dead' by medical personnel, but the person is later revived—and the person afterward tells of having had a remarkable experience while 'dead': meeting a 'Being of Light,' experiencing a 'Life Review,' being told to 'return to life' to accomplish some purpose, and so on.

I am quite familiar with all the objections to using NDEs as 'evidence' for life after death, such as: the fact that similar experiences can be produced by drugs (including those given to a dying patient for pain relief, such as ketamine), or by direct stimulation of certain parts of the brain. NDEs have also been attributed to lack of oxygen, as well as the neurochemical response of the 'dying brain,' etc. I am also aware that, although advocates may identify various 'common elements' of NDEs (consisting of six elements, or fifteen, or even more), no individual 'experiencer' has recounted *all* of these 'common elements,' and many report having had only a few of them. In fact, if you were to make a spreadsheet matrix—with column headings of all the individual 'elements' potentially experienced during an NDE—then added the data from all of these 'experiencers' into this matrix, there would probably be much more *dissimilarity* than *similarity*, when comparing the experiences of different individuals. And of course, there is also the obvious fact that—since the person was ultimately revived—the 'experiencer' was not *really* 'dead'; which, by definition, is a condition one does not *return* from.

These objections are all valid, in at least some cases. Nevertheless, I find it quite interesting that, if we were nothing more than our physical bodies, *why* would we have such experiences? What would be the 'evolutionary advantage' of being able to have such experiences (particularly in the days before modern medical resuscitation was possible)? Why isn't a person's experience simply *nothingness*, once respiration ceases and the heart stops beating, rather than there being a continuation of consciousness—with this period of unconscious 'nothingness' ending, once the physical body is revived? The notion that our consciousness can continue almost uninterrupted, despite an extreme medical condition of the physical body, seems to me suggestive of at least the *possibility* of 'life' after physical death. (And of course, nearly all such 'experiencers' believe NDEs are virtually *proof* of life after death; and their lives are often substantially altered, as a result of the experience.)

I wrote an entire book (*The Gift of God Is Eternal Life*) on the topic of Hell, Conditional Immortality, and Universalism, so I'm not going to deal with those topics here. But suffice it to say that even life in a 'Hellish' environment *would*, of course, be a 'life after death'—as would a finite period of conscious punishment, followed by eternal annihilation. But I remain unpersuaded that there is any valid reason (including 'God's justice') for a theistic God to preserve a person for all eternity simply for the purpose of tormenting him or her. (Even if this 'torment' is primarily the individual's own self-regret, rather than being placed in a literal 'Lake of Fire,' etc.)

The theological notion that one's free will is somehow 'frozen' at the time of death, so that repentance and change are no longer possible, also seems inconsistent to me. If there are evil beings, such as a Hitler or Stalin—who seem irredeemably 'set in their evil ways'—annihilation strikes me as a more appropriate fate, than an eternity of conscious torment; who would really *want* Hitler to live forever, while he was cursing and blaspheming God (or 'Providence')? (Although, along with Universalists, I might wonder if—perhaps after a few thousand years to "think their misspent lives over"—even many of the worst of persons on Earth might yet be 'redeemable.')

To recapitulate: to say that I am 'living' after my physical death, I suggest that I would need to have some continuity of consciousness being carried forward from my current life. But this continuity would *not* have to encompass every single detail of my earthly life as it is contained in my physical brain. So I think it's entirely possible that all the information and experiences contained in my physical brain could *die*, along with my physical body—but if the essential *essence* of myself were somehow preserved, this would constitute a legitimate 'life after death.'

But of course, the question is: **How** would this 'essence' be able to be preserved? I must admit that I really don't have the slightest idea; and

I'm unwilling to invoke 'spiritual bodies' or other speculative concepts in order to try and disguise my acknowledged ignorance.

Still, I don't think (and I've actually changed my opinion on this, over the years) that the idea of our surviving bodily death is incoherent or incredible—particularly not given some of the things we've learned from contemporary science. For example: The universe is filled with moving photons, that were emitted literally *billions* of years ago from very distant stars. If photons (as well as other forms of energy) can 'live' for billions of years, is it impossible to conceive that a bundle of energy constituting our personal 'essence' could also continue, perhaps indefinitely?

Remember that 'Quantum Entanglement' suggests that actions affecting physical entities in one place, can instantaneously affect physical entities in a very distant place; and also remember that String Theory postulates *physical dimensions* that we cannot perceive. Suppose that there was an 'energy-being' (or 'spiritual being,' if you prefer that term) which is a *copy* of our 'essence,' that exists in a 5th, 9th or 10th physical dimension that we cannot perceive directly. My physical body in our *present* 4-dimensional world could then utterly dissolve, while my 'essential copy' continues, somewhere else. (NDEs, as well as any of a wide variety of other 'spiritual' experiences, might be attributable to us being able to briefly become *aware* of this other dimension.)

It should also be noted that a 'life after death' would not necessarily have to constitute an ***eternal*** life—that is, a life that would *never, ever* end. While this suggestion may generate a chorus of disagreement, I personally don't have any particular objection to the idea of an individual post-mortem life coming to an end, at some point in the future. (I can definitely imagine running out of things to *do* after, perhaps, a mere 400 trillion years or so.)

Suppose that our 'life after death' ended (or, that we became a 'drop in the cosmic ocean') after, say, one thousand years (a 'millennium,' in biblical theology). Or, better: perhaps after 10,000 (or even 100,000) years—after you had had time to read all the books, learn to play all the musical instruments, talk to all of the interesting people, and visit all of the exotic places you never had time to, while living on Earth. If your life ended at such a point, you might well view it as having been 'fulfilled.'

Or suppose that we stretched this existence out into not thousands, but *millions* of years: we would then probably want to explore the universe, if only to get a 'change of scene.' But after exhaustively exploring a few hundred thousand exoplanets, would we eventually reach a point of feeling, "Ahh, this planet is also boring; frankly, if you've seen a million solar systems, you've seen 'em all"? In such a case, becoming a 'drop in the cosmic ocean' might be very *desirable...*

A major aspect of the tragedy of death in this world is that it often seems to occur far 'too soon'! The child who dies of cancer; the wife who dies during childbirth; the young parent who dies while her/his children are still young and very needful of parental love; the honest hardworking person who dies just months or days before retirement; the beloved family member who we wish we could have seen 'just one last time,' and so on—such situations cause much of our trauma over death. But the notion of one's life coming to an end after, say, eighty years on this earth, is not inherently 'tragic.' The conclusion, "He/she lived a good, long life," is a satisfactory consummation for most of us. And if we *were* to have that opportunity to reunite with our loved ones after death, that would be even *more* satisfactory—even if it did not continue *forever.*

But, for the sake of contrast, let's suppose that the materialists are correct, and that we really are nothing beyond our physical bodies; and that, once the physical body is dead, our life is over—forever. That doesn't inherently seem to be a condition to particularly fear, or regret. Certainly, one could object to one's death occurring right *now,* before we had an opportunity to say 'goodbye' to our loved ones, tidy up our financial affairs, etc. But still, I see no valid reason to want to 'Rage, rage against the dying of the light' (as Dylan Thomas's poem, *Do Not Go Gentle Into That Good Night,* suggests). Falling asleep at night is normally a *comforting* experience; not one to be feared, or resisted. Death, under the materialist theory, would probably be much like falling asleep, without waking. Our minds may initially be racing with thoughts when we first lay down to try to go to sleep; but ultimately, sleep comes upon us—just as death might come, perhaps, with a sense of resignation, and *acceptance…*

After the death of others, we can at least find some comfort in realizing, "They are no longer suffering, or having to deal with the many problems of this world. They are finally 'at rest.'" And if some of us had erroneously believed that we would live on after our deaths, and it turns out that we don't, so what? One presumably isn't going to have a conscious 'realization' of that fact, or experience a sense of regret; there would just be nonconscious nothingness.

But still, was living life as a dogmatic materialist so overwhelmingly *wonderful* that those who are believers in life after death have truly 'missed out'? Are the joys of believing in the Multiverse and 'A Universe from Nothing' truly so stupendous that they outweigh the benefits of all other belief systems—including the hope of being reunited with our deceased loved ones? In fact, I would think that it's far more likely that believing "This life is not the *end"* gave the believer in life after death much more comfort and reassurance than was had by the hardheaded skeptic, who boastfully advocated living a "life without comforting illusions!" (Which, incidentally, is an acknowledgement that such beliefs are indeed 'comforting.')

After death, according to the materialist, both materialist and believer are simply dead, and forever gone; so the materialist doesn't even get the satisfaction of telling the believer, "See? I told you so!"

Perhaps a less dogmatic skeptic could echo Tom Paine, when he testified, "I *hope* for happiness beyond this life." Paine said 'hope'—not 'believe,' or 'know.' I would suggest that the *hope* of a life after death—and the possibility of an ultimate *reunion* with loved ones—is certainly of great value to the grieving ones left behind after a tragic death. Would a dogmatic materialist really *want* to take away such a comforting hope? What would even be the point of such 'evangelization'?

Sometimes, even one's most fervent beliefs may be best *unarticulated...*

8. Does Life Have "Meaning"?

During my junior and senior years in college (after I had discovered Existential Philosophy), I frequently told friends and fellow students, "Life is meaningless." I recognize now that a major part of the attraction that this pessimistic expression had for me was that the phrase genuinely *shocked* my hearers (which I took a kind of perverse pleasure in causing).

That particular expression is not one to which I any longer assent; nor have I, for about four decades—but I think that the expression still conveys a certain degree of truth, to the extent that it suggests that there is not necessarily just *one* 'meaning' or 'purpose' or 'goal' of life— which applies universally to everyone, in every context and situation.

A number of my friends in high school and college (this was in the mid-1970s) were convinced that 'the Rapture' was going to take place 'within one generation after the return of the Jews to Israel'; which, seeing that these friends were all of the 'Pre-Tribulation, Premillennialist' view, meant that they figured that the Rapture had to occur not later than seven years before the end of a 40-year 'generation' after the 1948 founding of the State of Israel—in other words, not later than 1981 (1988 – 7 = 1981). According to this chronology, the (post-Rapture) 'End of the World' had to occur by 1988.

Obviously, it didn't happen. Even if you start counting a 40-year 'generation' from 1967 (when the Israelis captured Jerusalem during the Six-Day War), it still didn't happen. And even if—following Psalm 90:10—you consider a 'generation' to be *seventy* (or perhaps eighty) years, we still seem to be running out of time (from 1948) for the Pre-Trib Rapture to happen. But of course, you might instead consider a 'generation' to be *120 years* (based on Genesis 6:3)—which potentially can take you up to the year 2087 (1967 + 120)—by which point nearly all of us will be dead. (Personally, I conclude that this entire line of reasoning is simply *wrong.*)

But such interpretations can give sincere persons an intense evangelistic fervor (at times, nearly bordering on panic!). The famous American preacher Dwight Moody (1837-1899) exhibited this when he said, "I look upon this world as a wrecked vessel. God has given me a lifeboat and said, Moody, save all you can." And, if you accept Moody's presuppositions—namely, that those individuals who don't get 'saved' in this lifetime, are going to experience *eternal conscious torment*—this kind of attitude makes perfect sense, and is even kind of benevolent. (How would we view someone who sincerely believed that we were dangling over an eternal pit of fire, but didn't even try to *warn* us?)

Of course, most Christians have a much broader perspective on the purpose of our life here. For example, the *Westminster Shorter Catechism* (considered authoritative by many Presbyterian and Reformed churches) states its first question as: "What is the chief end of Man?" And the answer is, "Man's chief end is to glorify God, and enjoy him forever." A Catholic, on the other hand, might say something like, "The meaning of life is to prepare to be with God in Heaven."

Other religions have somewhat similar, but also somewhat different, perspectives. Orthodox Judaism might suggest that the purpose of life is "to elevate the physical world (*Olam HaZeh*) and prepare it for the world to come (*Olam HaBa*)—the Messianic era." Most Muslims would probably say that the meaning of life is more like, "To know, serve and worship God, our Creator, under His terms and conditions." Hinduism would probably be more likely to suggest that our purpose should be "to know and attain union with God." (Whereas a Scientologist might argue, "The goal of life can be considered to be *infinite survival*.")

By way of contrast, various psychologists, 'Self-Help' authors, and TV hosts may propose that the meaning of life is "investing in something larger than the self"; or perhaps, "To become the best version of yourself"; or even, "To leave the world a better place than how you found it." The American Humanist Association's *Manifesto III* recommends that we "lead ethical lives of personal fulfillment that aspire to the greater good of humanity." Philosopher and social reformer Jeremy Bentham formulated the 'Utilitarian' principle, according to which we should seek "whatever brings the greatest happiness to the greatest number of people."

Other viewpoints abound. Evolutionary biologists may suggest that our goal should be the replication of our DNA, and thus the survival of our genes. On a more 'financial' level, Malcolm Forbes (the publisher of *Forbes* magazine) is said to have coined the phrase, "He who dies with the most toys wins." (Not surprisingly, Forbes led a rather extravagant and materialistic lifestyle.)

It seems to me that the various worldly interpretations of our goal/ meaning/purpose are about as diverse as *we* are. For some people, their *career* may be their 'purpose'; for other people, their *family* may be the primary motivating factor; for still others, it may be a quest for knowledge, or the pursuit of art and creative expression. When it comes to life goals, clearly 'one size *doesn't* fit all.'

But it's also true that—for some of us, in some situations—life can actually be something that seems *burdensome;* to the degree that we might even want to take our own life. Probably all (or nearly all) of us have occasionally entertained passing thoughts of suicide. It may happen because of some 'external' factors, such the loss of a job; divorce; death of a loved one, and so on. The unhappy person may simply agonize, "I just want this *pain* to *be over!*" (Such an unhappy person is presumably expecting death to be a permanent *extinction* of the self.)

But of course, it's far from certain that death is simply 'extinction.' (I think of this every time the media tells a news story of some deranged person who randomly kills members of a crowd, or schoolchildren, and then kills himself; presumably, such monsters wouldn't kill themselves if they expected to *live on*, after killing themselves.) Most of the world's major religions (including, perhaps surprisingly, some branches of Buddhism) have a concept of an afterlife that is quite *unpleasant*—a 'Hell,' if you will; and persons committing suicide are sometimes said to end up there.

As I've written previously, I don't believe in the traditional Christian notion of a Hell consisting of 'eternal conscious torment'; but if there *is* some kind of life after death, it is certainly possible that it could include an existence that is much less *pleasant* than a 'heavenly' one would be. It wouldn't have to constitute a 'Lake of fire,' or include 'weeping and gnashing of teeth,' 'unbearable thirst,' or any of the other stark images found in the Gospels. Perhaps it would simply be a period of solitary reflection on the pain that you had caused *others* by your suicide: the family members and friends left behind, your responsibilities that are now imposed on others. It might also involve reflection on your lack of *appreciation* for all the 'good' that you had been given in life—and the sobering realization that now, you can't 'go back' and try to 'fix' things.

But of course, it's also quite possible that there *is* no kind of life after death; and that, at death, you really *do* simply cease to exist— forever. I find it interesting that, nowadays, such a perspective has become increasingly commonly-held, and is often promoted as being the 'rational, scientific outlook' on life. In this perspective, life is often viewed as being essentially 'random,' a 'chance event,' or just a 'fluke' in the 'cosmic Monte Carlo game.' We may or may not be the only planet that has intelligent life on it—but in this recommended 'rational, scientific outlook,' there was certainly no intention, forethought, or 'purpose' involved in our being here: non-living chemicals just somehow assembled themselves into living ones; the 'cosmological constants' and 'physical laws' that made life here possible may have been nothing more than simply one possibility in an infinite number of 'quantum wave function collapses.' Nothing will preserve human life after death, and our entire solar system is destined to simply come to an end some several billion years hence; and thus, everything we know is destined to simply end up on the cosmic 'scrap heap.' (And it may, or may not, be 'recycled' into another universe, later.)

But those scientists, philosophers, skeptics, and other pessimists who hold such views certainly have not *proved* these concepts, nor conclusively refuted all of the alternative views. But, just for the sake of argument, let us suppose that these pessimistic views are indeed true: are any of us significantly *harmed* by not accepting them?

According to this skeptical viewpoint, everyone from 'Traditionalist' Roman Catholics, to Jihadi Muslims, to Evangelical fundamentalists, to Deistic scientists, to fervent supporters of atheistic and materialistic evolution (charter members of the 'Richard Dawkins Fan Club,' so to speak) ultimately *dies*, and that's it: no rewards, no punishments, no regrets, no happy memories—just nothingness, forever.

If we were to ask such a skeptical proponent, "Why would I ever *want* to accept, or even *consider,* your world-view?" they might detail some of the more *extreme* 'sacrifices' that some religious believers may subject themselves to. (Celibacy, vows of poverty, extreme fasting, etc.) But the vast majority of modern religious believers are *not* depriving themselves of all possible creature comforts, in order to live alone in the desert, or to send all their money away to support overseas missions; they are *not* practicing celibacy, and may not be avoiding meat during Lent, either; they are mostly not spending 70 hours a month in 'witnessing' (as Jehovah's Witnesses 'Pioneers' do). For whatever 'sacrifices' most modern believers *do* make for their religion (a significant weekly donation placed in the Offering Plate, for example), they may feel themselves as having been *well-rewarded* for them.

And even those who *are* engaging in genuinely 'sacrificial' services (who, for all we know, may very well be silently reciting Second Timothy 4:8, and eagerly anticipating receiving their 'crown of righteousness' in Heaven when they die) may feel themselves as quite well 'repaid' for their sacrifices: They may testify, "I experience such peace and joy when I'm sharing Christ with an African or Indonesian child"; or "I feel *good* when I give 35% of my paycheck to my church, because they are doing so much *more* with it than *I* could have done'; or "by entering the Catholic priesthood, I feel that I am not just sharing my love with *one* person [a wife], but am sharing it with my entire congregation'; or "I used to work 80 hours a week for a corporation, just to help them make more money—but now, I'm working even harder, but for something that has genuine *meaning* and *purpose* behind it!"

Those who have studied philosophy have probably recognized this line of argument I am presenting as being a variation of 'Pascal's Wager,' that was proposed by the French philosopher and mathematician Blaise Pascal in his *Pensees* ('Thoughts'). I don't think Pascal's argument (basically, "You lose nothing if you believe in God and He doesn't exist; but you lose *everything* if you don't believe, and He *does* exist") is very effective as an **apologetic**; that is, as a way of persuading unbelievers to become Christians. For one thing, one cannot simply 'become a Christian,' as one could place a bet on the roulette table; a genuine conversion isn't just a simple matter of 'choice.' If you have firm intellectual reservations about Christianity or religion, for example, you can't just 'decide' to make them go away. (Yes, I know some Evangelicals will probably disagree with me, here.)

But I think Pascal's revised argument has considerable 'defensive' value for *religious believers*, who are being confronted by unusually antagonistic skeptics. The believer can say to the skeptic, "Look: if you're right, *both* of us are just going to die eventually, and disappear into nothingness. If I prefer giving 10% of my paycheck to my church, and you'd rather spend the same amount of money on tailgate parties for your favorite football team, so what? I don't find at all persuasive your 'multiverse' and 'many worlds' counter-arguments to the evidence I see for cosmic 'fine-tuning.' And even though you have 'alternative theories' for things like Near-Death Experiences, and divine healing, I have my own counter-arguments to *your* arguments! And, frankly, when I look at your life, I don't see a lot there that *attracts* me; so I'm quite content to just stay as I am."

The notions that 'the universe *came from nothing*'; that 'it was just *chance* that life happened to evolve from nonliving chemicals; time is the *hero* of the plot'; that 'the universe is just a meaningless and wasteful happenstance, that will ultimately burn itself out and collapse back into a bunch of black holes'; that 'if we eventually destroy the ecological balance of our planet, it'll just be another dead planet among quintillions of others,' etc., are frankly not particularly *appealing.*

If, indeed, there was very persuasive *evidence* backing up such unattractive notions (such as geologists and geochemists had, when arguing that the world and universe were much older than a simplistic reading of the Genesis account in the Bible would suggest), that would be one thing. But if their arguments are mostly based on hypothetical theories involving 'possible superpositions of quantum wave function collapses,' indecipherable mathematics, some rather speculative evolutionary concepts, and are also reliant on snarky critiques of some of the more 'off-the-wall' religious believers, there is no need for most of us (who believe that we *have* had experiences of the 'spiritual'; and think that the world we see around us is *not* exclusively the product of 'chance,' but shows considerable evidence of *design*) to want to adopt such a skeptical position.

One's life 'purpose' or 'goal' gives most of us sufficient reasons for carrying on, despite the not infrequent unpleasantness and pain of many of our earthly situations. It's understandable to feel anger and depression after the breakup of a marriage or long-term relationship; or about losing a job you had faithfully held for many years; or of having medical and physical problems which left you substantially unable to care for yourself, and so on. For such reasons, it makes sense to try to adjust one's goals in life to things that are achievable, and largely subject to one's own control. Goals like 'trying to make a better life for my children,' 'trying to make my spouse as happy as possible,' 'supporting charitable works as much as I can,' etc., are both worthwhile, and achievable.

Bertrand Russell opined in his 'What is an Agnostic?' essay that "Throughout the animal kingdom, animals ruthlessly prey upon each other. Most of them are either cruelly killed by other animals or slowly die of hunger. For my part, I am unable to see any very great beauty or harmony in the tapeworm." While Bertrand Russell is one of my very favorite philosophers, I think that this statement is a gross exaggeration. Animals in the world (those who are not being hunted by humans, at least) often feed and water themselves in a rather leisurely fashion; many of them seemingly have a great deal of time for rest and 'recreation.' (Observe the harbor seals sunning themselves in San Francisco Bay, for one example.)

If a wild animal is ultimately taken down by a stronger and faster predator, at least these animals didn't have the kind of *self-aware consciousness* that we humans have, so their suffering was not prolonged. And the bodily damage caused by parasites such as tapeworms is certainly far less than the damage caused by murders, rapes, ecological carnage, etc., that we *humans* cause to each other—but I note that Lord Russell wasn't proposing to get rid of human beings, on that account. (And by the way: tapeworms *are* rather remarkable creatures, in that they can grow their bodies to extraordinary lengths; and if a part of their body is damaged, it can grow back. Just avoid contaminated water, and undercooked meat, to keep free of them.)

There is certainly much in our world that is painful, unjust, and hateful. There are certainly natural disasters such as hurricanes, and wildfires; there are fatal diseases, that may even strike young children. But it is certainly within our power as human beings to have established a social order that would make such events much *less painful* than they currently are. In a better and more equitable social order, we wouldn't have caused the 'Climate Change' and 'Global Warming' which exacerbate wildfires; and we could have had our populations more evenly distributed and farther away from the coastlines, so that fewer of us were living in areas subject to hurricanes and floods. And even when disasters occurred, we could act swiftly to resettle and financially reestablish displaced families. When an occasional child was born with a harmful genetic condition, we could have established a long 'Waiting List' of parents who want to give such a 'special' child the extra care and attention it needs, if the birth parents are unable to do so. It's not the fault of Nature, nor of the physical universe, that our existing social, political and economic order is in such a mess.

But suppose that, in the end, our lives are (as Shakespeare's *Macbeth* observed) nothing more than "sound and fury, signifying nothing": so what? Even religious believers (nearly all of them, at least) think this is the fate of *animals;* and when it comes to the fate of *insects* (much less *bacteria*), no one supposes that they have any prospects of 'eternal life' to motivate and comfort them. Yet even such lowly creatures can live, feed, and reproduce (and even frustrate we 'superior' humans who are trying to *swat* them!). If we *don't* live eternally—and in this respect are therefore no different than all the other creatures—would this automatically make our lives 'meaningless'?

Simply having the use of our five senses is a tremendous blessing: To smell blooming flowers in the spring, to taste a delicious meal, to listen to a treasured piece of music, to sit and watch a lovely sunset, and to feel the gentle touch of a loved one, can be *indescribably* precious experiences; it is unfortunate that we often don't truly *appreciate* them, until one of our senses is taken from us. If we can't have such blessed experiences 'forever,' they do not thereby lose their value; if anything, it should make them even *more* precious to us. If we are no more than ants (or even bacteria) on a 'cosmic' scale, what difference does that make? We can still find love, happiness, and contentment in the lives that are given to us.

If I knew that my life was ending within the next fifteen minutes, I would naturally have a multitude of regrets: for not having spent more time with my loved ones, of not having provided more for our family financially, and for having 'wasted' so much precious time in unimportant matters. But I think my dominant emotion would *not* be regret, and self-recrimination. I think that I would reflect on the fact that I *have* found lasting love in my life; I *have* been able to express myself creatively; and my life *has* been relatively free of the extreme kinds of pain that many others have had to endure. I would be thankful for my many blessings, and I would hope that the last emotion I experienced before the end was a profound sense of:

Gratitude

PART B
TWELVE LAY
SERMONS

(Although I am not a Christian, and I basically only attend a church service for a wedding or funeral, I think it is somewhat unfortunate that the 'sermon' or 'homily' that many people attended to at least once a week is disappearing from our culture. Although far too many sermons preached in churches were poorly-prepared and boring, a good weekly sermon could be a very effective way of making us *thoughtful* about our lives, and our values. So I am here [in the spirit of Thomas Henry Huxley] providing some examples of what I might have said, if I ever found myself standing in front of a church congregation some Sunday morning.)

1. In the Image of God

Genesis 1:26-27, in the familiar words of the King James translation, reads: "And God said, Let us make man in our image, after our likeness: and let them have dominion over the fish of the sea, and over the fowl of the air, and over the cattle, and over all the earth, and over every creeping thing that creepeth upon the earth. So God created man in his own image, in the image of God created he him; male and female created he them."

Of course, we modern people are aware of the potential gender-discriminatory implications of God creating 'man,' and of 'him' being made in the image of God. Accordingly, many modern translations and paraphrases replace the generic term 'man' with other terms: such as 'humankind,' 'human beings,' 'humanity,' or 'humans.' But all translations agree that "male *and* female he created them," and that we were created "in the image of God." But just what does "in the image of God" mean, or imply? To find out, we need to continue reading in the next chapter—which contains a somewhat different account of the creation. I'm now reading from the New Revised Standard Version.

Scholars have also long noted that in Chapter 1, the word used for 'God' is *Elohim,* whereas Chapter 2 uses the term, *YHWH Elohim,* or 'LORD God,' with 'LORD' in all capital letters. In the account in Chapter 2, "no plant of the field was yet in the earth and no herb of the field had yet sprung up"; and "the LORD God formed man from the dust of the ground," and then "planted a garden in Eden."

So in Genesis 1, plants and trees were created on the third day, *before* humans—who were created as 'male and female' on day six. But in Genesis 2, the man Adam was seemingly created *before* plants; and after their creation, he was then placed in the Garden to till it. ('Adam,' by the way, is simply the Hebrew word for 'man.')

The text continues, "Then the LORD God commanded Adam, 'You may freely eat of every tree of the garden; but of the **tree of the knowledge of good and evil** you shall not eat, for in the day that you eat of it you shall die.'" It's interesting to note that Adam was *not* forbidden to eat of the 'tree of life,' which is mentioned in verse 9; it's also interesting that Eve hadn't yet been created, when this command was given.

Chapter 2 (v. 18-20) then has God saying, "'It is not good that the man should be alone; I will make him a helper as his partner.' So out of the ground the LORD God formed every animal of the field and every bird of the air, and brought them to the man to see what he would call them; and whatever the man called every living creature, that was its name. The man gave names to all cattle, and to the birds of the air, and to every animal of the field; but for the man there was not found a helper as his partner."

Of course, passages like this may give us pause: Did God really expect that Adam might find a suitable 'partner' from among the cattle, birds, and other animals? Some people will simply want to throw out the Bible entirely, on the basis of rather simplistic interpretations of such passages. But I would suggest that there may actually be some profound *wisdom* contained in these verses, if we look more deeply into them.

God then caused Adam to sleep, removed one of Adam's ribs, and He created a 'wo-man' from it. This 'wo-man' was not until later given the name 'Eve': which in Hebrew means, 'life-giver.' We are then told, "Therefore a man leaves his father and his mother and clings to his wife, and they become one flesh." Of course, neither Adam nor Eve had an earthly 'father or mother' to leave; so this passage is obviously reflecting the cultural needs of a later era. Now, however, we are getting to the real point of the story that I want to focus on: what it means for people to be made "in the image of God."

Let us note that in 2:25, the text says, "the man and his wife were both naked, and were not ashamed." Many of us have heard, and perhaps even some of us were sternly taught, that sexual intercourse was the 'Original Sin.' Well, Original Sin was clearly *not* having sexual intercourse, since in Genesis 1:28 God had told Adam and Eve, 'Be fruitful and multiply.' And of course, in chapter 2, God only forbade eating the fruit of the tree of knowledge of good and evil; he hadn't forbidden sexual intercourse. So in the Genesis account, it was their *disobedience* of God's command not to eat of that one tree, that was the transgression.

We are told that Adam and Eve were originally naked, but they were not ashamed; in this respect, they were like animals. Dogs don't wear clothes—except, say, when human beings put 'dog sweaters' on them in the winter—and they don't seem to have any sense of *shame* about this unclothed condition. On the contrary, dogs not infrequently *lick* their 'private parts' in public, and male dogs may also try to grab one of your legs, and … well, you get the idea. The point is that animals such as dogs aren't in the least *embarrassed* about being naked. So human beings in the Genesis story were originally like the animals, in their nakedness.

And, since Adam and Eve were not forbidden to eat from the 'Tree of Life,' it's not clear from the Genesis text that this status was ever intended to *change*. Adam and Eve might have just wandered around forever, eating fruit from the various trees, and being 'fruitful and multiplying.'

It's also noteworthy that there was no **meat-eating;** in Genesis 1:29, God gives humans "every plant yielding seed that is upon the face of all the earth, and every tree with seed in its fruit," and 2:16 only allows them to "eat of every *tree* of the garden"; so Adam and Eve would apparently have been *vegetarians.* And, interestingly, even the *animals* were only given "every *green plant* for food," according to Genesis 1:30.

But then, in Chapter 3 the serpent, who "was more crafty than any other wild animal that the Lord God had made," asks Eve if God had really said that they can't eat of 'any' tree in the garden; and she replied that God said, "You shall not eat of the fruit of the tree that is in the middle of the garden, *nor shall you touch it,* or you shall die." A prohibition by God against 'touching it' was not stated in Genesis 2, by the way; so is Eve 'adding' this, or was she told this at some other time, that was not recorded for us?

The serpent then tells Eve that if she eats of the tree of knowledge of good and evil, she will not die; and that "God knows that when you eat of it your eyes will be opened, and **you will be like God, knowing good and evil**." So Eve ate of the fruit of the tree; and then she gave some to Adam, who also ate. The text, by the way, doesn't say that the fruit eaten was an *apple*—notwithstanding the famous logo of Apple Computers, in which the apple has a bite taken out of it.

But after they both ate, "the eyes of both were opened, and they knew that they were naked." So they made clothes for themselves out of fig leaves. And then, "They heard the sound of the Lord God walking in the garden at the time of the evening breeze, and the man and his wife hid themselves from the presence of the Lord God among the trees of the garden. But the Lord God called to the man, and said to him, 'Where are you?'"

Now, Bible literalists usually suggest that this appearance of God was a 'theophany,' which is commonly defined as "an explicit appearance of God to a person." That's possible, of course; but it's also possible that the author's point was *not* to describe the Creator of the universe as a physical being, who likes to take a walk in the garden in the evenings, when it's cooler—but rather, the author is using this image to make a point in his story. In fact, such descriptions of God in the Bible should usually be viewed as an 'anthropomorphism,' which is basically creating a concept of *God* in **our** image, rather than *us* being created in **God's** image.

At any rate, for their actions, the serpent is condemned to crawl on its belly; women will henceforth experience pain in childbearing, and Eve is told that her husband "shall rule over you." Adam was condemned to have to toil to get bread to eat, and he would also be bothered by thorns and thistles as he worked.

Now, I would like to point out that nothing in the Genesis text suggests that this crafty serpent was *Satan*; that is a later interpretation—mostly by Christians, who in the Book of Revelation called Satan "that ancient serpent" (Rev 12:9, 20:2), and have also interpreted Ezekiel 28:13—"You were in Eden, the garden of God"—as referring to Satan. But actually, it seems curious that God would 'punish' *all* serpents—remember that 'normal' serpents can't *speak,* and they *naturally* crawl, rather than walk—if this serpent wasn't really 'one of their own,' but was actually Satan in disguise, and actually the one who deceived Eve.

As we saw earlier, in Chapter 3, the serpent tells Eve, 'God knows that when you eat of it **your eyes will be opened**, and you will be like God, knowing good and evil." And Eve observed that "the tree was to be desired **to make one wise**." And so she and Adam ate of the tree. This is the part of the story that Christian theologians have since called 'The Fall,' and some of them attribute all subsequent bad and unpleasant things in the world, to this primeval event.

We should note, however, that prior to their eyes being 'opened' after eating the fruit, Adam and Eve were *not* 'wise,' nor did they know 'good and evil'—because to know good and evil was to **be like God.**" They were aware, certainly, that they had been *told* by God not to eat of that tree, but they seemingly didn't have what we might call an 'ethical' or *moral sense*—a sense of knowing 'right' and 'wrong.' And this, I would suggest, is primarily what the text means by describing us as being made "in the image of God."

The Genesis text tells us that when God confronts them about their actions, they both try to shift the *blame:* Adam blames Eve—and, by implication, God—when he says: "The *woman* whom **you** gave to be with me, *she* gave me fruit from the tree, and I ate." Then Eve argues defensively, "The serpent *tricked me*, and I ate." So although both of them now try to shift or deflect the 'guilt' of their own actions, their very reactions show that, after having had their eyes 'opened,' they now possess at least the beginnings of this 'moral sense.' Now, they can feel shame, they are aware of their nakedness, and they have a sense of guilt—which they try to deflect to someone else.

When you are training a pet dog, and the animal does something we told them not to do, we may firmly scold them, saying, "Bad dog!" We might even smack the dog on the nose with a rolled-up newspaper. But do our pets really feel 'bad'? In other words, do they have a *conscience* or *moral code,* that they realize they violated, by their prohibited actions? I don't think so.

The dog may understand, in effect, "If I chew up that couch, or if I go to the bathroom on the rug, I'll get hit and yelled at"—and it may modify its future behavior, accordingly. But is there in the animal a genuine sense of having done something **wrong**, with this realization being the cause of their future change of behavior? In other words, can animals engage in what Christians call 'repentance?' I ask again, does a 'bad dog' really *feel* 'bad'? Or is this changed behavior just a matter of *conditioning,* such as animal trainers teach us to use?

I could be wrong, of course. A lot of pet owners will swear that their animals seem 'embarrassed' after doing something 'wrong'; they may even post cute videos of such an animal on YouTube. But in my opinion, a 'bad dog' doesn't really feel *bad,* in the sense that we mean when we tell a child, "Why did you hit your sister or brother? That was a *'bad'* thing to do!" We want children to develop this *moral sense;* and even our legal codes treat 'juveniles' differently from 'adults,' because we acknowledge that it takes *time* for young people to fully develop this moral sense.

Next, "the Lord God made garments of skins for the man and for his wife, and clothed them." I think it's interesting to note that, since all creatures were originally intended to be vegetarians, God now makes garments of *skins* for Adam and Eve—which presumably involves the *death* of the animal.

God then admits in Genesis 3:22, "See, the man has **become like one of us**, knowing good and evil." So the text seemingly acknowledges that it is 'knowing good and evil' that makes humans 'like God.' Adam was apparently intelligent enough when he was first created that he was able to think up names for all of the animals; yet he didn't know what 'good and evil' were—and thus he was not 'like God.'

God drove the couple out of the garden, and placed an angel called a 'Cherubim' to guard the entrance to the garden with a flaming sword, so that the tree of life was forever inaccessible to them. The text, by the way, is sufficiently vague in its geographical details, that we don't know *where* this garden was supposed to have been located, on our modern maps; probably somewhere is Mesopotamia, which was mostly in our modern Iraq and Kuwait.

Not until Genesis 9:3, after the Flood in the time of Noah, does God give humans permission to eat *meat*—and there is no additional restriction placed on this, except that "you shall not eat flesh with its life, that is, its ***blood***." This is the first mention in the Bible of meat needing to be drained of blood before its consumption—which is very important in the Jewish dietary laws, which are known as 'Kosher' regulations. So, humans are now being given more *complex* rules to follow.

An important 'moral' point is then made in Genesis 9:5-6: where God tells Noah, "I will require a reckoning for human life. Whoever sheds the blood of a human, by a human shall that person's blood be shed; for in his own image God made humankind." So, our being made in God's image also requires us to follow a code of *social justice,* and to carry out the appropriate penalties.

The 18th century Swedish naturalist Carolus Linnaeus, in his very influential 1735 book *Systema Naturae,* identified three 'kingdoms' in Nature: the Animal, the Vegetable, and the Mineral. We humans are certainly part of the 'Animal Kingdom,' in Linnaeus's system. And I happen to think that it's very important that we be concerned with the *welfare* of our fellow animals—such as when animals are being abused, or when there are species that are in danger of extinction. One doesn't have to belong to PETA, to have a proper concern about animal welfare.

Yet, we are also unmistakably *different* from the other animals. No other animals create technology, such as computers and cell phones; no other animals build churches, or cathedrals; no other animals have symphony orchestras, or football fields. And no other animals seem to even have a complex symbolic *language,* such as we have. The 'ape language' experiments of the 1960s, '70s, and '80s, as well as John Lilly's similar attempts to communicate with dolphins, were mostly quite disappointing. Apes, for example, do not seem to be able to progress beyond the level of a small child, in their use of American Sign Language, or other symbolic forms of communication.

Psalm 8:5 tells us that we humans have been made "a little lower than the angels." Unlike the angels, however, we don't 'live forever'— at least, not in our physical bodies. But we *are* also 'higher' than the animals, because we know what 'good and evil' are; we have a 'moral sense,' as well as sense of 'shame,' that are critical parts of what we call our *conscience.*

Let me conclude by once again posing the question, "What does it mean, to be made 'in the image of God'"? Well, it *doesn't* mean that we *look* like God, physically. God isn't a majestic-looking man with a long beard and gray hair, two arms and two legs, who sits on a throne in Heaven; that is *anthropomorphism,* which I mentioned earlier. Principally, Genesis tells us that to be in the 'image of God' means to know what 'good and evil' are; to have a *moral sense.*

How important is knowing what 'good and evil' are? Let us imagine, for a moment, that the Genesis story had included no tempting serpent; and that Adam and Eve had eventually eaten of the tree of life, and were able to live forever—except that, by not having eaten the 'forbidden

2. What are the Heavens Telling Us?

I'd like to focus our attention on two Psalms: Psalm 19, and Psalm 8. The first verse of Psalm 19 reads, "The heavens are telling the glory of God; and the firmament proclaims his handiwork." (NRSV) The 'firmament' in this verse is simply the sky: the 'vault' or 'arch' in which the stars seem to reside—which, to us, appears to be more or less like a *dome,* placed over the earth. Most of us have probably experienced going outside at night, and being very impressed by the stars above. That is the kind of emotion that is being expressed in Psalm 19: a sense of awe, and wonder.

Under ideal conditions, there are a little over 4,500 stars which are potentially visible on a very dark night, to those of us living in this hemisphere; although if we live in a city—particularly a well-lighted one, or one with polluted air—we may only be able to see a few hundred, and perhaps just a few dozen, stars at night.

But the stars visible to the naked eye aren't even the tip of the iceberg. With the invention of the telescope, utilized by scientists ever since Galileo, the vastness and deep complexity of the heavens became much clearer. We discovered that the stars are actually *suns,* like our own Sun—and that actually, they are often much *bigger* than our Sun, which is simply an average-sized star. We later thought ourselves to be situated in a 'galaxy' that we named the 'Milky Way,' based on its appearance as a hazy band of light. And up until the 20th century, we thought that our galaxy contained all of the stars in the entire universe.

But the American astronomer, Edwin Hubble (1889-1953), using the newly-developed Hooker Telescope at the Mount Wilson Observatory, discovered that what used to be called 'spiral nebulae'—which had previously been thought to be just clouds of dust and gas—were in fact too distant to be part of our galaxy; and, upon more precise study, they were found to be entire galaxies of their own.

Since 2017, astronomers have suggested that our universe may contain as many as two trillion galaxies; and that's entire *galaxies,* not simply individual stars. Our Milky Way Galaxy is estimated to contain anywhere from 100-400 billion individual stars. Multiplying that figure by two trillion galaxies, yields a number of stars that is … well, truly staggering; and it makes us realize that the few thousand stars that we can see with our naked eyes are a nearly infinitesimal part of the whole.

For many of us, this realization only serves to increase our sense of awe at the universe in which we find ourselves. As Psalm 8 says, "When I look at your heavens, the work of your fingers, the moon and the stars that you have established; what are human beings that you are mindful of them, mortals that you care for them?"

And this sense of wonder is greatly magnified when we also take note of the fact that the universe proceeds in accordance with regular, predictable 'laws.' Sir Isaac Newton, one of the greatest scientific minds of all time, accounted with great precision for the movement of all the planets in our solar system in his very important book, the *Principia*— the 'Mathematical Principles of Natural Philosophy.' He concluded this book with the statement, "This most beautiful system of the sun, planets, and comets, could only proceed from the counsel and dominion of an intelligent and powerful Being ... This Being governs all things, not as the soul of the world, but as Lord over all; and on account of his dominion he is wont to be called Lord God.... The Supreme God is a being eternal, infinite, absolutely perfect...."

The English poet Alexander Pope (1688-1744) wrote a famous epitaph for Newton after his death: "Nature and Nature's laws lay hid in night: God said, 'Let Newton be!' and all was light."

I find it fascinating that, in recent years, scientists have discovered a great deal more about the physical 'constants' that operate in our universe. Such discoveries have actually been turned into a powerful argument for the existence of God, that is often called the 'Fine-Tuning' argument. The idea is that, if many of these physical 'constants' in our universe had been even *slightly* different, our universe, as well as our world, would not have been possible.

Some of these 'constants' include: the relative strength and range of the force which is holding electrons in orbit around the nucleus, and binding protons and neutrons together in an atom's nucleus; the precise degree of the electric charge of the electron; the ratio between the masses of the proton and the electron; the balance between the electromagnetic and gravitational forces, which control the initial formation, and then the stability, of the stars; the Earth's distance from the Sun, making it neither too hot, nor too cold here; the Earth's tilt on its axis, which provides our 'seasonal' changes, and so on.

The theoretical physicist Freeman Dyson (1923–2020), who was not a Christian, acknowledged in his book, *Disturbing the Universe,* "There are many … lucky accidents in physics. Without such accidents, water could not exist as liquid, chains of carbon atoms could not form complex organic molecules, and hydrogen atoms could not form breakable bridges between molecules… I do not claim that the architecture of the universe proves the existence of God. I claim only that the architecture of the universe is consistent with the hypothesis that *mind* plays an essential role in its functioning."

Of course, not all scientists agree with Dyson's conclusion. The prominent evolutionary biologist Richard Dawkins wrote in his best-selling book, *The God Delusion:* "This conclusion is so surprising, I'll say it again. If the odds of life originating spontaneously on a planet were a billion to one against, nevertheless that stupefyingly improbable event would still happen on a billion planets. The chance of finding any one of those billion life-bearing planets recalls the proverbial needle in a haystack. But … any beings capable of looking must necessarily be sitting on one of those prodigiously rare needles before they even start the search… however small the minority of evolution-friendly planets may be, our planet necessarily has to be one of them."

So, while Dawkins admits that the possibility of life arising on our planet is "stupefyingly improbable," and a "prodigiously rare needle," he suggests that since there are so unimaginably *many* stars out there—and presumably, also planets orbiting many or most of those stars—this vast number makes even such wildly improbable events statistically possible.

That's conceivable, I suppose. But I wonder what Dawkins would say if *Christians* were the ones proposing such a billion-to-one theory? Since he writes books with titles like 'The God *Delusion,*' I suspect that he would be quite *contemptuous* of such a proposal.

Frankly, rather than pin my life and hopes on such a billion-to-one shot, I'm inclined to think that the existence of so *many* of these 'finely-tuned' constants strongly argues that they are, in fact, *not* just 'lucky accidents'—but instead, these finely-tuned constants are a clear indication that they were *intended*. And in fact, that they suggest there is an 'Designer,' underlying the cosmos that we see.

And thus, I think we can all heartily agree with the Psalmist who wrote in Psalm 8: "O Lord, our Sovereign, how majestic is your name in all the earth!"

3. Revenge, and the Rivers of Babylon

You may know that in the biblical accounts of the history of the nation of Israel, the 'glory days' of kings David and Solomon were immediately followed by internal unrest among Solomon's sons. This resulted in the division of the nation, in about 930 BCE, into two parts: 'Israel' in the north, and 'Judah' in the south; the city of Jerusalem, which contained the Temple, was in Judah.

In about 722 BCE, the Assyrians conquered the northern kingdom of Israel, and forced its inhabitants to leave their homes and scatter into the world, where they soon lost their distinct identity as Jews. These exiles are sometimes referred to as the 'Ten Lost Tribes' of Israel.

The southern kingdom of Judah, however, continued on, until it was conquered by Babylon under King Nebuchadnezzar—the king who is well-known from the Book of Daniel—in about 600 BCE. Its inhabitants were, likewise, forced to move: this time, to Babylon. This latter deportation is the background for Psalm 137; of which I'd like to read the first few verses, from the King James Version:

> By the rivers of Babylon, there we sat down, yea, we wept, when we remembered Zion. We hanged our harps upon the willows in the midst thereof. For there they that carried us away captive required of us a song; and they that wasted us required of us mirth, saying, Sing us one of the songs of Zion. How shall we sing the Lord's song in a strange land?

'Zion' was originally a ridge between two valleys in Jerusalem; the term was eventually used to refer to the entire city of Jerusalem, and thus symbolized the entire southern kingdom of Judah.

In our own times, when millions of refugees from the Syrian Civil War are seeking asylum and refuge; or, closer to home, when tens of thousands have fled from cartels and corrupt governments in countries like Venezuela, Guatemala, El Salvador, and Honduras, we can perhaps feel considerable empathy for the Jews—who were forced by an invading army to leave their homelands—and for their bitter tears, as they remembered Zion, their homeland; and as they were mocked by the conquering Babylonians, who demanded that their captives sing them songs about their lost homeland.

The biblical prophets Jeremiah and Ezekiel were living during this time, which is known as the 'Babylonian Captivity.' Jeremiah is often called 'The Weeping Prophet' (see Jeremiah 9:1 and 13:17), due to his sorrowful predictions of the coming destruction of Jerusalem, in the biblical book that bears his name. The Book of Lamentations also recounts Jeremiah's sorrow *after* the destruction of Jerusalem and its Temple by the Babylonians. Let's continue reading in Psalm 137, which illustrates the longing that the Jewish people felt for their homeland:

> If I forget thee, O Jerusalem, let my right hand forget her cunning. If I do not remember thee, let my tongue cleave to the roof of my mouth; if I prefer not Jerusalem above my chief joy.

Around sixty years later, in about 539 BCE, the Persian king, Cyrus the Great, conquered Babylon. Not long after that, King Cyrus graciously permitted the Jewish people who wished to return to their homeland in Judah, to do so; the biblical books of Ezra and Nehemiah tell this story.

About six hundred years later, the Jews living in Judah were once again forced to leave their homeland, after they lost their ill-advised war against the superior Roman army, which ended with Israel's defeat in 70 CE. The Jews were thus scattered among the nations, an event now known as the 'Diaspora.'

But I think it's very interesting that, even during their long years of exile, the Jewish people continued to passionately hope to one day return to Jerusalem. In fact, at the conclusion of the Passover 'Seder' or 'feast,' which is celebrated annually by Jewish families, they conclude the ritual with the statement, "Next year in Jerusalem." So, like the author of Psalm 137, they were hoping to someday be able to return to their ancestral home. And of course, when the State of Israel was formed by a United Nations mandate in 1948, the Jewish people once again had a nation of their own, in their ancestral land. So a Jewish person living now *can* celebrate the Passover festival in Jerusalem—as they had hoped for so many years.

But alas, our Psalmist was not living in this later period. Psalm 137 is one of a number of Psalms that are technically known as 'imprecatory Psalms'; that is, Psalms which include some rather severe *curses* against others. And thus, he prays:

> Remember, O Lord, the children of Edom in the day of Jerusalem; who said, Rase it, rase it, even to the foundation thereof. O daughter of Babylon, who art to be destroyed; happy shall he be, that rewardeth thee as thou hast served us. Happy shall he be, that taketh and dasheth thy little ones against the stones.

In military conquests back in biblical times, it was not uncommon for the invading armies to slaughter children—particularly male children, who otherwise, might one day grow up to become part of an enemy army. The conquering soldiers would just grab a baby by its legs, and then smash the skull of the poor child against a stone! With the technique, one bloodthirsty soldier could decimate an entire nursery in just minutes.

While Psalm 137 is perhaps the most extreme illustration, there are other similarly violent sentiments found in other Psalms; for example:

> Psalm 35:3-8: Draw out also the spear, and stop the way against them that persecute me... Let them be as chaff before the wind: and let the angel of the Lord chase them. Let their way be dark and slippery: and let the angel of the Lord persecute them... Let destruction come upon him at unawares; and let his net that he hath hid catch himself: into that very destruction let him fall.

> Psalm 59:13-15: Consume them in wrath, consume them, that they may not be... And at evening let them return; and let them make a noise like a dog, and go

round about the city. Let them wander up and down for
meat, and grudge if they be not satisfied.

Psalm 109:9-13: May his children be orphans, and his
wife a widow. May his children wander about and beg;
may they be driven out of the ruins they inhabit. May
the creditor seize all that he has; may strangers plunder
the fruits of his toil. May there be no one to do him a
kindness, nor anyone to pity his orphaned children. May
his posterity be cut off; may his name be blotted out in
the second generation.

Psalm 139: 21-22: Do not I hate them, O Lord, that
hate thee? and am not I grieved with those that rise up
against thee? I hate them with perfect hatred: I count
them mine enemies.

Psalm 140:10: Let burning coals fall upon them: let
them be cast into the fire; into deep pits, that they rise
not up again.

When someone has done something against you, it is a perfectly
natural reaction to hope for something similarly bad to happen to them.
We may find ourselves praying, perhaps guiltily, "Get that guy, God!
Take him down!" This seems to be the attitude of the Psalmists, in those
cases I've just quoted. Even the apostle Paul, in his letter to the Galatians,
said of those who were causing dissension in the congregation about the
doctrine of circumcision, "I wish those who unsettle you would castrate
themselves!" (Gal 5:12)

But we, in modern times, seemingly have a big problem: namely,
that the sentiments expressed in these Psalms don't seem… well, very
'Christian'! After all, in the Sermon on the Mount in Matthew 5, Jesus
advised us:

You have heard that it was said, 'You shall love your
neighbor and hate your enemy.' But I say to you, **Love
your enemies and pray for those who persecute you,**

so that you may be children of your Father in heaven; for he makes his sun rise on the evil and on the good, and sends rain on the righteous and on the unrighteous. For if you love those who love you, what reward do you have? Do not even the tax collectors do the same? And if you greet only your brothers and sisters, what more are you doing than others? Do not even the Gentiles do the same? (Mt 5:43-47)

Some people, seeing the contrast between Old Testament passages like Psalm 137, and New Testament passages like Matthew 5, will conclude that "The Old Testament God is a God of Wrath and Vengeance; while the New Testament God is a God of Love"—but this is surely an exaggerated picture. There are many passages in the Old Testament about God's love, such as Nehemiah 9:17: "you are a God ready to forgive, gracious and merciful, slow to anger and abounding in steadfast love." Likewise, there are lots of passages in the New Testament about God's wrath, such as Romans 1:18: "For the wrath of God is revealed from heaven against all ungodliness and wickedness of those who by their wickedness suppress the truth."

Having a violent response to those who do violence against us and our loved ones is, unfortunately, quite 'natural.' But the fact is, that returning violence with violence is often counterproductive. Mahatma Gandhi and the Rev. Martin Luther King Jr. led multitudes of people to freedom, using the principles of nonviolent resistance. And, while such techniques were probably more effective against the British Empire and 'Christian' Americans living in the Southern states, then they would have been against either Nazi Germany or Stalin's Russia, these nonviolent techniques remain a far better ideal to strive towards, for modern Christians.

So I think that we can shake our heads at the author of the last part of Psalm 137, and say to him, "Taking revenge against the infant children of the Babylonians will *not* truly make you 'happy'; in the end, only *love* can make any of us happy."

4. Curse God and Die: The Problem of Suffering

The Book of Job is one of the most puzzling books in the Old Testament, as well as one of the most controversial. Bible literalists will often suggest that it was one of the earliest-written books in the Old Testament, whereas most modern critical scholars tend to think it is one of the most recent.

Among the puzzling passages in the book—and I'm using the New Revised Standard Version—is a reference in 40:15 to a creature called 'Behemoth,' followed by a reference in 41:1 to a sea creature called 'Leviathan.' A few translations suggest these creatures are a 'hippopotamus' and a 'crocodile,' respectively, but such translations are quite doubtful: we are told of Leviathan, for example, that "From its mouth go flaming torches; sparks of fire leap out. Out of its nostrils comes smoke, as from a boiling pot and burning rushes." (41:19-20) For our purposes, however, I propose to ignore such questions, and simply take the book as it is written.

The Book of Job is a most interesting and relevant book, however, because it addresses—at some length—issues that all of us have surely had: namely the problem of suffering, and questions such as, "Why does God allow evil in the world?" and "Why do bad things happen to good people?"

The first chapter of Job explains that Job was "blameless and upright, one who feared God and turned away from evil." He had seven sons and three daughters, thousands of ranch animals, and 'very many servants.' After his children had held a feast, Job would even offer sacrifices for them, saying cautiously, "It may be that my children have sinned, and cursed God in their hearts." So Job sounds like an all-around 'good guy,' right?

But then we come to verse 6, where we are told: "One day the heavenly beings came to present themselves before the Lord, and *Satan* also came among them." Satan? You mean 'Lucifer,' the *Devil*—the ultimate 'bad guy'? Yep, that's him. Although the New Testament has several dozen references to 'Satan,' he only appears four times in the Old Testament, apart from these first two chapters of Job. And the word translated as 'Satan' basically means 'Accuser,' or 'Adversary.' So:

what is Satan doing among the 'heavenly beings'—other translations call them 'sons of God' or 'angels'—who were 'presenting themselves before the Lord'? The book of Job never tells us.

God asks Satan, "Where have you come from?" and Satan explains that he has been walking around all over the earth. God then says to him, "Have you considered my servant Job? There is no one like him on the earth, a blameless and upright man who fears God and turns away from evil." So here, we have it directly from the mouth of God: that Job is "blameless and upright."

But Satan cynically points out how wealth much Job has, and then suggests to God, "But stretch out your hand now, and touch all that he has, and he will curse you to your face." So Satan—the Accuser, the Adversary—has proposed to God a *test* of Job. And then, amazingly, God replies to Satan, "Very well, all that he has is in your power; only do not stretch out your hand against him!" So, incredibly, we are told that God allows Satan to do as he wishes with Job's possessions, as long as he does not harm Job directly.

And so, Job is soon grimly informed that essentially all of his possessions have either been stolen or lost, and that all ten of his children have died in an accident. But, notwithstanding all these tragedies, Job simply states resignedly, "Naked I came from my mother's womb, and naked shall I return there; the Lord gave, and the Lord has taken away; blessed be the name of the Lord." And we are then told, "In all this Job did not sin or charge God with wrongdoing."

We have an English expression, "the patience of Job," and this passage is an excellent illustration of such patience. I doubt that very many, or even *any* of us, would have responded similarly, if we had lost all of our *children*, in addition to all of our possessions.

We continue in Chapter 2, where Satan is again presenting himself with the 'heavenly beings' before God, and God tells him that Job "still persists in his integrity, although you incited me against him, to destroy him for no reason." So, once again, God calls Job "blameless and upright," and even states that he was "incited against" Job by Satan "for no reason." But Satan again challenges God, "stretch out your hand now and touch his bone and his flesh, and he will curse you to your face." And, astonishingly, God again tells Satan, "Very well, he is in your power; only spare his life." Satan then inflicts "loathsome sores on Job from the sole of his foot to the crown of his head."

So now, even Job's wife has apparently had enough, and she says to him, "Do you still persist in your integrity? Curse God, and die." Yet Job replies to her, "You speak as any foolish woman would speak. Shall we receive the good at the hand of God, and not receive the bad?" And we are again told, "In all this Job did not sin with his lips." At this point, Satan—thankfully—drops out of the story.

But then, Job has three 'friends' who "sat with him on the ground seven days and seven nights, and no one spoke a word to him, for they saw that his suffering was very great." (2:13) But finally, Job "cursed the day of his birth," and he laments, "Why did I not die at birth, come forth from the womb and expire?... Or why was I not buried like a stillborn child, like an infant that never sees the light?" (3:1,11,16)

Job's 'friends' basically place the blame on Job for his own troubles. Zophar tells him, "For you say, 'My conduct is pure, and I am clean in God's sight.' But O that God would speak, and open his lips to you... Know then that God exacts of you less than your guilt deserves.'" (11:4-6) Eliphaz asks him, "Is it for your piety that he reproves you, and enters into judgment with you? Is not your wickedness great? There is no end to your iniquities." (22:4-5) And Bildad suggests, "How then can a mortal be righteous before God? How can one born of woman be pure? If even the moon is not bright and the stars are not pure in his sight, how much less a mortal, who is a maggot, and a human being, who is a worm!" (25:4-6)

With 'friends' like these, who needs 'enemies'? But remember, however, that those of us who have read the first two chapters of the Book of Job know that it was God himself who twice called Job "blameless and upright"!

Job finally replies, "I will say to God, Do not condemn me; let me know why you contend against me... How many are my iniquities and my sins? Make me know my transgression and my sin. Why do you hide your face, and count me as your enemy?" (10:2-3, 13:23-24) And Job gets fed up with his so-called 'friends,' and tells them, "As for you, you whitewash with lies; all of you are worthless physicians. If you would only keep silent, that would be your wisdom!" (13:4-5)

But Job also confesses, "For I know that my Redeemer lives, and that at the last he will stand upon the earth; and after my skin has been thus destroyed, then in my flesh I shall see God." (19:25-27) This is one of the rare verses in the Old Testament that clearly suggests a life after death—probably in the form of a resurrection of the dead, rather than as an 'eternal soul.'

Next, a young man named Elihu joins them, and he "was angry at Job because he justified himself rather than God; he was angry also at Job's three friends because they had found no answer, though they had declared Job to be in the wrong." (32:2-3) Elihu defends the goodness of God, and proclaims His majesty.

Ultimately, however, it is God who answers Job from out of a whirlwind, saying, "Who is this that darkens counsel by words without knowledge? Gird up your loins like a man, I will question you, and you shall declare to me. Where were you when I laid the foundation of the earth? Tell me, if you have understanding. Who determined its measurements—surely you know!" (38:1-5)

And God then proceeds to lay out in great detail all of the things about the world and the universe about which Job is ignorant—and after this devastating verbal onslaught, Job can only meekly reply, "See, I am of small account; what shall I answer you? I lay my hand on my mouth... I know that you can do all things, and that no purpose of yours can be thwarted... therefore I despise myself, and repent in dust and ashes." (40:3-4; 42:1-6)

God then commands Job's friends to offer for themselves a burnt offering, and tells Job to pray for them, explaining to these friends, "for I will accept his prayer not to deal with you according to your folly; for you have not spoken of me what is right, as my servant Job has done."

Then, after this has been accomplished, God "restored the fortunes of Job ... and the Lord gave Job twice as much as he had before." Job has another ten children—still seven sons, and three daughters—and "Job lived one hundred and forty years, and saw his children, and his children's children, four generations. And Job died, old and full of days." (42:10-17)

So, is this a 'happy ending' to the story of Job? No; not to me, at least. The book just leaves too many questions unanswered. Personally, I doubt that very many parents would feel themselves 'made whole' after having tragically lost all their children in an accident, by simply being given another 'complete set' of them.

And let me state clearly that I definitely *don't* think that the Book of Job contains anything like a literal *transcript* of conversations that actually took place in Heaven, or anywhere else. We should note that in the Hebrew Bible—that is, the Bible of the Jewish People, which Christians call the 'Old Testament'—the book of Job is placed in the *Ketuvim* or 'Writings,' along with books such as Psalms, Proverbs, and the Song of Songs; it is *not* placed with the 'historical' books, such as Judges, Samuel, and Kings.

So we needn't think that God was literally deciding Job's fate on the basis of a 'challenge' that Satan issued to him; this is a book of *literature,* that is making its point through telling a *story:* much as Jesus often taught by using parables. But I think there are some points that we can draw from this book, that may be of help to us.

First of all, let us note that Job clearly *wasn't* being 'punished' for anything he did—his tragedies had nothing to do with anything he had done; and in the book, God himself admitted this more than once. We all know from experience that sometimes, "bad things *do* happen to good people"—and this reality is echoed in the Book of Job. So accusations of *guilt* are very often a completely *incorrect* response to a tragic situation that befalls someone.

Secondly, many of us believe firmly that "Everything happens for a *reason*"; thus, when something terrible happens, we may agonize over it, asking ourselves, "Why did God give me cancer?" or "Why did God take my child, or my spouse?" In such anguished outcries, we are desperately seeking an *answer; a* 'Why?' in response to our deep and heartfelt pain.

But the simple fact is that, in many situations, there may not *be* any 'Why' for such trials that come upon us; or at least, none that we will ever learn, in this lifetime. So, although our contracting a serious disease, or losing a loved one, may indeed ultimately prove to be an occasion for profound learning and spiritual growth on our part, I don't think we can truly say that this tragedy happened *for* that reason—as if God was putting us through some kind of 'test,' that we can either pass or fail.

And thirdly and finally, I would simply observe that Job *never received an answer* to his many questions! Although his material wealth was ultimately more than restored, and he was given another group of children—perhaps even a *better-behaved* group than the first ones, so that he no longer needed to offer sacrifices for them, after one of their parties—Job was never told about the dialogue between God and Satan, much less given any *other* reason or justification for his suffering. But nevertheless, Job basically remained faithful to God throughout his trials; and ultimately, he once again found happiness, and lived a long and fulfilling life.

So in the end, I think that the Book of Job is simply counseling us to persevere, and remain true to ourselves during times of trial; and to not agonize over them, by trying to find some hidden 'meaning' behind our suffering. Job might have taken the early advice of his wife and cursed God—expecting to be struck down dead immediately afterwards—but he didn't; and thus, his example of steadfastness during trials can be a worthwhile example for us.

Our worldly wealth and loved ones may or may not be restored to us; but the 'patience of Job' may nevertheless be the best attitude to maintain during our own times of tribulation.

5. Is a Living Dog Better than a Dead Lion?

Our text today—using the New Revised Standard Version—is from the book of Ecclesiastes, which begins by explaining that it is "The words of the 'Teacher.'" The Hebrew word translated as 'Teacher,' is *Qoheleth*, which is also frequently translated into English as 'Preacher.' The book of Ecclesiastes has traditionally been attributed to Solomon, one of King David's nineteen sons, who was the wisest king of Israel. The book describes its author as "the son of David, king in Jerusalem" (1:1), and later adds, "I, the Teacher, when king over Israel in Jerusalem...'; so we are certainly intended to think of the book as containing the words of Solomon. But we should note that much of the book is written in the third person, as if by someone who has later edited or 'gathered together' these sayings. At any rate, for our purposes today, I will ignore such technical questions, and simply refer to the author or authors as the 'Teacher.'

The book takes a very 'philosophical,' and surprisingly pessimistic view of life. He says, "I, the Teacher... applied my mind to seek and to search out by wisdom all that is done under heaven; it is an unhappy business that God has given to human beings to be busy with. I saw all the deeds that are done under the sun; and see, all is vanity and a chasing after wind. And I applied my mind to know wisdom and to know madness and folly. I perceived that this also is but a chasing after wind. For in much wisdom is much vexation, and those who increase knowledge increase sorrow." (1:12-18)

The Teacher recounts his many acts: "I made great works; I built houses and planted vineyards for myself; I made myself gardens and parks, and planted in them all kinds of fruit trees. I made myself pools from which to water the forest of growing trees. I bought male and female slaves, and had slaves who were born in my house; I also had great possessions of herds and flocks, more than any who had been before me in Jerusalem. I also gathered for myself silver and gold and the treasure of kings and of the provinces; I got singers, both men and women, and delights of the flesh, and many concubines." (2:4-8)

But this activity did not bring him happiness: "I thought the dead, who have already died, more fortunate than the living, who are still alive; but better than both is the one who has not yet been, and has not seen the evil deeds that are done under the sun." (4:2-3) He laments, "There is a vanity that takes place on earth, that there are righteous people who are treated according to the conduct of the wicked, and there are wicked people who are treated according to the conduct of the righteous." (8:14) He continues, "under the sun the race is not to the swift, nor the battle to the strong, nor bread to the wise, nor riches to the intelligent, nor favor to the skillful; but time and chance happen to them all." (9:1)

He often waxes poetical, as in a famous passage that was turned into a popular song—first by folk singer Pete Seeger, and later by the rock group, The Byrds: "For everything there is a season, and a time for every matter under heaven: a time to be born, and a time to die; a time to plant, and a time to pluck up what is planted; a time to kill, and a time to heal; a time to break down, and a time to build up; a time to weep, and a time to laugh; a time to mourn, and a time to dance; a time to throw away stones, and a time to gather stones together; a time to embrace, and a time to refrain from embracing; a time to seek, and a time to lose; a time to keep, and a time to throw away; a time to tear, and a time to sew; a time to keep silence, and a time to speak; a time to love, and a time to hate; a time for war, and a time for peace." (3:1-8)

He summarizes (if I may momentarily switch to the King James Translation): "a man hath no better thing under the sun, than to eat, and to drink, and to be merry"; he later adds that "wine gladdens life, and money meets every need." (10:19) So apparently, the Teacher reaches a conclusion of something like, 'Party On!'

Nevertheless, the book ends on a reasonably 'orthodox' conclusion: "Fear God, and keep his commandments; for that is the whole duty of everyone. For God will bring every deed into judgment, including every secret thing, whether good or evil." (12:13-14)

Ecclesiastes is definitely a highly interesting book, particularly for those of a 'philosophical' turn of mind. But that's actually not the topic of this sermon: rather, it is the Teacher's thoughts about death, and what happens afterward. He says, "For the fate of humans and the fate of animals is the same; as one dies, so dies the other. They all have the same breath, and humans have no advantage over the animals; for all is vanity. All go to one place; all are from the dust, and all turn to dust again. Who knows whether the human spirit goes upward and the spirit of animals goes downward to the earth?" (3:19-21)

Later, he adds, "whoever is joined with all the living has hope, for **a living dog is better than a dead lion**. The living know that they will die, but the dead know nothing; they have no more reward, and even the memory of them is lost. Their love and their hate and their envy have already perished; never again will they have any share in all that happens under the sun... there is no work or thought or knowledge or wisdom in Sheol, to which you are going." (9:4-6, 10)

'Sheol,' by the way, is just the common grave; the place where all people—good and bad, including patriarchs such as Jacob and David—go to, after death.(See, for example, Genesis 37:35, Job 14:13 and 17:13; Psalm 49:15 and 89:48; and Hosea 13:14.)

But is it really true that "the dead know nothing"? That "they have no more reward"? And that "never again will they have any share in all that happens under the sun?"

To be sure, there are some purportedly 'Christian' groups, such as the Jehovah's Witnesses, who teach that when we die, we *all* enter a state of unconsciousness, which some call 'Soul Sleep.' Such groups rely on certain biblical 'proof texts,' largely utilizing these passages from Ecclesiastes, as well as a few other parts of the Old Testament, to make their case.

But relying primarily on books like Ecclesiastes and Job to establish points of *doctrine* is a flawed methodology. Let us remember that the Teacher of Ecclesiastes also recommended that we should "eat, drink, and be merry," and that "money meets every need"; but those sentiments certainly do not reflect anything like 'mainstream' Christian teaching.

The doctrine of 'Soul Sleep' is also certainly not traditional Christian teaching. On the contrary, the Christian church has always taught that humans have an eternal *soul,* that goes to be with God after death; but also, that one day, there will be a 'resurrection of the dead,' in which our souls will be united with a spiritual *body.*

To be sure, this doctrine was not fully articulated or understood until New Testament times; and particularly, not until after the disciples came to have faith in Jesus' resurrection. Still, in the later books of the

Old Testament, there are some passages hinting at this future doctrine, such as Isaiah 26:19, which tells us, "Your dead shall live, their corpses shall rise"; Ezekiel 37:12 likewise says, "Thus says the Lord God: I am going to open your graves, and bring you up from your graves, O my people; and I will bring you back to the land of Israel"; and Daniel 12:2 also informs us, "Many of those who sleep in the dust of the earth shall awake, some to everlasting life, and some to shame and everlasting contempt."

What does the church teach about the fate of the Christian after death? In the New Testament, Philippians 1:21-23 says, "For to me, living is Christ and dying is gain… I am hard pressed between the two: my desire is to depart and be with Christ, for that is far better." Second Corinthians 5:8 states, "we would rather be away from the body and at home with the Lord." And perhaps most famously, Jesus—while dying on the cross—tells the repentant thief, "*today* you will be with me in Paradise." (Lk 23:43) So, while the New Testament doesn't give us very much *detail* about the post-death state, at the very least it is certainly portrayed as 'being with Christ.' The fourth gospel likewise portrays Jesus as having told his disciples, "because I live, you also will live." (Jn 14:19)

The Christian doctrine of life after death is certainly not a 'peripheral' teaching; Paul—perhaps echoing the 'Teacher' of Ecclesiastes—wrote in First Corinthians 15:32, "If the dead do not rise, Let us eat and drink, for tomorrow we die!" And, to be sure, this 'live for the moment' philosophy seems to be the perspective of an increasing number of people, in our modern world.

But I often think that the general decrease of a belief in life after death has also had some very 'negative' consequences, in our society. Think of all the tragic murders that we have seen in the last decades: where evil people will shoot up schools, churches, workplaces, clubs, peaceful demonstrations, and any other place or occasion where people are gathered. It is not uncommon for such shooters to take their own lives when they are finally surrounded by the police—or to, more or less, allow themselves to be killed by the police: 'suicide by cops,' some law enforcement professionals call this.

What do such deranged persons expect to happen to them after their deaths? Presumably, they expect *nothingness,* a state of non-being. One doubts that they would take their own lives if they anticipated going directly into a condition of 'everlasting contempt,' as Daniel 12 puts it.

For someone with a belief in post-death 'nothingness,' the pessimistic beliefs of the Teacher of Ecclesiastes make perfect sense. And even Paul admits, "if Christ has not been raised, then our proclamation has been in vain and your faith has been in vain… If for this life only we have hoped in Christ, we are of all people most to be pitied." (1 Cor 15:14, 19)

But let us remember: the Teacher of Ecclesiastes lived *prior* to the New Testament proclamation. And that proclamation gives Christians firm grounds for *hope* of living on after our deaths; hopes of being reunited with lost loved ones—and hopes of this world not simply being a 'vale of tears,' which is followed by eternal nothingness. And that message of hope is one that this sorrowful world could benefit greatly from hearing from Christians, as well as from Jews, Muslims, and other persons of faith.

6. The Bible, Morality, and Social Justice

The Bible is the all-time best-selling, and most widely-printed book; perhaps 6 billion copies of it have been printed. In a distant second place is *Quotations from Chairman Mao Zedong,* with close to one billion copies having been printed. Third place goes to the *Quran,* with about 800 million copies having been printed. But of other books in the 'Top Ten,' four of them are closely related to the Bible: namely, the Church of England's *Book of Common Prayer,* John Bunyan's *Pilgrim's Progress, Foxe's Book of Martyrs,* and even the *Book of Mormon.*

However, there are any number of people today who are strongly opposed to the Bible, for a variety of reasons. One common objection is that the Bible is supposedly "irrelevant to today's pressing issues, such as political and economic matters, which it pointedly ignores. It therefore supports the status quo, including the growing economic inequality in most societies."

But I wonder if the people who hold such opinions have ever read the Book of James in the New Testament, which says in Chapter 5: "Come now, you rich people, weep and wail for the miseries that are coming to you. Your riches have rotted, and your clothes are moth-eaten. Your gold and silver have rusted, and their rust will be evidence against you, and it will eat your flesh like fire. You have laid up treasure for the last days. Listen! The wages of the laborers who mowed your fields, which you kept back by fraud, cry out, and the cries of the harvesters have reached the ears of the Lord of hosts. You have lived on the earth in luxury and in pleasure; you have fattened your hearts in a day of slaughter. You have condemned and murdered the righteous one, who does not resist you." I'm quoting today from the New Revised Standard Version, by the way.

The prominent atheist Richard Dawkins said in his book, *The God Delusion,* that "The God of the Old Testament is arguably the most unpleasant character in all fiction: jealous and proud of it; a petty, unjust, unforgiving control-freak; a vindictive, bloodthirsty ethnic cleanser; a misogynistic, homophobic, racist, infanticidal, genocidal, filicidal, pestilential, megalomaniacal, sadomasochistic, capriciously malevolent bully."

Yet it's interesting that even Professor Dawkins also wrote in his

2012 essay, 'Why I Want All Our Children to Read the King James Bible,' that the Bible "*should* be read"; however, he adds the qualification that it should be read "only as a great work of literature… [and] not a guide to morality."

Of course, Dawkins is one of the most prominent evolutionary scientists in the world. But I wonder: does he endorse the view of many evolutionists of previous generations, who promulgated the *Eugenics* movement: which advocated the involuntary *sterilization* of close to 100,000 persons in this country alone, who were deemed 'unfit'? Or does he accept the viewpoints of the 'Social Darwinians,' who believed that rich people were obviously 'superior' to poor people, as was demonstrated by their material prosperity? I suspect that Dawkins would strongly reject the views of some of *these* 'evolutionists.'

It seems to me that Professor Dawkins is being unfairly 'selective' in his reading of the Old Testament. For example, since there are, at most, a handful of verses in the Old Testament that Bible literalists cite as being opposed to *male* homosexuality in general, calling the Old Testament God 'homophobic' is clearly an exaggeration. The Old Testament has more verses than that condemning the eating of *pork*—so would Dawkins call it 'porkaphobic'?

But Dawkins is also ignoring the fact that many verses from the Old Testament—particularly from the Prophets—have been cited as a primary source of inspiration by a variety of contemporary advocates for social and political justice. Martin Luther King Jr., in his famous 'Letter from a Birmingham Jail,' for instance, cited the prophet Amos, quoting Amos 5:24, "Let justice roll down like waters and righteousness like a mighty stream." Even more famously, toward the conclusion of his epochal 'I Have a Dream' speech, Rev. King quoted Isaiah 40:4-5: "Every valley shall be exalted, and every mountain and hill shall be made low: and the crooked shall be made straight, and the rough places plain: And the glory of the Lord shall be revealed, and all flesh shall see it together."

Would Dawkins and other Bible critics reject the sentiments of the prophet Zechariah, who said, "Thus says the Lord of hosts: Render true judgments, show kindness and mercy to one another; do not oppress the widow, the orphan, the alien, or the poor; and do not devise evil in your hearts against one another." (7:9-10)

Or what about the counsel of Jeremiah, who tells us, "Thus says the Lord: Act with justice and righteousness, and deliver from the hand of the oppressor anyone who has been robbed. And do no wrong or violence to the alien, the orphan, and the widow, or shed innocent blood in this place." (22:3) Or how about Isaiah, who told the people, "learn to do good; seek justice, rescue the oppressed, defend the orphan, plead for the widow." (1:17)

I think it is also important to point out that verses like these are supporting and defending those who are the most *powerless* in modern society: the poor, the orphan, the widow, the alien. These biblical prophets are strongly condemning those who oppress such persons, who rob them, who cheat and defraud them. The prophets strongly advocate justice, and oppose violence; they preach righteousness, mercy, and kindness—and they attribute all these sentiments as based in, and originating from, their God. So I would ask Richard Dawkins: Are such as these truly the sentiments of a 'capriciously malevolent bully'?

And such verses are hardly limited to the Old Testament. Let us recall Jesus' formulation of the Golden Rule: "In everything do to others as you would have them do to you; for this is the law and the prophets." (Mt. 7:12) This principle is beautifully illustrated by Jesus' Parable of the Good Samaritan, in which a man who had been viciously attacked and robbed by thieves, is compassionately rescued and taken care of by a Samaritan man, had never even seen him before.

Jesus spurned worldly riches, telling the rich young ruler who approached him, "If you wish to be perfect, go, sell your possessions, and give the money to the poor, and you will have treasure in heaven; then come, follow me." When the rich man went away 'grieving' after hearing this, Jesus told his disciples, "it is easier for a camel to go through the eye of a needle than for someone who is rich to enter the kingdom of God." (Mt 19:21-24) So tell me: Is that "supporting the status quo," or endorsing "economic inequality"?

In another parable, Jesus described as 'righteous' those persons to whom he could say at the Last Judgment, "Come, you that are blessed by my Father, inherit the kingdom prepared for you from the foundation of the world; for I was hungry and you gave me food, I was thirsty and you gave me something to drink, I was a stranger and you welcomed me, I was naked and you gave me clothing, I was sick and you took care of me, I was in prison and you visited me." (Mt 25:34-36)

Jesus' disciple John told his fellow believers, "How does God's love abide in anyone who has the world's goods and sees a brother or sister in need and yet refuses help? Little children, let us love, not in word or speech, but in truth and action." (1 John 3:17-18)

So I heartily agree with Professor Dawkins that all of us should read the Bible: whether in the King James Version, or in a more modern version. But I think that we need to read the *entire* Bible, and try to grasp its many messages in their entirety, rather than just plucking out a few verses that may sound shocking, when divorced from their historical context.

And I would also strongly suggest that the Bible, in both Testaments, has a great *deal* to tell us about 'social justice' *and* morality!

7. Do Not Be Like the Hypocrites

Our biblical text this morning is from the Sermon on the Mount, in the Gospel of Matthew; I'm reading Chapter 6, verses 1-8, from the New Revised Standard Version:

> Beware of practicing your piety before others in order to be seen by them; for then you have no reward from your Father in heaven. So whenever you give alms, do not sound a trumpet before you, as the hypocrites do in the synagogues and in the streets, so that they may be praised by others. Truly I tell you, they have received their reward. But when you give alms, do not let your left hand know what your right hand is doing, so that your alms may be done in secret; and your Father who sees in secret will reward you.
>
> And whenever you pray, do not be like the hypocrites; for they love to stand and pray in the synagogues and at the street corners, so that they may be seen by others. Truly I tell you, they have received their reward. But whenever you pray, go into your room and shut the door and pray to your Father who is in secret; and your Father who sees in secret will reward you. When you are praying, do not heap up empty phrases as the Gentiles do; for they think that they will be heard because of their many words. Do not be like them, for your Father knows what you need before you ask him.

I think we all have seen people who "practice their piety before others, in order to be seen by them.'" For example, think of the white Hollywood celebrities who have adopted orphaned black babies—which would, seemingly, be a very good and generous thing to do—but then call a *press conference* to introduce them to us; and at the same time, to get free *coverage* of their charitable acts on TV news and entertainment shows. Or think of all the TV stars who make a generous donation to

AIDS research—and then are very careful to be *photographed* while doing so. Or the singers and rappers who invite the media to film them passing out turkeys to poor families at Thanksgiving and Christmas.

Or what about the Pop stars who appear at a 'Benefit concert' for victims of a hurricane—stars who, it's true, may not get *paid* for their appearance; but who nevertheless get a lot of 'free publicity'? Or what about the rich people—of all political parties—who announce that they are making a large donation to some 'political' cause during a lavish occasion, where they are surrounded by hundreds of the 'beautiful' people, who fervently applaud them for their actions?

Jesus said, "Do not be like the hypocrites." So: are such modern occurrences as I've just mentioned, valid examples of precisely what Jesus was condemning? Well, let me first suggest that we need to be very careful before we reach such a conclusion, because Jesus also advised us to "judge not, lest you be judged." (Mt 7:1) We cannot see what was truly in the hearts of famous and prominent people who perform such acts of charity; so it would be unfair to assume that they had predominantly *selfish* motives.

But Jesus also gave us some very specific examples, that will perhaps aid us in our interpretation of his words. Jesus gave a very interesting illustration about charitable giving, that I quoted earlier: he advised us to "not let your left hand know what your right hand is doing, so that your alms may be done in secret." Now, if only *one* of our hands knows what we're doing, and the other hand has no idea, that's pretty darn *secret!* So I would guess that Jesus would probably say that holding a press conference to announce our giving of alms, would not be a good idea.

Jesus says of such people, "They have received their reward." What does that mean? When I was quite young—and rather puritanical, I must admit—I used to think that Jesus was talking about a *negative* 'reward,' such as their 'eternal condemnation' after death, or something similarly horrible. But that can't be the correct interpretation: the word 'received' is in the *past tense*—so it's not something that's still waiting for them in the future.

Now, I think that what Jesus was actually saying, was that for someone who does something 'good' primarily to receive the praise and adulation of people, that praise and adulation *is* their 'reward,' and it's all they're going to get—they're not going to be given some 'special' place or reward in Heaven, for having done such 'good deeds' here on earth. They *do* indeed get a 'reward': but the reward is the just the praise and adulation that they were seeking... and that's *all* they get.

We should also note that seeking publicity for a 'good deed' may have some honorable motivations behind it. Some celebrity may want to use his or her fame to help bring some comparatively little-known charitable cause to greater public attention. The average person, for example, may not know about programs that allow American families to adopt needy children from other countries; or, the average American citizen may not know the grave seriousness of the threat of AIDS in Africa. A famous person appearing at a press conference may give some much-needed and much-appreciated *publicity* to a very worthwhile cause.

And of course, *publicly* performing our 'good deeds' may well be a two-sided coin: you can just as well be *criticized* for doing something 'good,' as be praised. A critic of the Hollywood stars who adopted the orphaned African baby may think cynically, "Oh, they're always off making movies, so they'll never even be *home* to 'raise' that child; they'll just turn the child over to the care of some nanny." Or about a star who donates money to some charitable cause, the critic may sneer, "Well, if I made as much money as they do, I would have donated a lot *more* than a lousy fifty-thousand bucks! And besides, it's also a tax writeoff for them, so big deal!"

Such practical uncertainties would, however, suggest one significant advantage in *God* being the one deciding whether or not our actions are hypocritical; since, presumably, God is perfectly *objective* when judging our motives. Proverbs 21:2 tells us, "All deeds are right in the sight of the doer, but the LORD weighs the heart."

To be sure, there is nothing inherently or even particularly wrong about wanting to be recognized for any 'good deeds' that we do. For example, if my wife doesn't happen to notice that I did the laundry for us this week (without being *asked* to do so), I may feel myself moved to quietly point it out to her; and, although I feel gratified when she then thanks me for doing this, I know that I would have felt better if she had just *noticed* my good deed 'on her own,' without the necessity of my bringing it to her attention—because that kind of 'spoils it.' And of course, there's nothing particularly wrong with making sure that your *boss* knows when you do something exceptional at work; but just understand, that while such actions may help get you a raise or a promotion at work, they aren't going to get you into *heaven!*

And, ironically, Jesus is *not* advising us to be *completely* 'selfless' in our actions—to a degree that we would refuse to accept *any* kind of 'reward' for having done something good; on the contrary, he specifically said that "your Father who sees in secret will *reward* you." So Jesus is apparently suggesting that we, as Matthew 6:20 advises us, "store up for yourselves treasures in *heaven*, where neither moth nor rust consumes and where thieves do not break in and steal."

Now, what about prayer? How do you feel about people who make a point of prominently praying *in public*? Politicians, for example (particularly during election years), may make a point of being photographed in front of a church, and holding a Bible—even though they haven't set foot in *any* church for years, much less cracked open a Bible.

And what about the people who are trying to get prayer re-introduced into the public schools? Well, let me first point out that no one can, or *would*, try to stop a public school student from going off by him or herself, and praying; in fact, that seems to be more or less what Jesus recommended to us about prayer: "go into your room and shut the door and pray to your Father who is in secret." Somehow, I don't think that a public school teacher reading off some school board-approved 'nondenominational prayer' before class is the kind of prayer that Jesus had in mind.

What about people who seemingly actually measure *on a clock* the amount of time they spend daily in prayer? "I spend thirty minutes on my knees every morning," such a person may proudly inform us. Is that what Jesus suggested? Well, I would observe that the Lord's Prayer— the 'model' prayer he gave to his disciples—is actually very short; you can repeat it in less than one minute. Yet it is a sterling example of covering everything that a prayer *should* cover.

You may wish to give a simple prayer of thanks to God, when

something good happens; or you may spend hours in agonized prayer, if you are wondering why some tragic event has struck someone you love. But remember: it's not the "many words" that matter, according to Jesus, but the attitude of one's heart.

And long, drawn-out prayers really aren't even necessary. Jesus told us, "your Father knows what you need before you ask him." So there is no need to give God an exhaustive accounting of every single bill that you need to pay, or every physical ailment that you want relief from; he already knows.

So, in conclusion: "don't be like the hypocrites"; just be honest and humble—and "your Father who sees in secret will reward you."

8. The Great Commandment

Many of the stories about Jesus in the Gospels have two, three, or even four versions, depending on which Gospel you read; and the account of Jesus giving us the 'Great Commandment' is no exception. Today, I'm using the version from Mark 12:28-31, which probably has the earliest version of the story, where we read in the New Revised Standard Version:

> One of the scribes came near and heard them disputing with one another, and seeing that he [Jesus] answered them well, he asked him, "Which commandment is the first of all?" Jesus answered, "The first is, 'Hear, O Israel: the Lord our God, the Lord is one; you shall love the Lord your God with all your heart, and with all your soul, and with all your mind, and with all your strength.' The second is this, 'You shall love your neighbor as yourself.' There is no other commandment greater than these."

Some people who refer to Jesus stating this 'Great Commandment' don't realize that he didn't 'invent' this commandment, but was actually quoting from the Old Testament; and he is actually quoting *two* commandments, not just one.

The first commandment is found in Deuteronomy 6:4-5, which says, "You shall love the LORD your God with all your heart, and with all your soul, and with all your might." 'Might,' in this case, means 'strength'—love God with everything that you've *got,* in other words. Matthew's version of this incident (22:34-40) quotes Jesus as saying, "heart, soul, and *mind*"; the version in Luke 10:25-28, for comparison, says we are to love God with our "heart, soul, strength, *and mind.*"

I think it's very interesting that when Jesus quotes this commandment from Deuteronomy, he apparently renders the last part of it, "and with all your *mind.*" The Greek word used in our Bibles for 'mind' is *dianoia,* whereas 'might' or 'strength' is *ischus.* So all three 'Synoptic' Gospels quote Jesus as more or less adding to the quotation from Deuteronomy that we should love God with our *minds,* as well as with our hearts and souls and strength. So much for the idea that 'faith' is supposed to just be an unthinking, blind *acceptance* of doctrines.

The second commandment cited by Jesus is found in Leviticus 19:18, which says, "You shall not take vengeance or bear a grudge against any of your people, but you shall love your neighbor as yourself."

The *setting* for Jesus' statement of the Great Commandment is different in the three synoptic Gospels, as well: In Mark, the scribe, seeing that Jesus "answered them well," asks his question in apparent sincerity. Whereas in Matthew's version, a lawyer—who was himself one of the Pharisees—asked his question to 'test' Jesus. And in Luke, it isn't even *Jesus* who quotes the two commandments: a lawyer wanted to test Jesus, and asked him, "what must I do to inherit eternal life?" And Jesus in turn asks *him* which commandment is the greatest? After the lawyer gives the proper answer, Jesus tells him, "You have given the right answer; do this, and you will live." Luke's Gospel then segues into the parable of the Good Samaritan, which provides an excellent example of 'loving our neighbor.'

According to Orthodox Jewish scholars, there are 613 'commandments' in the *Pentateuch*—the first five books of the Bible—which are collectively known to Jews as the *Torah:* which means 'Law' in Hebrew. There are commandments in the Torah about all kinds of topics, such as the requirements for worship in the Temple; there are commandments about what you have to do in order to keep 'ritual purity'; there are commandments about giving money to God; there are commandments about how to properly observe the Sabbath, as well as various annual festivals; there are commandments prohibiting idolatry; there are also commandments about family matters, and various legal issues.

We should understand that the Torah constitutes less than one-fourth of the entire Old Testament; which means that there are far more than 613 'commandments' or 'injunctions' that are contained within the *entire* Hebrew Bible. And of course, Christians are also asked to follow the various commandments which are found in the *New* Testament, as well. It can be very confusing to keep all of them straight, much less to try and follow all of them. But that's why it's fortunate, that Jesus simplifies it for us, in the Great Commandment.

Did Jesus say that the most important commandment was the need to sacrifice animals in the Temple? No, he did not. Did he say the greatest commandment was to give one-tenth of your money to the priests working in the Temple? No. Did he say that the most crucial thing was to make absolutely sure that you did no 'work' on the Sabbath? No. Did he say that what is essential is having your sons circumcised on the eighth day after birth? Or making sure that you gave your wife a 'bill of divorcement' before you can leave her? Or did he say that the most important commandment was for men to not sleep with other men? No; certainly not.

What Jesus focused on was *love:* and not just our 'other-worldly' love for God—but also including our very practical, 'this-worldly' love for our brothers and sisters right here. I think it's *very* significant that, out of all the 613 commandments in the Torah, Jesus identified two of them dealing with *love* as being the most important. But how was this love to be exhibited? Let me read part of one of Jesus' parables recorded in Matthew 25:34-40:

> Then the king will say to those at his right hand, 'Come, you that are blessed by my Father, inherit the kingdom prepared for you from the foundation of the world; for I was hungry and you gave me food, I was thirsty and you gave me something to drink, I was a stranger and you welcomed me, I was naked and you gave me clothing, I was sick and you took care of me, I was in prison and you visited me.' Then the righteous will answer him, 'Lord, when was it that we saw you hungry and gave you food, or thirsty and gave you something to drink? And when was it that we saw you a stranger and welcomed you, or naked and gave you clothing? And when was it that we saw you sick or in prison and visited you?' And the king will answer them, 'Truly I tell you, just as you did it to one of the least of these who are *members of my family*, you did it to me.'

The Greek word *adelphos*, which is translated here as 'members of my family' in the New Revised Standard Version, is rendered as 'brethren' in many other translations. Now, some interpreters think that when Jesus said this, he was only talking about our fellow Christians; in other words, they are suggesting that Jesus is commending the 'righteous' for helping out *other Christians*—but he wasn't asking us to help out someone that we just happened to encounter on the streets, or elsewhere.

Well, I don't necessarily agree with that interpretation. I think the writers of the gospels would have used the word 'disciple' or *mathetes* if that's what was originally meant by Jesus. 'Disciple' is used, for example, in Matthew 10:42, where Jesus said, "whoever gives even a cup of cold water to one of these little ones in the name of a *disciple*—truly I tell you, none of these will lose their reward."

In the parable of the Good Samaritan in Luke 10:25-37—which, remember, directly follows the story of the Greatest Commandment in Luke's gospel—Jesus talks about the Samaritan having pity and helping a total stranger, who had been attacked and left for dead by robbers... and who had just been ignored by two members of the 'priestly' class!

This stranger wasn't a 'disciple' of Jesus; he was just a person in need. After reciting this parable, Jesus asked his questioner, "Which of these three, do you think, was a *neighbor* to the man who fell into the hands of the robbers?" And the man replied, "The one who showed him mercy." And Jesus said to him, "Go and do likewise." So I think it is most likely that, to Jesus, *all* of God's children were his 'neighbor,' his 'brethren,' and the 'members of his family.'

So Jesus is telling us that the preeminent commandments are: Number One: to love God, and to love him with all our heart, soul, mind, and strength; but also, to love our neighbor, even as we love ourselves.

"Love God, and love your neighbor"; that's a pretty good summary of the message of Jesus. That's short enough to fit on one of those 'WWJD' bracelets that some Christians wear, which stands for 'What Would Jesus Do?' If someone ever asks you, "What do you Christians believe?" and they don't want a long, drawn-out answer, you can just tell them, "We believe that we should love God, *and* love our neighbor."

Those two commandments, "love God and love your neighbor,"

are inseparable; and Jesus said that they are superior to all of the other commandments: including the ones about building Temples, sacrificing animals, giving one-tenth of our goods to the priests, not eating pork, and all that other 'legalistic' stuff.

So what are we to do with these two commandments? After telling the parable of the Good Samaritan, Jesus told his questioner, "Go and do likewise." So that should be our mission: in this discouraged, broken-hearted, and depressed world, that seems to have no hope. Love people with the kind of love that God shows toward us.

9. Repentance, and Forgiveness

The first words that were spoken by the adult Jesus to the public are given in the gospel of Matthew (4:17): "Repent, for the kingdom of heaven has come near." (NRSV)

Just what did Jesus mean, by asking people to 'repent'? The Greek word translated as 'repentance' in the gospels is *metanoia;* this term basically means to have a change of mind, but it's much more comprehensive than just changing our minds: repentance involves a serious transformation of our thoughts, attitudes, outlook, and behavior.

When we do something wrong, most of us have been told ever since early childhood, that we're supposed to say, "I'm sorry." Now, the word 'sorry' can easily be used without it implying any genuine *repentance* whatsoever. Suppose we tell a child, "Tell your sister that you're *sorry,* for having hit her!" The child may speak those words out loud, but be secretly thinking, "But she hit me *first!"* and not in the least feel any genuine sorrow.

Today, we often no longer even say the words, "I'm sorry"; frequently, we may just say something noncommittal, like "My bad." Now, I suppose that, in theory, saying "My bad" *is* one way of admitting a certain degree of *responsibility* for something. But, as with saying that we are 'sorry,' there is no necessary connection with the kind of 'repentance' that Jesus advised; in fact, such expressions can be used as a way to just casually dismiss our hurtful actions as unimportant.

For example, we might say angrily to someone, "Fine, all right—*my bad,* okay? I already said I was sorry; so can we just forget about it, and move on?" What is *missing,* if we agree to 'just move on'? Well, for one thing, we're missing the *repentance* that Jesus spoke about; we're missing the requirement of making any *changes* in ourselves.

It's true that modern psychoanalysis has often tried to get us to move *beyond* feeling 'sorry' for things that we've done. All of us can quote 'Pop' psychologists—or even preachers—that we've seen on TV, who confidently advise us not to "waste our time regretting the past."

But I think it's interesting that the eminent psychiatrist Karl Menninger, in his book, *Whatever Became of Sin?* wrote the following:

Is no one any longer guilty of anything? Guilty perhaps
of a sin that could be repented of or atoned for?... I believe
there is 'sin' which is expressed in ways which cannot
be subsumed under verbal artifacts such as 'crime,'
'disease,' 'delinquency,' 'deviancy.' There *is* immorality;
there *is* unethical behavior; there *is* wrongdoing. And
I hope to show that there is usefulness in retaining the
concept, and indeed the word, **sin**...The assumption that
there is sin... implies both a possibility and an obligation
for intervention. Presumably something ... which can
be reparative, corrective... and that something involves
me and mercy—we want them, too.

And that's the focal point of 'repenting': one can then be *forgiven*, if
one sincerely wants to change. But I think it's interesting that Jesus' own
disciples were often depicted in the gospels as not being particularly
'forgiving.' In Luke 9:52-56, for example, we are told:

And he [Jesus] sent messengers ahead of him. On their
way they entered a village of the Samaritans to make
ready for him; but they did not receive him, because
his face was set toward Jerusalem. When his disciples
James and John saw it, they said, "Lord, do you want
us to command fire to come down from heaven and
consume them?" But he turned and rebuked them.

Of course, perhaps Jesus' most famous teaching about forgiveness
is found in Matthew 18:21-22, where Peter asked Jesus, "if my brother
sins against me, how often should I forgive him? As many as seven
times?" But Jesus said to him, "Not seven times, but, I tell you, *seventy
times* seven times." In other words, there is essentially *no limit* to our
obligation of forgiveness.

There is, however, a 'catch,' which Jesus explains in Luke 17:3-4:
"If another disciple sins, you must rebuke the offender, and **if there
is repentance**, you must forgive. And if the same person sins against
you seven times a day, and turns back to you seven times and says, 'I

repent,' you must forgive." So you don't 'forgive' a person who keeps doing something wrong again and again... *unless* there is that sincere element of *repentance*—of genuinely turning away from wrong, of transformation, of change.

And the Peter of the gospels is a person who really *needed* forgiveness. You will remember that, notwithstanding Peter's boast during the Last Supper that he would *never* deny Jesus, yet that very night, he did—three times. And when Peter realized what he had done, we are told that "he went out and wept bitterly." (Mt 26:69–75) But of course, Jesus *did* forgive Peter—who certainly 'repented,' and became the most stalwart and courageous *advocate* for Jesus in the early church.

We're told in Luke 23:34 that when Jesus was being crucified, he called out, "Father, forgive them, for they don't know what they're doing." So Jesus even pleaded with God to forgive those who were crucifying him. I'm afraid that if most of *us* had been present at the crucifixion, we might have expected (or wanted!) him to instead pronounce *judgment* upon the Roman soldiers, and command them to "Repent, and release me, or you will be destroyed!"

Jesus advised practicing forgiveness to everyone who listened to him. In Matthew 6:14-15, which is part of the Sermon on the Mount, Jesus said, "For if you forgive others their trespasses, your heavenly Father will also forgive you; but if you do not forgive others, neither will your Father forgive your trespasses."

Perhaps surprisingly, there are only a few times in the gospels when it is recorded that Jesus told the *people in general* to 'repent.' But there are many occasions when he told his *followers* to 'forgive.' Maybe the reason for this difference is that we cannot *control* the behavior of someone that we advise to 'repent'—but we *can* change our *own* behavior, and we can forgive those who have wronged us.

I think that the ultimate example of forgiveness is found in the story of the thief on the cross. In Matthew's account, we are told that both of the criminals who were being crucified along with Jesus mocked him—even as they themselves were being crucified! But in the account in Luke, we are told that one of the men 'repented,' saying to the other, "we indeed have been condemned justly, for we are getting what we deserve for our deeds, but this man has done nothing wrong." Then he said, "Jesus, remember me when you come into your kingdom." And Jesus told him, "Truly I tell you, today you will be with me in Paradise."

Imagine that: This man had done something deserving of capital punishment by crucifixion, which was the most cruel form of execution that the Roman world knew of. Yet Jesus, even in the very last hours of his life, showed that such a man *could* be forgiven, and even enter Paradise!

Of course, it's much better to not 'put off' repenting until the *last minute,* so to speak. For one thing, delaying 'repenting' until you are essentially on your *death bed* basically is an admission that you've wasted your entire previous life. And of course, who knows whether or not your 'repentance' is really *sincere?* Think of Mafia gangsters who may donate money to the church, have their kids baptized, confirmed and married in the church, and so on: perhaps they are thinking that, "No matter how many people I may have hurt or killed, I can say a few 'magic' words at the last minute of my life, and still go to Heaven." Frankly, that sounds pretty 'risky' to me.

The message of Jesus is clearly a message of forgiveness; and we *should* forgive others, as we ourselves wish to be forgiven. Now, it's perfectly true that if you forgive someone—perhaps an estranged parent, or a rebellious child, that you haven't spoken to in years—they won't necessarily *accept,* much less *appreciate,* your 'forgiveness.' That's fine; we can't control their reactions—yet we *should* be the ones at least making the *offer.*

We can control our *own* change of heart, however, and make the decision to 'repent' and change ourselves—but also to *ask* forgiveness of anyone whom we've wronged. Again, they may not be willing to forgive us—particularly if we've put off our own repentance for far too long; that's something that we can't control. But if we sincerely 'repent,' and change our ways, the path leading to reconciliation with those we've become alienated from will be much more likely to succeed.

And *reconciliation* is something that most people in this broken, hurting world desperately need.

10. All are One in Christ Jesus

Our reading is from Paul's letter to the Galatians, in the New Revised Standard Version:

> Now before faith came, we were imprisoned and guarded under the law until faith would be revealed. Therefore the law was our disciplinarian until Christ came, so that we might be justified by faith. But now that faith has come, we are no longer subject to a disciplinarian, for in Christ Jesus you are all children of God through faith. As many of you as were baptized into Christ have clothed yourselves with Christ. There is no longer Jew or Greek, there is no longer slave or free, there is no longer male and female; for all of you are one in Christ Jesus. (Gal 3:23-28)

In this statement, Paul says that Christians are no longer 'imprisoned' under the Jewish law, which was our 'disciplinarian' until Christ came. Now, Christians are "in Christ Jesus ... children of God through faith."

Let's break down Paul's statements. First of all, he says that "As many of you as were baptized into Christ have clothed yourselves with Christ." But what about professing Christians who *haven't* been baptized? Are they not included? Or what about people who were baptized in one form, rather than in another? For instance, the Catholic Church, the Eastern Orthodox Church, the Episcopalian Church and the rest of the Church of England, plus most Churches in the Reformed tradition—such as Lutherans, and Presbyterians—typically baptize *infants,* shortly after birth; while those following the Anabaptist tradition— '*ana*-baptist' means '*re*-baptism'—including Southern Baptists, Pentecostals, and many other Evangelicals, baptize only those persons who are old enough to make a 'profession of faith.'

Furthermore, people in some denominations may be baptized according to different 'modes': infants are typically baptized by sprinkling a few drops of water on the infant's head; children or adults may be baptized by 'affusion,' or *pouring* some water over the convert's head; or, as with most Evangelicals, baptism may be administered by full bodily immersion in water.

Is baptism a crucial doctrine? Well, it certainly is considered to be at least *very important* by a number of denominations. But I think we should all note that in his first letter to the Corinthian church, Paul was upset over the fact that baptism was becoming a source of quarrels and division in the church. So he told the church at Corinth, "I thank God that I baptized none of you except Crispus and Gaius, so that no one can say that you were baptized in my name. (I did baptize also the household of Stephanas; beyond that, I do not know whether I baptized anyone else.) For ***Christ did not send me to baptize but to proclaim the gospel.***" (1 Cor 1:14-17) So Paul didn't seem to be as strict about baptism as a lot of modern denominations are; and he even drew a distinction between *baptism* and 'preaching the gospel.'

Paul also said that "There is no longer Jew or Greek." Now, in the historical context from which Paul was writing, the word *Hellen,* which is translated as 'Greek,' most often referred to non-Jewish Greek-speaking persons—who were not limited to persons originating from the country of Greece. All of the New Testament books were written in Greek, for example, by persons who were in all likelihood born and raised as Jews. But many persons in the Roman Empire spoke Greek, since the Greek language and culture had been spread widely throughout the world by the conquests of Alexander the Great in the 4th century BCE. And of course, Paul himself spoke Greek, and he wrote all his letters in Greek—yet in his letters, he clearly intends 'Greek' to mean someone other than a born-and-raised Jew such as himself.

A somewhat different yet also related Greek word is 'Gentile,' or *ethnos,* which basically means 'non-Jew.' English New Testament translations may use these two words as somewhat overlapping, such as in First Corinthians 10:32 and 12:13, where some translations render the word *hellen* into English as 'Gentiles,' while a larger number of translations render it as 'Greeks.' At any rate, Paul's point seems to be that there should be no divisions in the church between those who are Jews, and those who are not.

Paul rejects another 'division,' when he says, "there is no longer slave or free." The whole issue of 'slavery and the Bible' is a complex one, that we don't have time to go into today. But for now, suffice it to say that the kind of 'servants' and 'slaves' that are mentioned in the Bible were not even remotely comparable to the persons cruelly subjected to 'chattel slavery' in the American South, prior to Emancipation. Under Southern 'chattel' slavery, slaves were treated as *property*, and they had no rights: slaves could be sold and resold, inherited, whipped, or even killed, just as the owner of a horse could do with his horse whatever he pleased.

"The 'servanthood' mentioned in the Bible was more comparable to the 'indentured servitude' that was common in early days of our country: when people would contact to work for someone for a set period of time—perhaps until the cost of their passage from Europe to this country was paid off—but after this period, they were free; yet even while they were working as 'servants,' they were still fully human beings, with rights. So those professing 'Christians' in the 16th through 19th centuries who tried to use the Bible to justify their evil practice of slavery were absolutely wrong—not only *morally,* but *theologically* and *historically!*

At any rate, Paul's point is that there should be no distinction in the Church between 'servant' and 'free.' In fact, in Paul's letter to Philemon—which all scholars agree was written by the apostle Paul—Paul actually advises a runaway servant named Onesimus to return to his master Philemon, who was in turn advised by Paul to accept Onesimus back, as a 'brother' in the faith. Paul was certainly not advising, say, a 1st century Frederick Douglass or Harriet Tubman to return to a state of chattel slavery; but he *was* advising Philemon that he should now treat his returning servant as a *Christian brother,* and not as a 'slave.'

The final example Paul gives is this: "there is no longer male and female; for all of you are one in Christ Jesus." Of course, this matter is still quite controversial in the Christian church, with some prominent preachers and teachers loudly and enthusiastically quoting Paul in Ephesians 5:22-24, where he reportedly wrote, "Wives, be subject to your husbands as you are to the Lord. For the husband is the head of the wife just as Christ is the head of the church... Just as the church is subject to Christ, so also wives ought to be, in everything, to their husbands."

Now, I think it's interesting that the people who love to cite verses 22-24, don't nearly as often like to quote verse 25, "Husbands, love your wives, just as Christ loved the church and gave himself up for her." Let us ask ourselves, how did Christ act toward his own disciples, who were the forerunners of the church? Did Jesus ever order Peter to get up, go get him a jug of wine, bring him a blanket, and then just *shut up* for the rest of the evening? Did Jesus ever sarcastically ridicule and put down John, or any of the other disciples? And can you even imagine Jesus ever *striking* one of his disciples? No, quite the contrary; Jesus told his disciples firmly that "whoever wishes to be great among you must be your servant, and whoever wishes to be first among you must be your slave." (Mt 20:20-26)

As we all know, there is still great 'division' within the Christian church on the role of women in the church: Can women be ordained to the ministry? Can women preach, and teach men? Our particular church and denomination, of course, place no restrictions whatsoever on what women can do: they can serve, teach, preach, minister, be ordained, serve as bishops, or anything else. We feel strongly that this is the correct interpretation of Paul's statement, "there is no longer male and female." Yes, things were different in the culture of the 1st century church; but *we* are not living in that culture. Other Christians may disagree with us on this issue, and that's their prerogative; but we're not going to change our position.

Now, there are certainly some questions that Paul *didn't* answer in this passage from Galatians, that we might fervently wish he had dealt with. For example, what about Gays and Lesbians? Or Transgender persons? Are Christians to be "one in Christ Jesus" with our many LGBTQ family, friends, and neighbors?

Well, I think that we should first probably acknowledge that the Old Testament law was not particularly sympathetic to *male* homosexuality; although, curiously, Leviticus 18:22 and 20:13 say nothing about *Lesbians,* nor do any other passages in the Old Testament. But we should also note that the Old Testament was likewise quite unsympathetic to people who ate pork, or shellfish like shrimp and lobster. Here, I think it's important to recognize that laws given to the Israelite nation are not necessarily applicable in the New Testament era, or in contemporary culture. For instance, we don't sacrifice animals as a sin offering, and our men don't all travel to Jerusalem three times a year for the Jewish 'Pilgrimage' festivals.

In the New Testament, the question really hinges on how one translates two Greek words, *malakos* and *arsenokoite*; again, that's a larger issue than we have time to really go into today. For now, I would simply point out that First Corinthians 6:9 uses both words; and if you compare the various translations of just these two words by using an online website such as biblegateway.com, you'll see that this issue isn't nearly as simple as some would like to make it.

Now, it's perfectly true that Paul didn't say in Galatians 3, "there is neither gay nor straight." But by the same token, neither did he say, "there is neither Black nor white"; or "Latino or Anglo"; or "native-born or immigrants"; or "Republican or Democrat"; or even, "skinny or obese." But we must remember that Paul lived in the first century CE, not the twenty-first century; he spoke about the matters that were pressing issues in his own day and time. But I still think we can utilize the principles found in Galatians and elsewhere, as well as the teachings of Jesus, to give us some direction.

Paul was strongly opposed to those Christians who were creating divisions in the church on issues such as circumcision; whether they should follow the Jewish dietary laws; and observing or not observing Jewish feast days. Paul also strongly condemned Roman worship in the temples of their idols; yet in First Corinthians 8:10, he did not prohibit Christians from entering such a temple, and even eating meat that had literally been offered to *pagan gods* shortly before! (And let us also note that the early church, in Acts 15:29, had strongly advised Gentiles *against* eating meat that had been offered to idols.) So clearly, there was some *diversity* in the church on such issues.

It's also true that Paul didn't say, "there is neither Muslim nor Christian." But I think there is some guidance here from the teachings of Jesus. In Jesus' day, orthodox Jews were staunchly opposed to the *Samaritans.* The Samaritans had built their own Temple to worship in on Mount Gerizim (Jn 4:20), rather than using the Temple in Jerusalem; and they had significant religious and political differences with orthodox

Jews. Yet Jesus used a 'Good *Samaritan*' as the admirable example for us to emulate, in one of his most famous parables.

Even in Old Testament times, there are mysterious figures such as Melchizedek: who was 'the priest of the most high God,' and he blessed Abraham (Gen 14:18-20). Melchizedek was praised in chapters 5 to 7 in the Book of Hebrews in the New Testament, and Jesus is even said in Hebrews 5 to be "a priest forever, according to the order of Melchizedek." So one could apparently be a "priest of God" *before* anyone had later created categories such as Jew, Christian, Muslim, Hindu, Sikh, or whatever.

In conclusion, remember that, in his teaching about the 'Great Commandment,' Jesus told us to love God, and to love our neighbors as ourselves: he summarized, "for this is the law and the prophets." (Mt. 7:12) The witness of Christians to the world is often sabotaged by all the 'divisions' we build between ourselves; but also, and more importantly, by the fact that we often seem to not be following the *Law of Love* in the 'Great Commandment.'

I would suggest that we should focus ourselves more on loving God and our neighbors, and less on dividing ourselves, according to doctrines that are capable of different interpretations.

11. Negatives, and Positives

I'm reading from the King James Bible: in Paul's letter to the Philippians, he says in conclusion:

> Finally, brethren, whatsoever things are true, whatsoever things are honest, whatsoever things are just, whatsoever things are pure, whatsoever things are lovely, whatsoever things are of good report; if there be any virtue, and if there be any praise, think on these things. (Phil 4:8)

Christians are sometimes looked upon very *negatively* by non-Christians; and these non-Christians' opinions are often reinforced by the way that some Christians are portrayed in the media. The mass media—often hoping to boost their ratings by focusing on controversy—frequently gravitates toward covering the most 'extreme' actions and opinions, since these are supposedly the most 'newsworthy.' The media will often give wide coverage to professing Christians who are loudly protesting same-sex marriage or abortion, while the media typically ignores the far larger numbers of Christians who are simply meeting quietly to worship, and who are assisting people in their neighborhoods who are needing help.

It's not surprising that non-Christians may have strongly critical views of Christians, if all they know is what they see and read in the mass media. For one example, there was a Baptist minister named Fred Phelps—who, thankfully, passed away in 2014—who founded the Westboro Baptist Church in Kansas; nearly all of its members are part of Phelps' immediate family, including his thirteen children. Although Phelps was once a lawyer who, quite admirably, took on a number of civil rights cases, and was even praised by some local civil rights organizations, Phelps later led his congregation down the path of outright *hatred* toward Muslims, Jews, and—most harshly—against Gays.

Phelps and his followers would actually show up at the funerals of Gay men who died of complications associated with AIDS, and they would hold up signs reading, 'God Hates Fags.' In fact, to this very day, that hateful phrase is the URL address of their website! Just imagine how a grieving family and friends would feel at a funeral, after seeing purported 'Christians' holding up such signs, during a memorial ceremony for someone they dearly loved.

Westboro Baptist members have also held up disgusting signs at the funerals of dead American veterans, reading, 'Thank God for Dead Soldiers,' because they argued that such deaths were a 'punishment' from God, for America's 'immorality.' The Westboro Baptist Church is, thus, quite rightly regarded by civil rights organizations as a 'hate group'—in the same class as the Ku Klux Klan. Just imagine: what might some non-Christians think, after seeing such a vicious hate group portrayed in the media as a 'church'?

Another kind of negative perception that non-Christians may have about Christians is based on a theological concept known as the 'Rapture.' According to this doctrine, Jesus could return to the Earth at any time, at which time he will 'take up to Heaven' all *true* Christians. The Rapture doctrine has only been around since it was largely invented by John Nelson Darby in the 1830s, but it has greatly gained popularity since the 1948 establishment of the State of Israel, which some Bible teachers—like Hal Lindsey—interpret as being the major 'sign' that we are now supposedly living in the 'End Times.'

This Rapture doctrine gained much attention from the general public following the publication of the hugely popular 'Left Behind' novel series, written by Tim LaHaye and Jerry Jenkins. Three 'Christian' movies starring Kirk Cameron were then made based on these books; and more recently a much less 'evangelistic' *Left Behind* movie—with a bigger budget, and starring Nicholas Cage—was released.

You have perhaps seen a bumper sticker on some cars, or you might even have been in such a vehicle, which warned you, "In case of Rapture, this car will be UNMANNED!" The idea behind this bumper sticker is that millions of Christians around the world could suddenly 'vanish,' and those non-Christians 'left behind' supposedly won't be intelligent enough to see the connection between the sudden disappearance of millions and millions of 'true' Christians, and the rapid rise of a satanic 'One World Government'—which the non-Christians will purportedly and very unwisely embrace. (Personally, I think that seeing the Rapture *bumper sticker* on thousands of 'abandoned' cars will be enough to tip off those 'left behind' about what is *really* going on.)

Not surprisingly, the Rapture concept has been ridiculed in such Hollywood films as *This is the End,* starring Seth Rogen and James Franco, and *Rapture-Palooza,* starring Craig Robinson and Anna Kendrick.

The concept of this 'Rapture' paints an extremely *pessimistic* view of the world's future. It would seem that, if this doctrine is true, working towards world peace, or fighting 'global warming' and 'climate change,' are basically just a waste of time and energy, because the world is soon going to be taken over by Satan anyway. And why should we worry about carbon dioxide emissions today, when the entire world will be destroyed, and then recreated by God, just a few years from now? Christians holding such views can easily be perceived by their fellow citizens—citizens who may be working very hard to make our world a *better place*—as being nothing but otherworldly 'escapists'!

Yet another negative perception of Christians that some people have is that we are 'too judgmental': they suggest that we have ignored Jesus' admonition, "Do not judge, so that you may not be judged" (Mt 7:1), as well as the statement in Psalm 75:7, that "*God* is the judge." We've probably all seen the tattoo that some NBA players have, "Only God can judge me."

We Christians, to be sure, sometimes seem to be too eager to condemn people; and some professing Christians—such as Fred Phelps, once again—appear to be only too happy to confidently declare who *is* 'saved,' and who *isn't.* For example, Phelps preached a sermon on June 17, 2007 entitled, 'Ruth Graham is in Hell'; he was speaking about the wife of evangelist Billy Graham, after she had passed away the preceding Thursday.

Who among us is so wise, as to know for certain the eternal destiny of *anyone?* In his sermon of May 4, 2020, Pope Francis said that "Christ's death justifies everyone: Big, small, rich, poor, good and bad... 'But did he die for that wretch who made my life impossible?' He died for him too...The Lord died for all. And also for people who do not believe in Him or are of other religions... He died for everyone, He justified everyone." Many conservative and 'traditional' Catholics were quite upset by this sermon, since it could be interpreted that Francis was advocating the doctrine of 'Universalism'—the doctrine which suggests that, eventually, *everyone* will be in Heaven.

I don't personally think that Francis was preaching Universalism; I think he was, rather, just echoing Romans 5:18: "Therefore just as one man's trespass led to condemnation for all, so one man's act of righteousness leads to justification and life for all." But again, it's interesting to note that some professing Christians apparently have no hesitation about asserting that some persons are eternally lost, and are even now experiencing eternal conscious torment in Hell—and in some cases, these Christians even seem to be quite *satisfied* about this situation!

My point is that if *Jesus* told us not to 'judge' one another, isn't either asserting or suggesting that a given person is worthy of eternal Hell making the *ultimate* kind of 'judgment'? And isn't it supposed to be up to *God,* not us, to make such a determination? Given these situations, can any of us be very surprised that some non-Christians will accuse us of being 'too judgmental'?

And of course, when professing Christians get involved in *politics,* it can create an entirely new degree of opposition, such as if Christians seem to be identified with one particular political party; or if Christians seem to be dogmatically blind to any military excesses that might be carried out by, say, the State of Israel; or if Christians seem to be opposing women's rights or LGBTQ rights, this is naturally going to alienate a lot of people.

So I think we shouldn't be surprised when some non-Christians are disappointed, and even offended, when they find out that we are Christians. They may be thinking, "Oh, so you're one of those intolerant bigots I saw on TV!"; or "All you Christians clearly *hate* the Palestinian people!"; or "You're trying to legislate what I can do with my own *body!"*

How should we react to such opposition? Well, I suppose that we might remember that Jesus said, "Blessed are you when people hate you... for surely your reward is great in heaven." (Lk 6:22-23) But such an 'otherworldly' attitude, sometimes, can actually *reinforce* the stereotypes that people may have of us.

But another, and I think *better* reaction that we can have, is the one that Paul exhibited, in the verses from Philippians that I quoted earlier: "whatsoever things are true, whatsoever things are honest, whatsoever things are just, whatsoever things are pure, whatsoever things are lovely, whatsoever things are of good report; if there be any virtue, and if there be any praise, think on these things." We can focus on *positive* things, *encouraging* things, rather than just *arguing* with people, or appearing to condemn them.

Now, I'm certainly not suggesting that we should *ignore reality;* sometimes, we can be upset because there's good *reason* to be upset! We can be 'righteously indignant' for completely justifiable reasons. In fact, we surely can't look at this troubled, hurting world through rose-colored glasses, and pretend that 'everything is beautiful,' when it obviously isn't.

And Christians certainly can, and *should,* be involved in political issues. But the 'cookie cutter' approach—such as when individual churches and parachurch organizations distribute *Voter Guides,* telling you how you 'should' vote, as a Christian—just isn't the right way. The early church wasn't a *monolithic* community; and even more emphatically, the *modern* church can't be one. But I think that we should be very hesitant to 'break fellowship' with other Christians, on matters that we can, in good conscience, disagree about.

Paul in Philippians isn't encouraging otherworldly 'escapism.' He is suggesting that we Christians who are meeting together should encourage one another, by reminding ourselves about inspiring examples of truth, honesty, justice, purity, beauty—about *good things* in general. We should normally leave church on Sundays feeling encouraged and inspired, rather than angered about various political events in the world. That way, when and if we *are* unjustly criticized by others, we will be in a better position to deal with it, and not have it upset us—because we have chosen to "think on *these* things."

12. Joy to the World?

Christmas is the most popular holiday in the world. More than 2.2 billion people worldwide celebrate it, including 95% of Christians. But it is not just *Christians* who observe the holiday: more than 80% of atheists, agnostics, and other freethinkers celebrate the holiday. The infamous atheist, Madalyn Murray O'Hair, was a big fan of Christmas: complete with Christmas carols, and a Christmas tree. In all, about 93% of all Americans celebrate the holiday.

Furthermore, even in countries like Japan—where only about 1% of the people profess to be Christians—Christmas is widely celebrated with decorations, parties, family get-togethers, and such. In Communist China, where the government officially claims that only 1-2% of the people are Christians—although that number is surely 'low,' since many Christians in China fear identifying themselves publicly—even there, Christmas has become a 'big thing' in the cities, where there are Christmas trees, lights, decorations, and Christmas music playing in department stores. There's even a Chinese version of 'Santa Claus,' who is called *Shèngdàn Lǎorén* or 'Father Christmas'—and he looks pretty much like the bearded guy dressed in red and white that we're all accustomed to.

Christmas in our country is a time for decorating public areas, stores, and offices. About 76% of American households put up a Christmas tree; and we even see cars and trucks sporting 'Reindeer antlers.' Christmas shopping has now become a crucial component of our national economy. The day after Thanksgiving—traditionally the day that Christmas shopping officially begins, although merchants keep trying to move that day up *earlier* each year—is known as 'Black Friday,' because businesses that have been losing money all year, and thus operating 'in the red,' may make enough profit during that first weekend and the following holiday season, to put themselves back 'in the black.'

Christmas is also a big 'media sensation,' as well. In 2019 alone, media companies such as the Hallmark Channel, Lifetime, Netflix, Disney, UPtv, OWN, ION, BET, and others released about *one hundred* original 'made-for-TV' Christmas movies. Several cable channels actually broadcast nothing but Christmas movies 24/7, starting in mid-to late November. And when you add in all of the Christmas TV specials; the live concerts by 'seasonal' acts like Mannheim Steamroller and the Trans-Siberian Orchestra; plus the hundreds of Christmas music albums released by Pop artists ranging from Bob Dylan, to Jim Brickman, to Snoop Dogg, to Twisted Sister, it can be literally overwhelming.

For many of us, Christmas is, as the popular song says, 'The Most Wonderful Time of the Year.' It is definitely a time for *Joy*. For most people who celebrate the holiday, it is a time for decorating, and cooking special meals; for getting together with family; for exchanging presents; for reconciling with those we may have become estranged from; even for falling in love—the notion of falling in love during the holiday season being a common theme in many of those made-for-TV Christmas movies. And the concept of 'Peace On Earth' is always an appealing one—particularly in times, like now, when we still have troops overseas who are at risk; and we are witnessing various kinds of protest movements here at home.

But there is a question I would like to pose to many of the people who are celebrating Christmas: namely, *why* is this season so 'special'? Why are concepts like Love, Joy, Peace, and Reconciliation so seemingly *appropriate* for this particular holiday? Why don't we express the same kind of sentiments on, say, St. Patrick's Day? Why don't we get together with our families and exchange presents on Labor Day? Why don't we cook special holiday-themed meals on Arbor Day?

Now, don't worry: I'm not going to go off on a rant about a perceived need to 'Keep Christ in Christmas.' I'm also not going to weigh in on the question of whether or not there is a 'War on Christmas' being waged in our country. But I *would* like to read a short passage from the Bible: from the Gospel of Luke, Chapter 2, and verses 8-14; I'm reading from the King James Version:

> And there were in the same country shepherds abiding in the field, keeping watch over their flock by night. And, lo, the angel of the Lord came upon them, and the glory of the Lord shone round about them: and they were sore afraid. And the angel said unto them, Fear not:

for, behold, I bring you good tidings of great joy, which shall be to all people. For unto you is born this day in the city of David a Saviour, which is Christ the Lord. And this shall be a sign unto you; Ye shall find the babe wrapped in swaddling clothes, lying in a manger. And suddenly there was with the angel a multitude of the heavenly host praising God, and saying, Glory to God in the highest, and on earth peace, good will toward men.

And yes, this *is* the same passage that Linus read to Charlie Brown, in the beloved special, *A Charlie Brown Christmas.* If you recall that program, Charlie Brown agonizes over the increasing commercialism during this season, and about the meaning of Christmas, until he finally breaks down and cries out, "Isn't there anyone who knows what Christmas is all about?" And Linus's reading of this biblical passage both answers, and satisfies Charlie Brown.

I think it's interesting that Lee Mendelson, the producer of the Charlie Brown special, and its animator Bill Melendez, wrote a book about the process of creating that special: and in it, they reveal that Charles Schulz, the creator of the *Peanuts* comic strip, was warned by Melendez against including this Bible passage in the show, on the grounds that, "We can't do this, it's too religious." And this was way back in 1965; a straightforward Bible passage like that could certainly never be included in a *modern* holiday special. But Charles Schulz replied, "Bill, if we don't do it, who else can? We're the only ones who can do it." So the passage from the Gospel of Luke was included, and this special continues to be lovingly rebroadcast every year.

In this biblical passage, we find many of the concepts which are closely associated with Christmas: Joy, Peace on Earth, and Good Will. In many of the 'classic' Carols that are associated with Christmas, we also find these concepts, as well as other related ones: *Hark, the Herald Angels Sing* tells us that the coming of Jesus means, "God and sinners reconciled." *It Came Upon a Midnight Clear* repeats the message of the angels: "Peace on the earth, good will to men." *Silent Night* assures us that we can "Sleep in heavenly peace." And let us not forget the triumphant affirmation, *Joy to the World!* Somehow, to me, the secular song, *Joy to the World,* performed by Three Dog Night and others, falls vastly short of the classic carol written by Isaac Watts and Lowell Mason.

But it's true that it's not always as easy for many of us in the modern world, as it was for Charlie Brown, to just listen to a biblical passage read to us by a friend, and be satisfied. Many people nowadays not only don't believe, but don't even have any respect whatsoever, for the Bible; and many others can't just accept *everything* in the Bible at face value. But does that mean that such persons cannot share in the joyful atmosphere of this holiday—in the fabled 'Spirit of Christmas'?

Certainly not. Decorating our houses, offices, public buildings, and stores with evergreen trees, lights and garland is simply something that makes us *happy.* Giving presents to loved ones—particularly children— is always an occasion for happiness and celebration. Getting together with family and friends for a fine meal is certainly a time to rejoice. And falling in love is *always* 'in season.' But likewise: if there is someone with whom we need to reconcile... well, Christmas is certainly as good a time as any to do it—why put it off for another year?

But even if someone doesn't take the biblical story about the birth of Jesus in a woodenly 'literal' sense, isn't it still a moving and beautiful story? The inspirational tale of a long-awaited promise being fulfilled, by a child who was born in the humblest of circumstances, yet was recognized and honored by both influential 'Wise Men' and humble shepherds, with loving parents watching over this child, who will raise him to one day become the 'King of Kings'?

We can tell someone we love them on Valentine's Day; we can express religious devotion on Easter; we can reconcile with a parent on Mother's Day or Father's Day; we can give someone we love presents on their birthday; we can decorate our houses on Halloween; we can be thankful for the many blessings we have on Thanksgiving. But Christmas is the one time of the year when *all* of these activities seem appropriate.

Christmas is also special because, unlike most holidays, it isn't just limited to a single day: Christmas lasts for an entire *season!* Even before merchants got into the act, Christmas *was* historically celebrated for a season, beginning with the four Sundays of Advent leading up to

Christmas; and then from Christmas until the feast of Epiphany, twelve days later; and, for some, even continuing up to the festival of Candlemas, on February 2ⁿᵈ. It's very appropriate and 'traditional' to look forward to Christmas Day with anticipation, and even to 'count down the *days*' until it arrives.

Of course, a Christmas celebration is something that should never be 'forced' on anybody. There are some Christians who consider Christmas to be a 'pagan holiday,' and who are strong, and sometimes quite vocal, in their refusal to observe it. When encountering such a person, I like to remember the Apostle Paul, who wisely advised us in Romans 14:5-6, "Some judge one day to be better than another, while others judge all days to be alike. Let all be fully convinced in their own minds. Those who observe the day, observe it in honor of the Lord." There is no need to argue with someone whose feelings are different than ours about observing, or not observing, the holiday.

Similarly, we may have family members, friends, coworkers, and neighbors who are Jewish, Muslim, Hindu, or atheist. There is no need to greet such a person with "Merry Christmas," when simply saying "Good Morning!" is as appropriate, and not offensive.

But for those of us who *do* love, and eagerly anticipate this holiday, let us agree to enjoy it to the fullest! So now, let me simply wish all of you a very "Merry Christmas"!

PART C
THINKING ABOUT IT

(I have sometimes thought it would be fun to write a short weekly column for one of the 'free' newspapers that are available at grocery stores, laundromats, etc. While I have never pursued this idea *seriously,* I have here, just for fun—or perhaps as a 'thought experiment'—written a few 'rough draft' columns.)

1. Distractions

"I don't have *time* to think about such things!"

That's the way that a lot of us feel. And that's a completely reasonable thought, if we're running late for work or class; or if we have to pick up the kids or grandkids at school; or if we have urgent bills that must be paid, otherwise the electricity or heat might be turned off.

But imagine that a social scientist, or a 'Time Management' consultant, was studying our daily activities for a week or two, and preparing a written report; would the final report really show that we literally had *no* 'free time' available? Or, rather, would it show that we were actually spending surprisingly large amounts of time on activities that, when examined, are rather trivial? Or, to put it more bluntly, that we have quite a lot of 'wasted time'?

Time spent doing nothing in particular is not necessarily 'wasted time'; it may be much-needed 'down time' after a stressful day at work—time that we take to unwind and 'recharge our batteries' after our regular daily activities. And, to be sure, creative persons may sometimes find *inspiration* during such deliberately 'unfocused' periods.

But we also might be surprised (and even dismayed) to see the amount of time we spend doing things that are rather pointless. Watching television programs (particularly those containing the national average of *fifteen minutes* of commercials per hour!) is a noteworthy example. We may sit listlessly in our recliners, only half-watching commercials about prescription drugs we will never take (including the government-mandated warnings, being read so quickly as to be nearly unintelligible); automobiles we will never buy or lease; insurance policies we will never take out; restaurants we will never eat at; beverages we will never drink, and so on.

The advent of cell phones (with Internet access) has added a new layer of complexity to our idle time: while we *may* spend time on the phone in meaningful conversations with our loved ones, we may also spend too much time just looking at 'notices' forwarded to us via social media: perhaps of animals doing something mildly amusing; or anonymous persons spreading rumors of impending catastrophes (which never come about, and are immediately forgotten after their 'deadline' has passed); of unconfirmed 'news items' attributed to persons speaking 'off the record'; of the daily activities of famous persons (including members of the 'royal family' of some other country), and so on.

A characteristic of such unplanned activities is that they are, generally speaking, *distractions;* they 'accomplish' little or nothing of value, yet they occupy our time, in ways that are relatively unmemorable.

If such activities were of genuine value, they would not be 'distractions'; but to the extent that they take away our time that could more profitably be put to other use, they are pointless—and contribute to a general sense of boredom and lethargy, to which we are all at times subject.

One way of redeeming some of our 'lost time' is to bring a certain level of *intention* to these scattered moments; to give them purpose, and a focus. I would suggest that we can use such time to ponder various issues or questions—the kind that we often protest we 'don't have time' to consider.

2. Context

We all find ourselves existing in a specific context.

We were born. We remember little or nothing of our earliest years, but we were in fact born at a precise time: a time that was not in the Paleolithic era, or during the great dynasties of Egypt and China; not in the Greek or Roman era, and not in Christian Medieval times; not in the midst of eighteenth-century rationalism, nor even in the early 20th century—we are here, *now.*

We find ourselves in a certain social setting: probably a family of one kind or another, but perhaps in a more 'communal' situation (including foster care). We may have been brought up by one or two of our parents, and/or by other relatives (such as grandparents, aunts/ uncles, older siblings); or we might have had a non-family caregiver. These persons may have been with us since birth, or they may have come into our lives at some point, and later departed from us—perhaps due to death, divorce, remarriage, societal intervention, and so on.

The others around us might also include siblings, extended family, neighbors, and friends. Our home environment may have been loving and supportive, or it might have been harsh and abusive; probably, it included varying mixtures of such elements. It might have been quite stable, or it might have been subject to frequent disruptions, because of persons entering or leaving our social circle, or because of physical relocations, such as moving to different cities, states, or countries.

We are also living in specific economic circumstances. We might have been born into a condition of relative deprivation, or into one of comparative wealth; or, we might have found ourselves somewhere in-between the extremes. Our economic circumstances may have largely 'sealed us off' from various avenues and options (such as attending an 'elite' college or university), or they may have provided us with a very wide variety of educational choices and job opportunities.

We now find ourselves in a specific geographical location: a city, town, or village, which is part of a larger state or province, which in turn is part of a larger nation or other political subdivision. This political subdivision is itself existing within a larger context, that may be called 'the West,' 'the Far East,' 'the Third World,' 'Sub-Saharan Africa,' 'Eastern Europe,' 'Polynesia,' the 'West Indies,' or something else. Where we were born has tremendous implications for our future life possibilities, and our consequent limitations.

There were presented to us opportunities for education: such as family members and others teaching us the alphabet or numbers when we were children; preschool; public schools, or private schools; private tutoring, as well as opportunities for self-learning (time spent in libraries; time using online learning programs, and so on). We may have continued to high school, and perhaps gone on to college. We might have had formal vocational education, or on-the-job training. And we may have reacted to our educational experiences by having developed a 'thirst for knowledge'; or, alternatively, we may have vowed to "never crack open another book, after I graduate."

After a certain amount of education (such as finishing high school, and then college), our various life paths begin to diverge greatly from our peers. Most of us enter the work force, or find some other means of financial support. We may encounter a romantic partner, and perhaps get married; we might have children of our own, and/or assimilate the children of our partner. We may begin to replace the friends from our youthful neighborhood and its school with people with whom we now share similar life paths, or that we have encountered through work.

It is worth noting that, although we certainly had various 'choices' and 'decisions' to be made along the way, **a large part of our *context* was something that we ourselves had little or no 'control,' or even *influence* over.** Our physical features (including our overall physical appearance, and even our height), and our general medical condition all have great implications for our future lives, but they are simply presented to us as 'facts of life'—as part of the background we simply must deal with.

But as we age, we have an increasing number of opportunities to influence our own circumstances. We may have a choice of more than one household in which to live; we may be able to select one school or another; we can choose to focus our educational attention on academics, sports, the arts, or other areas. And of course, how we spend our 'free time' is to a great extent subject to our own control.

But our next most important choices probably involve where (and *if)* we work, and who we spend our lives with. These two areas are crucial, in determining [1] whether we will ultimately find ourselves in a 'dead-end, soul-destroying job,' rather than a *profession* to which we truly feel 'called'; or [2] whether we will have a loving partner with whom we might wish to begin a family, instead of feeling ourselves 'trapped' in a 'loveless relationship'—with children or other dependents who we may find 'burdensome.' Remedying such unhappy life situations may be as relatively easy as simply changing jobs; or it may be as devastating and painful—and perhaps, nearly as impossible—as a contentious divorce, involving young children.

Change is always possible; but as time goes on, we become increasingly solidified onto the path we continue on. Still, **up to the very end of our lives, even major changes can be made**—particularly those made in a 'positive' direction, that mostly are affecting ourselves. We can embrace a healthier lifestyle; begin the process of recovery from addictions; try to reconcile with family members and friends; undertake additional education; rediscover a long-ignored skill (such as creating art, or playing a musical instrument); and much more.

And, by altering such matters, we can make *our* context not only better for ourselves, but also for those around us.

3. Responsibility, Blame, and Pride

There are some things in life that seemingly just 'happen to' us; there are other things about which we were mostly the causative agent; and of course, there are also many things that constitute a mixture or 'blending' of the two.

We have no **responsibility** for the family into which we are born, nor the economic conditions originally surrounding us. We may have to overcome very substantial hurdles or barriers to our progress—barriers which are seemingly insuperable. On the other hand, we *do* have a measure of responsibility for not making the most of opportunities that we *did* have. How many of us could not have made *more* of our educational opportunities, for example? (Even if there were some barriers we faced, that attempted to slow our progress.)

All of us face 'barriers' of one sort or another. For example, if one is born into a relatively 'privileged' household, there may be considerably higher *expectations* that are placed on us. We may face pressure (of varying degrees of intensity) that seeks to guide us into certain directions: whether in education; in religion; toward certain professions; and toward particular family and relationship choices. We might be the child of one or two well-known public figures, and accordingly find ourselves measured by a relatively 'high' standard—and bear the burden of social disappointment and rejection, if we do not exceed, or even reach, this high standard.

If born into a far less privileged position, we may find ourselves largely free of such high expectations (unless our parents/guardians used this as an incentive to push us even *harder!*)—but instead have to contend with, and overcome, unwarranted prejudices and stereotypes (e.g., "You're going to turn out just like your father/mother!"; "No one can make it out of this neighborhood, so don't even try...").

Successfully attaining a basic educational level; avoiding involvement with the criminal justice system; finding steady gainful employment; and establishing and maintaining loving and supportive familial relationships, might seem to be relatively 'minor' achievements to some people—but if these goals were achieved after having begun from a very 'negative' starting position, these may be quite admirable (and even very *inspiring!*) accomplishments.

But when we overcome barriers in our social environment, can or should we afterwards 'blame' individuals, institutions, or even entire societies for the difficulties we encountered? In some cases, this is certainly fully justified: a person who physically or sexually exploited us when we were young is certainly not entitled to any sympathy, for example. Persons who engaged in racial, gender, or other prejudices against us were certainly wrong, and worthy of our disdain—at the very least.

It is very natural to feel a certain measure of 'righteous indignation' when reflecting on wrongs that may have been done to us. But if we intend to move ourselves past and beyond such unjust barriers, devoting time to our grievances and the assigning of **blame** may not be the most helpful approach. In one sense, it leaves us temporarily fixated at the location of an improper barrier, when our time might be better spent leaving it far behind us, and largely forgotten.

We may fantasize about 'confronting' some hostile figure from our past, and presenting them with a detailed catalogue of their sins against us—yet even if they were to frankly and fully acknowledge their faults (which is rather unlikely, of course), would this really 'accomplish' anything for us? If our aim was to '*move on* with our lives,' might it not be better to bypass such confrontations?

Moving forward is a ***direction***, that takes us away from hovering around the past. As past injustices recede further into our historical background, they gradually become too small to clearly perceive: similar to looking in the rear view mirror of a vehicle, as we drive away from a place. In time, such incidents may no longer even appear to be worth our momentary notice.

Can we justifiably feel **pride** in ourselves, for our own accomplishments? Certainly. But this should also be tempered with the acknowledgement of the substantial degree to which 'our' accomplishments are not exclusively 'OURS.' I am not referring simply to the sort of cursory *thank yous* that, say, an author traditionally lists at the beginning of a book. I am thinking of the fact that none of us had to discover the principles of agriculture for ourselves, nor invent the wheel—much less figure out how to make steel, produce electricity, or build a computer.

We were taught an already-existing verbal and written language, for which textbooks had already been printed. We came into a world that already had a monetary system of exchange. This world already had established a system of social order, such that there are traffic rules to follow, certain days on which the garbage is picked up, and phone numbers we can call in emergency situations. (If any of us were magically placed into a prehistoric world, could we even survive?)

Each of us has had a large number of 'decision points' in our lives, in which we *could* have gone in one direction, but we actually chose to go in another. To the extent that we took a particular path (particularly if it was other than the 'path of least resistance') that proved fortunate, we can certainly allow ourselves a small smile of *satisfaction*, when we are reflecting on the significant events of our own past.

But then, it is time to move on—because frequently reliving past triumphs is simply taking time away from our future accomplishments.

4. Civilization/Society

In all likelihood, we live in a society that is, to greater or lesser degrees, 'civilized.' That is to say, we need not develop for ourselves a detailed code of conduct, that governs our relations to others; nor a system of law enforcement, nor a judicial system.

In ways almost beyond counting, this is advantageous to us. Early American settlers couldn't simply dial '911' when they encountered danger, or were injured. If their crops failed, supplies ran low, and game animals were nowhere to be found, they couldn't just drive to the nearest grocery store, and purchase food and supplies with a credit card.

Philosophers such as Jean-Jacques Rousseau and John Rawls have described our relationship with our society as a 'Social Contract': that is, we voluntarily agree to follow certain rules and standards, in exchange for the benefits that civilized society brings. Having a monetary system, for example, greatly facilitates transactions between different individuals. A common medium of exchange allows an agreed-upon item (such as a $20 dollar bill) to represent the 'stored value' of a certain amount of work, and its exchange allows people with very different needs and wants to all participate in civil commerce.

(It's interesting that even many individuals/groups in this country with a largely 'anti-government' stance usually agree to accept donations and payments for merchandise in *U.S. dollars*—even if they prefer to call them 'Federal Reserve Notes,' rather than 'dollars.')

Some rudimentary standards of social conduct have presumably been in place since the very earliest societies. For example, it is obvious that a community cannot allow one of its members to murder another member, or to steal from them. Prohibitions against lying to a judicial tribunal are also quite ancient.

That isn't to say that the demands and restrictions put upon us by civilized society may not be in some cases burdensome—particularly if we have specialized, or relatively uncommon aims and ambitions. A female desiring to enter a previously all-male profession (or a male seeking to take a 'historically female' job), or an individual whose gender identity/sexual orientation is disparaged by some persons, may expect to encounter various degrees of opposition.

In modern societies, these social standards are subject to various caveats, and frequent revision. Discrimination against certain ethnic communities—although it unfortunately still frequently occurs—is less universally and strongly supported by the force of law, than it once was. We have also come to temper some criminal punishments based on our growing knowledge of mental insanity, as well as various sociological factors that may mitigate guilt, in specific cases. Regulations of activities and products such as gambling, pornography, alcohol, marijuana and tobacco may be alternately loosened, or tightened. Our own society is accordingly becoming more diverse over time, and less homogeneous.

Hopefully, those of us living within a particular society are also becoming more willing to be 'civil' toward others, in areas that are not regulated by law or custom. Variations in such superficial matters as clothing, hair style, tattoos and piercings, etc. are nowadays... if not exactly *welcomed,* at least generally *tolerated.* Other differences, however, such as language, religion, nationality, political affiliation, and economic class, remain in many societies matters for potential antagonism, and division.

Of course, it is often the case that different individuals within a given society have different values and standards, which may lead to conflict with others. These incidents can be as relatively 'minor' as a neighbor who is playing their music too loud, or as 'major' as a factory that is polluting the municipal water supply. Most societies thus have developed formalized methods of conflict resolution, such as a court system.

But it is true that determining 'right and wrong,' 'guilt and innocence' in such cases, can often be a very complex and controversial process; and, as with all complex processes, errors can be made. A person who was just released from prison—after having been proved innocent by relatively new technology, such as DNA evidence—or a parent whose unarmed son or daughter was shot and killed by an inexperienced (or even prejudiced!) police officer can hardly be 'made whole' by simply later receiving a monetary award.

Some persons may find living in modern society to be *too* burdensome. And certainly, it *is* possible to live, to some degree, 'Off the Grid'—that is, living by oneself (or perhaps only with select family/friends), and attempting to avoid all contact with governmental structures—including public utilities, police departments, and especially the IRS.

But, of course, there are severe 'trade-offs' in conducting such a lifestyle—notably, not being able to go to a doctor or hospital when one becomes severely ill; or being forced to rely exclusively on your own resources, to protect you and your home from vandals and thieves.

Even among very well-prepared persons (such as so-called

'Preppers'), you may be quite well-armed inside your compound, and have at least a year's supply of food and water stored—but hostile invaders can still probably set fire to your home; or an attacking mob can use explosives to blow up your compound, leaving you and your loved ones to die inside. Living such an 'anarchic' lifestyle probably remains, thus, an option only for a small minority,

But there remains a less-extreme possibility of living in a comparatively 'asocial' way: by simply avoiding many of the common societal *expectations* of us (e.g., being a self-employed Gay Libertarian vegan Atheist, for example). Such possibilities function as an 'escape valve' of sorts, by permitting some individuals to largely retreat and/or 'drop out' of certain aspects of a society in which, after all, they were probably simply *born into,* rather than having consciously *chosen.*

The existence of such 'singular' individuals does not pose any inherent threat to the greater society. After all, a literal *majority* (i.e., 50% + 1) of the population has never read the most popular bestselling book, downloaded the most popular song, watched the most popular cable TV show, or bought a ticket to watch the #1 movie. No one is *compelled* to attend a particular church, watch football on TV on Sunday afternoons, or vote in an election; there is still considerable room for *individuality,* even in a mass industrialized society.

Like virtually everything in life, there are 'pluses' and 'minuses' about living in a civilized society. But the worldwide trend is clearly moving in the direction of indigenous cultures giving up (whether eagerly, reluctantly, or both) some of their 'traditional' ways, in order to become part of modern industrialized civilization—complete with cell phones, social media, and loud nightclubs.

Is there something *lost* in making such changes? Absolutely. But there are also *gains.* The seemingly idyllic suburban lifestyle seen on 1950s TV shows also reinforced racial and ethnic separation, gender stereotypes, and uncritical social conformity. We need to appreciate the good aspects of change, and avoid feeling overly sentimental about the past.

Let us simply hope that, as the rate of change increases, we do not forget how to be *civil*, in our civilization…

5. Home, and Environment

I happen to love the neighborhood I live in: It's safe, usually quiet, and our neighbors are friendly. I also love the city I live in; to me, it seems superior to the other cities/towns I've lived in, or visited. Likewise with the state I live in; I can't seriously imagine myself living in any other state. I also love the country I live in; I was born here, and have never been out of this country—but I also have no particular interest in traveling elsewhere.

Undoubtedly, I am unusually 'parochial' in these views. If I was asked to provide some strictly *rational* reasons for thinking my particular neighborhood, city, state, and country to be any 'better' than others (particularly given my very limited experience in traveling elsewhere), I would fail miserably.

Still, it is certainly desirable to feel 'comfortable' in the place where one lives; some people, unfortunately, don't have such an experience. Many young people can hardly wait to become older and financially independent enough able to move away from their 'boring' hometown; recent college graduates may be quite eager to move to another state (or country) in order to pursue their careers; and even native-born citizens of this country can grow discouraged, frustrated, and sufficiently angry with current events such that they wish to leave their native country— for good.

Of course, a long-distance relocation causes various social disruptions for us: family, friends, and familiar sights will be left behind. Children who have been forced to move from an environment they were accustomed to (with its friends, family, supportive teachers, etc.) can attest to the pain this can cause. Moving into a new area where one does not have any family and friends for support can make anyone feel terribly isolated, and even lead to bouts of depression.

Yet in some cases, such a change may also be viewed *positively:* it can be perceived as a chance for a 'fresh start'; to state anew with a 'clean slate.' All of us have done things that we would probably prefer to *forget*; and relocating to a place where people are unfamiliar with our 'back history' can be a welcome relief for some. In those cases, such changes of location may prove to have been very fortunate, and even life-changing.

But it may also be the case that the new location seemingly has the same problems that one was trying to escape; or, alternately, it simply has a *different set* of problems—but ones that are just as undesirable and frustrating as the ones we were trying to escape. In such a case, one could consider moving yet again; or even, to return to where one just came from. (Perhaps with the newly-acquired knowledge and experience that "the grass isn't always *greener…*")

If one is presently enduring a relatively 'toxic' life situation, relocation (if feasible both financially and practically) may be a virtual life-saving *necessity*. However, if one just relishes a 'change of scene,' it might be wiser to try instead to find a profession that requires a great deal of travel—which allows one to experience *both* the 'new' and the 'familiar'; by, say, 'coming home' after a long out-of-town trip.

But it may simply be the case that one is better off to try to become more *accepting* of where one lives. One can focus on trying to change one's own *attitude*, rather than desiring to change the external environment.

When we think about it rationally, is our living situation *really* as bad, or as unbearable, as we might sometimes suppose? By comparing our situation with that of many others, we might actually realize, "I guess I don't have it so bad, after all."

One might also discover that, by ceasing to try and *resist* one's environment, one can enter into a non-contentious relationship with it. It may not really be 'worth it' to try and resist, when one can simply 'go along,' and experience less frustration.

(Because, remember: there is no guarantee that any other place will actually be *better*.)

6. Citizenship

One may be living in a country, without necessarily feeling a special 'attachment' or 'connection' with it. Perhaps you are only living here because of your job, or to attend a particular school, for instance. In such a situation, you might reflect that "this country is okay to visit, but I wouldn't want to *live* here." To such a person, ultimately returning *home* will bring a strong sense of relief.

It is quite possible, however, to feel oneself not committed or attached to *any* particular country. The Greek philosopher, Socrates, once declared that he was "not an Athenian or a Greek, but a citizen of the world." (According to Plutarch's essay, *Of Banishment*.)

Wandering the world freely, without binding attachments to any particular nation, may appeal to some people—especially to those with independent temperaments. For such a person, whenever something objectionable takes place in the country where they are residing, they can comfort themselves with the thought, "That wasn't *me!*" Such a person may then choose to move on to another place: without feeling any remorse, or sense of loss. Some may compare this kind of attitude to a practice of avoiding romantic attachments: preferring to 'play the field,' rather than commit to a specific individual.

Yet there may be a significant value that is being *lost,* in avoiding such attachments. One's country can be a significant component of one's personal identity. One may feel pride, and a sense of acceptance, about the accomplishments of one's fellow countrymen. In many cases, this sense of identification is formalized by one's **citizenship** in a particular country.

Of course, in America, the vast majority of us become citizens more or less 'automatically,' simply by having been born here. This is certainly a convenience, as one then partakes of the benefits of citizenship, without needing to pass through the complex gauntlet of conditions that foreign-born persons applying for citizenship do. But we 'native-born' citizens may also find that, by not having had to *work* for our citizenship, we actually *appreciate* it less; it becomes something that we simply take for granted.

Permanent residents (i.e., 'Green Card' holders) in this country may ultimately decide to apply to become U.S. citizens. This process requires an interview, and passing a fairly detailed written test (which a lot of us 'born' citizens might have difficulty passing!). But such 'naturalized' citizens are often quite *proud* of their new citizenship—to a degree that makes the rest of us look like rather 'lukewarm' citizens.

It is true that citizens may, at times, experience a sense of repulsion or even *betrayal,* at certain acts which were 'officially' performed by our country; this is perhaps most frequently encountered in the area of foreign affairs—where the extent of our country's activities may be hidden from the citizenry, and not publicly revealed, until decades later, if at all.

In more extreme cases—such as being a German citizen during Hitler's rule; or living in a brutal totalitarian regime (such as the former Soviet Union)—one's sense of revulsion may be quite rational. But even in such cases, one might still say with resignation that "I'm still a proud German" or a "proud Russian"—*despite* the current regime—and simply vow to "hold on" until change eventually comes.

If we watch televised news reports of the citizens of another country vigorously, or even violently, opposing some actions undertaken by our country, we may feel defensive, saying, "Hey: it wasn't *me,* who ordered that!" But of course, as citizens, we are quite naturally perceived by 'outsiders' as being a supportive part of the country of which we are citizens. (We ourselves often engage in the same kind of 'stereotyping,' when we see the protesters in a particular country on TV, and we assume that these individuals are representative of the sentiments of that entire country.)

In the 1960s, the saying, "My country, right or wrong," was often used as an objection to the young protesters who were opposed to the Vietnam war. (To which the students' response was usually, "You should want to *change* this country, when it's wrong!") But of course, citizenship is to some extent a 'package deal'; one can't simply 'pick and choose' the things that one likes, and then 'opt out' of all the others.

One may not particularly *enjoy* serving on a jury, or being subject to the military draft; but those are among the 'duties' that come along with our citizenship. (Although some other *suggested* 'duties': such as, "Stay Informed of the Issues That Affect Your Community," and "Participate in the Democratic Process," can essentially be waived.)

One can also *renounce* one's citizenship. This seems like a rather extreme action, unless one has extremely strong objections to one's country of citizenship—particularly since one can certainly *live* in nearly any other country for an indefinite period of time. And in some cases (e.g., the United Kingdom, Canada, Mexico), you can even be allowed to have 'dual citizenship,' thus being formally attached to more than one country.

Or, again, one could also choose to become 'stateless': holding citizenship in no country at all. But by such a choice, one is also forfeiting the potential positive feelings that may come with acknowledging, and even accepting (perhaps even quite *proudly!*) one's citizenship.

For most of us—those who are reasonably satisfied with the country of our citizenship—enjoying the benefits of citizenship, while acknowledging the associated duties, is a better path to take.

But also, when our country seems to be heading down a wrong path, doing what we can to *change* it.

7. Patriotism and Nationalism

It is, for many or most of us, a source of happiness and pride to feel a sense of patriotism toward our own country. This sentiment may be expressed by proclaiming, "I'm *proud* to be an American!"; or by wearing a patriotic symbol (such as a flag pin on one's lapel), displaying the nation's flag in front of one's home, and so on.

The sentiment of patriotism is greatly reinforced when it is done in a *corporate* manner—such as when one is participating in a rally or march, along with hundreds or even thousands of basically like-minded individuals. The realization that, "I'm *not alone* in my feelings for this country!" can strike one almost as a 'revelation.'

Such emotions can be a strong motivating factor in a young person's decision to join the military service, and to courageously risk life, and physical/emotional well-being, in order to defend our country from threats to our safety and security. During the Vietnam War era, many members of our military forces were unfairly *hated* by those 'at home,' because of strong disagreement about the conflict these uniformed persons were serving in. Fortunately, in the last few decades, most of our citizens have learned to separate one's respect for those *serving* in the military, from the *political* ends to which they are being ordered to support.

One's sense of love and respect for one's country can sometimes create in us a sense of 'defensiveness,' as when we feel our nation is being unfairly criticized. But in such cases, we may need to temper our perhaps justifiable sense of 'outrage,' by realizing that many in our country (particularly our elected leaders) may be saying similarly harsh things about *other* countries—which remarks may well be strongly resented by *its* own citizens.

If I am a proud American citizen, and I encounter an equally proud Chinese, Mexican, or French citizen, there is inherently nothing about this situation that should create any kind of conflict between us. Even if our *nations* are presently in a state of conflict with each other, we can still act in a respectful and 'civil' manner to each other: as individuals with differing views, that are probably largely based on our differing backgrounds.

That is one of the salutary aspects of such 'international' events as the Olympic Games—where participants are expected to follow the general standards of 'sportsmanship,' rather than 'politicizing' the Games. Such activities can lead to creating sympathetic feelings between the ordinary citizens of different countries (regardless of the formal political perspectives of these countries).

There is also certain kind of 'multicultural' pride which can arise at international gatherings: where the citizens of many nations can show pride in their own country, while also demonstrating a spirit of openness and mutual respect toward the proud citizens of other countries. We can take steps toward feeling ourselves as *both* citizens of our own country, as well as being a 'citizen of the *world.*'

But—as with most 'good things' in life—it is quite possible to take even a strong virtue (such as patriotism) to an extreme. One can view another's pride in his or her own country as being in some way *threatening* to my own.

When taken to extremes, respectful and reasonable patriotism can evolve into undesirable forms of *nationalism*—of which we saw some vivid examples, in the Fascism which led up to World War II. The German national anthem, *Deutschland, Deutschland, über alles* ("over every other land," it may be translated) can be heard simply as a fervent expression of patriotism; or, as under the Nazis, it may have more sinister overtones.

Another person's country can certainly be the 'best for *them*,' without this denying that my own nation may be the 'best for *me*'—just as someone else's loving attachment to their *own* spouse is not in any way 'diminishing' my love for *my* spouse.

The world is a very diverse place; and, with modern communications, all of us are increasingly aware of countries other than our own. It is difficult to imagine any 'one' form of society and government as being uniformly appropriate for *all* peoples, throughout the world. (And many of the citizens of other countries do not look upon, say, contemporary American democracy, as the ideal for their *own* country to strive for.)

When we go out to a restaurant, we may choose from among national dishes such as Italian, Mexican, French, Chinese, Indian, Russian, Ethiopian, Turkish, Thai, and many more. The availability of such national variations is a good, and *enriching* aspect of our world; in a similar way, the path of mutual respect for each other's national pride is certainly the best attitude to have.

8. Family

It has been said, quite rightly (for example, by Atticus Finch, in *To Kill a Mockingbird*), that "You can choose your *friends,* but you can't choose your *family!*"

The family unit has traditionally been one of the chief cornerstones of a society. Although the classic 'nuclear family' (i.e., mother, father, children) seems to get the most discussion, one's 'extended family' (or lack thereof) can be crucial, and even *primary,* in the social development of a child.

In the unfortunate instance of some disastrous event—such as the death, or imprisonment of parent(s) or guardian(s)—a child now needing to live with loving grandparents, or an equally caring aunt/uncle, is normally much more reassuring and stable, than the child simply being cast upon the care of strangers, and subject to regulations and requirements of the state.

There is a significant emotional difference in growing up as an 'only child,' rather than growing up in a household with one or more siblings. While some commentators might perceive an only child as likely having grown up 'spoiled,' it is also possible that such a person will feel themselves *isolated* and less 'grounded,' since there is no sibling who can truly *empathize* with their social experiences at home.

Our relations with friends are often situational, and loosely sentimental; they can be ended without advance warning, and almost 'at will'; whereas a familial relation—at least formally—lasts until death. Those who grew up in a loving and supportive family situation, usually hope to provide such an environment for their own children. And even those who *didn't* have the blessing of such an environment, may firmly vow to provide their own children with "the kind of home environment that *I didn't have*."

One's family is often crucial to the definition of *who **we** are*. Bearing the 'Family Name' can be a tremendous blessing; but equally well, it can be perceived as a burden. One may be admonished by family members that "A [family name] doesn't act that way!" But on the other hand, bearing the family name can also grant one immediate access to benefits (in education, employment, etc.) that one did not have to earn for oneself.

Having a common 'genetic background' is perhaps the *least* important aspect of similarity among family members, when compared to the impact of family members having shared a *culture*, which has extended for much or all of one's lifetime (and even tracing back to previous generations). 'Coming home to meet the family' is always one of the key tests for a romantic relationship—because by being linked to a person romantically, you are also becoming linked to your loved one's family.

Those who have had supportive family members will likely exhibit a level of confidence and reassurance that others may not have. It is very comforting to have the knowledge that, in a bind, "I could always move back home with my parents"; or, "if I had to, I could borrow my brother's/sister's car for a couple of weeks"; or "my uncle said he can get me a job at his shop, if I get laid off."

Family relationships are ones that do not need to be *justified* to others. Our friends and coworkers may ask us, "Why do you sometimes hang out with *that* person?" But if the person in question is a family member, then that is all the explanation that need be given. And since one can't 'divorce' or (in most cases) legally disentangle oneself from a family member, we have to acknowledge that this relationship is a binding one.

And in some cases, one's family members may actually be able to be *more* honest and straightforward with you, than would someone (such as a coworker) whose ties to you are more tenuous. Your friends and coworkers—afraid of harming their relationship with you—may refrain from telling you that you seem to have a drinking problem, or that someone you're involved with "just doesn't *seem right* for you!" While a family member can often be honest—brutally honest, if need be—about their perceptions of your life, since "No matter what, we're still *family!"*

Family members can also be a strong source of comfort during times of sickness, or death. It is common for family members to 'pull together' at such times, to support and reinforce each other. It is a very helpful consolation to realize that, even though you are experiencing pain or loss, you still have members of a 'support network' that will always be there.

But of course, if family members can quite often be a genuine blessing, they can likewise be somewhat of a burden—and much more than 'somewhat' of a burden, in certain cases. Consider the anxiety one may experience in agonizing over whether or not to invite, say, a 'problematic' relative to an important event such as a wedding— fearing the very real possibility of this person creating a significant embarrassment. (E.g., the uncle who shows up drunk and belligerent, etc.) But along with such risks, can also come the possibility of *rewards;* having the firm support of one's family at crucial life events is always emboldening.

Of course, particularly in these days of increasing stresses being placed upon the 'traditional' family, increasing numbers of people today may largely grow up without having had the benefit of significant familial support. It is not surprising when such a person feels 'dragged down' by such a situation; but such a situation can also become an opportunity for one vowing to *overcome* such early limitations.

It is also quite possible to become *estranged* from family members—and there may be quite valid reasons for such estrangement. (Cases involving emotional and/or physical abuse are common examples.) But less serious reasons, such as "I always feel like I'm being *judged* by my family," or "They've written me off, ever since I changed religions," can be just as potent, as a justification.

But equally, in such cases, *reconciliation* is often a possibility. While simply 'forgetting the past,' and 'letting bygones be bygones' may not seem like viable alternatives, having a willingness to just begin anew, and trying not to let past infractions determine our future relations, can lead to at least some measure of reconciliation. And the result of having been able to repair 'broken' family relations will always leave one feeling more 'whole.'

In the end, in considering such broken relationships, it can also be helpful to remember that 'Life is short,' and that we might one day greatly regret being on our death bed, or attending a funeral, while realizing that we didn't at least make an *attempt* to reconcile—and even to try to make *amends* to those we ourselves may have hurt.

9. Education

The instinctual abilities 'built into' living creatures can be truly amazing—as anyone who's ever futilely chased an annoying fly with a swatter can attest. Although recent technological developments have made us aware that vast amounts of information can be stored in extremely small repositories, the relatively complex evasive behaviors that are possible for something as small as a gnat are nevertheless amazing.

However, while human babies are born with certain instinctual abilities (e.g., sucking; or grasping a finger), we humans have an enormously greater need than other animals to be *taught* things. And the things we need to be taught are of much greater complexity that those required for our mere physical survival.

The fact that we have developed both verbal and written languages is extremely helpful, in this regard. While we *could* rely solely upon non-verbal physical demonstrations to teach someone how to, say, peel and eat an orange, one certainly could not convey the complexities involved in a contemporary fruit farm's operations by such simple demonstrations.

Most modern societies have developed formalized systems of education, such as are carried out by their public school system. We in America basically consider that there is a certain 'core' curriculum, that any person who is to become a participating citizen in our country needs to know. To this end, we attempt (with varying degrees of success) to make available such schooling to all young people at no cost—and we even strive to *mandate* such 'elementary' education for minors.

But increasingly, given the rising complexity of modern society, such 'basic' educational levels may be insufficient. The kinds of assembly-line jobs (where a relatively brief tutorial was all that was required for a new worker) that used to be common are rapidly vanishing from our country, and a great many 'service-level' jobs (e.g., in the food service and hospitality industries) do not have a particularly bright long-term outlook. (As the Coronavirus pandemic demonstrated vividly.)

The level of technical expertise needed to perform many of the newly-created jobs of the present, and the projected future, is rising rapidly. And it is no longer the case that one can go to college for four years, and be confident that one has learned nearly all that one needs to know about a given profession. (Some college graduates would formerly vow to "never crack open another book" after graduating; that hardly seems like a recipe for success in the current job market.) Consider, for example, the degree to which nearly everyone nowadays needs to have a certain level of computer proficiency. Education in the modern world is increasingly something that must be pursued over one's entire lifetime.

But at the same time, computer software is also becoming much more 'user-friendly'; no one needs to learn to ponderously enter DOS commands, any more. We are increasingly able to utilize voice-activated technologies (e.g., Google Assistant; Apple's 'Siri'; Amazon's 'Alexa,' etc.) to spare us the bother of typing requests into a computer. Who would have predicted, just decades ago, that we would one day be able to use a device small enough to fit into a shirt pocket to access vast libraries of information?

But with this increasing simplicity, there are also disadvantages. The speed with which data can be accessed, retrieved, and presented in either a brief audible, or very short written form, can be enormously helpful for answering simple 'objective' facts (e.g., "How many U.S. Presidents are still alive?" or "What is the name of Beyoncé's new song?" or "How tall is Sylvester Stallone?"); but this brevity also encourages a certain level of *superficiality* in the answers we expect to receive; engaging in the kind of 'serious' research that once had to be done by poring through technical reference works in a library is *too slow* for many moderns, who would much prefer a 'sound bite' answer that can be retrieved almost instantly.

The advent of photographs, film, television, and the modern profusion of digital media, likewise, has both 'positive' and 'negative' aspects. On the one hand, while it is sometimes true that 'seeing is believing,' visual/auditory media can cause us to develop the impression that we are much more *knowledgeable* about a subject than we truly are; we may insist, "I *know* that's true, because I just *saw it* on TV!" (Forgetting that this bit of media may have been carefully manipulated, in order to deceive us.) And with the increasingly widespread use of social media throughout the world, such relatively fragmentary information (as well as misinformation, and deliberate lies) can be instantly shared with millions, by simply pressing a button or two.

When we have so many available options for educating ourselves today, it's a shame that we don't make considerably more *use* of them. It is ironic that, precisely when so much more information is being made readily available (e.g., entire books being converted to digital format, that can be downloaded in just minutes) at minimal or no cost, many of us prefer to use modern technologies to simply indulge our apparent obsessions with, say, the intimate details of the lives of celebrities.

But such obsessions are seldom *fulfilling,* intellectually; they may be compared to eating junk foods, versus a well-balanced meal. While one can subsist (perhaps indefinitely) on 'fast food,' and high-calorie snacks, ultimately one's body will require more. And our minds, as well as our bodies, are equally desirous of adequate nourishment.

Education at its best can be one of the most rewarding activities in life, since ideally, it fully engages our highly complex minds. Even as our bodies will feel at their best when we eat properly and exercise regularly, so our minds will remain most active and engaged when they are encouraged to more fully explore this marvelous world we are living in.

10. Employment

It is an unfortunate reality of life that often, what we most *love* to do, is not something that we can do *professionally*. A person may be extremely interested in, say, 17th century French Literature: but the opportunities for *employment* in such a field (particularly in this country) are quite limited. Similarly, fields such as entertainment (acting, music, dance) and sports simply have far too many people interested in them, relative to the 'professional' slots that are available. (Just think of the thousands of talented would-be actors, who are supporting themselves by bussing tables, or waitressing.)

The notion of one's work as a 'calling' (with its theological implications of one having been 'called' by God, into a certain profession) is not heard much today. Too many of us are simply 'getting by,' and doing something that we are largely disinterested in (and may even actively *hate*), in order to survive.

Psychologists and social scientists realize, of course, that all of us would be happiest to be doing something that we do well, are highly interested in, and are also able to earn a comfortable living while doing it. But a large number (the majority?) of jobs out there simply don't fit this description.

But for those who have creative impulses, modern technology has helped us out greatly in this regard. While one certainly needs, in one way or another, to be able to support oneself (you can't sleep on Mom's couch *forever*), it is certainly possible to earn a modest living through part-time work, while leaving you sufficient time to devote yourself to your *true* interests. I would actually suggest that **the future of much creativity belongs to the *part-time* 'artist.'**

Consider the outlook for someone who wants to be a musician these days. The outlook just a few decades ago could be very bleak, because recording studios were seemingly exclusively focused on acts that could potentially be 'popular,' and it was often nearly impossible for newcomers to break into the field, or even get their work recorded. (Making a cassette tape of your band playing in someone's garage just wasn't as 'cool' as being able to buy a commercial recording of a band, at a record store.) And increasingly, venues like bars and dance clubs switched from having 'live' musicians, to simply playing recorded music; so it became even harder for such musicians to find an audience.

But nowadays, although *commercial success* is still elusive to all but a very select few, an aspiring musician can now purchase a music sequencer for a relatively minor cost; digitally record himself or herself; add whatever 'virtual' instruments are desired; and even make a 'music video' version of a song—and then send it off electronically, throughout the world. Perhaps you can even make a few dollars by doing this; but even if not, you can still take great pleasure in your 'professional-sounding' product.

It is similar with print media, and aspiring writers. An 'unknown' person trying to get a non-commercial book published in the late decades of the 20th century faced a seemingly hopeless task. Publishers were often only interested in the 'quick sale,' and would rather 'remainder' thousands of unpurchased copies of a formulaic book, than try to identify and develop 'new' authors. Budding writers were not infrequently limited to handing out photocopied typescript copies of their 'unpublished' books.

But these days, nearly anyone can pay to have published a 'real' physical book—and it is even easier (and cheaper) to publish a 'digital-only version.' And if writing an entire book seems too daunting a task, one can simply start to write an online 'blog,' jotting down thoughts as one wishes, and sharing it with whoever might be interested.

Social media has likewise created amazingly vast opportunities for expressing one's creativity. Very little technology is required to produce one's very own 'TV show,' Podcast, or maintain a 'Website.' Even some surprisingly *esoteric* topics and people can actually achieve a substantial 'following' on social media (particularly on YouTube).

The rise of such outlets for creativity is particularly opportune today, since the jobs that many (most?) people have are largely things that they don't particularly 'like' to do. (Which, of course, is why we have to be *paid* to perform the jobs.) We may feel 'stuck' in a job that we truly *hate*—one that places us in a state of agitation, and literally counting the minutes until our workday is over. But if one can leave the job behind at quitting time, and then turn to one's *real* interests upon arriving home, this situation is much more bearable.

But even if we have a job that we are largely 'happy' with, there are surely substantial parts of it that we would not choose to do, were it not 'part of the job.' (E.g., "I basically love my job, except I can't stand all the stupid staff meetings we have to participate in"; "I love interacting with customers at the counter, but I hate having to log and then file away all of the receipts, after we close for the night.")

Even persons who have what would seemingly be 'dream jobs,' would probably acknowledge that there are nevertheless substantial *unpleasant* aspects to them; e.g., Presidents have to hold Press Conferences with hostile reporters; actors have to give repetitious 'promotional' interviews about their latest movie; sports stars have to sign autographs and pose for 'Selfies,' when they are trying to have a quiet dinner at a restaurant, etc.

The reality is that many jobs are ones that no one would *voluntarily* do, if they really had a choice. This includes physically-demanding jobs, that leave one exhausted and aching at the end of the workday, as well as mind-numbingly repetitive jobs—such as phone center employees, who may spend their entire day transferring people from one department to another, or being rudely hung up on.

The simple fact is that no one likely feels 'called' to, say, design the packaging for toilet paper; or to clean public restrooms after a football game; or to dispose of 'biohazard' materials placed in a hospital trash receptable. But *"someone* has to do it."

But there really are *no* areas of our lives that are entirely without a 'downside,' to offset their advantages. (Including raising children; what parent hasn't occasionally thought, "These kids are going to drive me *crazy!"*) We simply have to learn to "take the *good* along with the *bad*."

The best that most of us can probably hope to achieve is simply a kind of *balance* between our 'professional' and our 'personal' lives: so that whatever we do for a 'living,' it still leaves us enough time, and financial resources, to do as we wish with our non-work hours.

11. Loneliness

The Greek philosopher Aristotle said in his *Politics:* "that man is more of a *social animal* than bees or any other gregarious animals is evident… The proof that the state is a creation of nature and prior to the individual is that the individual, when isolated, is not self-sufficing; and therefore he is like a part in relation to the whole. But he who is unable to live in society, or who has no need because he is sufficient for himself, must be either a beast or a god: he is no part of a state." (Bk One, Pt. II)

Some people may prefer the solitary life: living out in the woods, or in the desert, with no immediate neighbors, and few if any disturbances. Thoreau famously wrote in *Walden:* "I have never felt lonesome, or in the least oppressed by a sense of solitude… In the midst of a gentle rain … I was suddenly sensible of such sweet and beneficent society in Nature… and in every sound and sight around my house, an infinite and unaccountable friendliness all at once like an atmosphere sustaining me… Every little pine needle expanded and swelled with sympathy and befriended me… that I thought no place could ever be strange to me again." ['Solitude']

Certainly, most of us can appreciate an occasional opportunity to 'get away from everyone and everything' for a limited period of time. But in general terms, most of us prefer to live in close contact with others.

But this is not always possible. We may be temporarily separated from others by our (or their) work, school, or other commitments. Our preferred companions may be traveling, or even imprisoned. When we are unable to be with those we are most close to, it is natural to feel an almost 'oppressive' sense of our solitude. But for most of us, such periods are only temporary; we are either soon reunited with our customary companions, or else we gradually develop new ones.

But for some people (and for nearly *all* of us, at times), such involuntary solitude seems to be *more* than just 'temporary.' We may feel a sense of disconnectedness from family, friends, coworkers, and all others. We may feel isolated, alienated, and unwanted. This sense of longing for human contact results in a profound experience of **loneliness**.

This condition may be due, in part, to our failing to live up to others' *expectations* of us. It may be due to involuntary physical or emotional conditions of ours, which may cause others to turn away from us in unease. And it can also be due to our own social and behavioral propensities, which can alienate and drive others away from us.

But whatever the reasons, there is no escaping the pervasive and debilitating sense of loneliness we may be left with. We might seek out the company of companion animals, such as dogs and cats; but despite the genuine love we may feel for, and from, such creatures, it remains true that we cannot experience the same kind of mutual 'communion' with animals that we can with another human. Such a simple matter as a *two-way conversation* is not possible with animals.

We can temporarily defer, and sometimes even escape our sense of loneliness through finding purposeful activities; a mind fully occupied with other activities cannot dwell on its own solitude. In time, one's sense of loneliness may simply be crowded out of one's mind, or forgotten. Religion and spirituality are an avenue of healing for many; yet even deeply spiritual people may report being 'Lonely, but never alone,' due to the spiritual presence or presence they may feel, even in intense times of loneliness.

Again, for most of us, such periods of profound loneliness are temporary, in nature. We may soon reconcile with others; we may develop new contacts at work, in social groups, or in our neighborhoods. We may begin to enlarge our circle of activities, and meet new people. In such cases, our period of loneliness may soon be nothing but a vague memory.

But while we are enduring a period of loneliness, it is surely best to not do anything to make our situation any *worse*; e.g., by indulgence in alcohol, or other drugs. Such avenues seldom provide any 'constructive' assistance, and will more likely simply result in making us even *more* truly isolated.

But since nearly all of us are 'social animals,' we can be assured that others similarly wish to avoid such a sense of isolation. The Internet, and various forms of social media, can also be wonderful tools for enabling us to tentatively 'reach out,' and communicate with others. Participation in a 'virtual' community can be a powerful first step toward establishing 'real,' personal contacts with others—and thus, to fulfilling the 'social' side of our selves.

Loneliness, of whatever form, need not be a continuing condition— if we are willing to reach out to others, and are also receptive to the efforts of others to reach out to us.

12. Friendship

The conventional wisdom holds that we can choose our friends, but can't choose our family. But to a certain extent, our friends are not simply a matter of 'choice'; there are all kinds of variables and 'chance' events involved in the selection of our friends.

For example, they typically have to live near to us (or *have* lived near to us for a time; in our hometown, or in college, for example); they might need to be a coworker at our mutual employer; or a member of another kind of social grouping, such as a club, team, church, mosque, or synagogue. And they must have at least *some* level of common interests, or mutual activities we both enjoy.

Many of our friendships, however, are also characterized by a certain degree of *transience,* because they can be—if not *ended,* at least drastically *reduced*—by any number of 'external' factors, such as: one or both of us getting a different job; graduating from school; or moving far away. Without the continued frequency of contact with a friend, the friendship may well recede into the background, within our list of acquaintances.

Many of our friendships are likewise *situational:* friendships in high school, or in a religious congregation, for example. If you see a very good friend from high school (perhaps at a Class Reunion) that you haven't seen for a number of years, after an initial rush of emotion at meeting once again, you may very well find that the two of you have grown far *apart* from each other, since you last met. Similarly, if one of you has since moved away from the religion you both used to share, this may even create a strong *barrier* between you. This is quite natural, since the external environment—that once helped bring the two of you together—is now no longer present, to support the friendship.

There are also many *degrees* which are possible within friendships. A very close friend may be a person in whom you feel you can confide *anything*—things that you might not be willing to tell even a spouse, or a close family member. But equally, a friend may be a person with whom you have gradually worked out the informal *parameters* of your relationship: you may have discovered, for example, that it is not fruitful to discuss politics or religion, with certain friends. You also may have some friendships that are based almost exclusively on some shared, but *limited,* characteristics: you may both be Five-Point Calvinists, members of the Green Party, fans of the symphonies of Havergal Brian, or collectors of rare school lunchboxes. You may realize that you share little or nothing else in common with such friends, apart from this limited common interest—but this one mutual interest still keeps you on friendly terms.

It is sometimes argued that friendships are (almost by definition) impermanent, and that only *family ties* are truly 'lasting.' Of course, there are many people who have deliberately and forcefully 'broken off' relations with family members (such as an abusive parent; an embarrassingly alcoholic sibling; a rebellious child, etc.), so this is certainly not an 'absolute.'

But, most often, it *is* true that friendships can be 'terminated' more easily than familial relationships. After a bitter argument, both parties (or one party, if the feeling is not mutual) may solemnly pledge to *never again* communicate with the other. And of course, in these days of social media, one or both parties may simply 'block' all communications from the former friend, with the touch of a button. Social media, in fact, has created a whole new definition of 'friend.' If someone brags that "I have 563 *friends* on Facebook," this hardly demonstrates anything even slightly resembling a 'close relationship' with such persons. (You can even 'follow' someone on, say, Instagram or Twitter, while secretly *despising* the person.)

You may find, over time, that you have grown *apart* from even very close friends. The shared memories of good times you have shared will remain, and you will likely always have a strong 'sentimental' attachment to these experiences, and to the person. But the social 'evolution' of both of you, as you move through life, may ultimately lead the two of you in quite different directions, which can be quite natural. If the two of you happen to meet in public, after not having seen each other for years, the initial 'reunion' can be very joyful; or, conversely, it can also be somewhat *awkward*. (You might even find yourself wondering, "Why was I ever friends with *this* person?")

But, hopefully, most or all of us *do* find some 'true' friends, of the *lasting* kind: such friends can provide the kind of emotional support that is not always provided even by a beloved spouse, or family member. You may, for example, feel able to act in a 'freer' manner with such friends, than with your family members. You may also have certain activities that you engage in with your friends, that you don't (or can't) do with family, or the other members of your social circle.

Perhaps the greatest tribute that you can give to a friend is telling them that "You aren't just a 'friend'—you're like *family!*" This implies that the bond between you is virtually *indissoluble*, and is a lasting part of your identity.

Friendship is a treasure, and a good friend is one of those things that can help make life beautiful.

13. Romantic Love

There are many forms of human love: the mutual love between a parent/ grandparent and a child; the love of siblings, and other close family members for each other; the love of close friends, particularly when these relationships have been long-lasting. But perhaps the highest and most exhilarating form of love is the mutual love between a *couple*— whether such a relationship is supported or sanctioned by societal forms (such as marriage), or not.

Romantic love (for want of a better term) is perhaps the most intense, most eagerly sought, and most celebrated form of love among humans. The notion of two people, bound together by a reciprocal spirit of love, perhaps pledging (and expecting) to retain their intensity of feeling for a lifetime, is a 'magical' one.

Of course, literature, poetry, and every form of media endlessly celebrate this form of love. So-called 'Romantic' movies typically end with the couple seemingly having both found their 'one true love.'

But romantic love tends to be somewhat cheapened and degraded, by the way it is presented in much of our culture. For example, does the phrase 'love' in much of popular music necessarily mean anything more than a (probably transient) physical attraction? A singer stating that "I *need* your love, baby," is probably not thinking about making a lifetime commitment to this other person.

In fact, the very notion of 'commitment' seems almost antithetical to 'love,' to many modern people, who may argue that "A marriage license is just a piece of paper, and a wedding ring is just a hunk of jewelry." While this is certainly true, in a strict literal sense, this argument ignores the fact that these items can also be powerful *symbols* (as well as reminders) of a deeper, and more lasting commitment.

Naturally, the 'commitment' aspect of romantic love can be *over*-emphasized, as well. While it is certainly true that "Love isn't *just* a feeling," if 'love' lacks such an emotional element (as can sometimes happen, particularly after a period of many years together), it may be difficult to distinguish such a commitment from, say, a simple sense of *obligation.*

I suspect that nearly everyone who has experienced a true and lasting romantic love will attest that (along with the love of a parent for a child) it is probably the most intense and important emotional experience possible in this life.

But, particularly in these changing times, it is not uncommon for persons to, apparently, 'fall *out* of love': a situation when couples break up, marriages are ended, and both partners go their separate ways—sometimes with their former intense feelings of love replaced by bitterness and resentment. The great liberalization that has taken place in our laws concerning divorce since, say, the 19th century, is a reflection of what has certainly been the case in society at large; namely, that for many of us, marriage no longer entails a "till death do us part" attitude.

It is perhaps not surprising that feelings of love within a relationship can rather swiftly turn to almost their polar opposite. The emotional openness that comes with love also leaves one *vulnerable*. (I sometimes imagine that when you truly love someone, you 'give away' a part of yourself—and that part does not necessarily *return* to you, if that love ends. So you will always feel yourself 'missing' something of yourself, when the relationship is over.)

We should note, however, that modern societies often impose considerable pressures upon couples, that make it increasingly difficult for them to stay together. Financial obligations are a common source of anxiety, and are in fact perhaps the most commonly-cited reason (apart from vague generalizations such as 'irreconcilable differences') for couples to break apart. When one factors in the stresses added by raising children, on top of work and other responsibilities, it is perhaps remarkable that *more* couples don't break up.

Statistically, the divorce rate in this country has dropped slightly since the 1970s; but it remains, however, much higher than it was, say, seventy-five years ago. For a couple entering into a first marriage today, perhaps 45% of such unions will ultimately end in divorce. (And the fact that a couple doesn't *divorce* doesn't necessarily mean that they have a 'good' relationship.)

Of course, the issue is further complicated by the fact that many modern couples (about two-thirds) live together for a time prior to marriage; or they may eschew formal matrimony entirely. And today, there is little or no 'social stigma' for couples cohabitating without being married. So, then, one might wonder, why even *bother* to get married? Why not simply be together when, where, and for as long as the partners please; but then simply separate, should it be the wish of one or both parties?

One reason, of course, is that a marriage *formalizes* a relationship—both for the two parties, as well as in the view of others. More 'practically,' it also provides a measure of legal and financial security, in the case of couples with children.

But increasingly, many individuals now choose to have children without even being part of an ongoing 'couple.' This trend, of course, may eventually cause problems (e.g., emotional, as well as financial) for both parent and child; but it can also lead to some insecurity on the part of the child about her/his identity, since it basically takes *two* participants to conceive a child. But in the end, the most important thing for a child is probably simply to feel secure and loved. Single parents can provide this reassurance quite well. as can unmarried couples, same-sex couples, and so on. So one no longer *has* to "get married, in order to have kids."

But to me, perhaps the best reason for marriage nowadays is to provide an opportunity for two partners to formally declare their mutual commitment to making the relationship work. It is a way of vowing to the other person, "I'm in this relationship for good. I'm not making any 'qualifications' or 'caveats' about my commitment; and I'm not entering into it with the thought that 'I can always get a divorce later, if I change my mind.'"

In short, marriage can be a firm declaration of love—and the intent to continue one's commitment to that relationship, for a lifetime. When such a declaration is mutual, it can indeed lead to all of the joyful results that the poets and songwriters have praised.

14. Freedom

Our National Anthem states that we Americans are living in "the land of the free." But interestingly, the terms 'free' and 'freedom' appear only infrequently in both the *Declaration of Independence* and the *U.S. Constitution*: e.g., as "freedom of speech" in the 1st Amendment, or in the reference to "Free and Independent States" in the Declaration. And, as we all know, at the time this country was founded, slavery was permitted (although only implicitly—unlike the *Constitution of the Confederate States*, which explicitly made slavery legal), and women were clearly 'second-class citizens.'

What do we mean by 'freedom,' anyway? Some may informally define it as something like, "being able to do whatever I want to do," but this definition is surely too vague. Would someone who wants the 'freedom' of being able to indiscriminately shoot—without being punished for it—members of a particular political persuasion, who are protesting in front of our State Capitol, be allowed this 'freedom'? Surely not.

Would I be able to walk into a mansion owned by a billionaire, and take up residence, without their permission? Could I take down famous paintings in museums, and either deface them, or else take them away and hang them on the walls of my own home? Could I walk into a grocery store, and destroy all of the food products that aren't vegan-friendly? Of course not. So we need a more practical definition of being 'free.'

Herbert Spencer wrote in his 1851 book *Social Statics,* that "every man may claim the fullest liberty to exercise his faculties compatible with the possession of like liberty by every other man." He added that "every man has freedom to do all that he wills, provided he infringes not the equal freedom of any other man." John Stuart Mill, in his 1859 book *On Liberty,* suggested that "the only purpose for which power can be rightfully exercised over any member of a civilized community, against his will, is to prevent harm to others. His own good, either physical or moral, is not a sufficient warrant..."

These statements express a commonly-expressed sentiment about freedom: that it applies to us *personally,* insofar as what we do does not affect others. This principle is seemingly unobjectionable, to most of us. However, it may be more difficult than it seems, to determine what *does*, and does *not,* affect others. Let's attempt to break 'freedom' down into its components.

Certainly, one component of being 'free' is freedom of *thought.* George Orwell, in his book *1984,* coined the term 'thoughtcrime' to describe thoughts that a person has, which are contrary to the politically 'acceptable' ones. But of course, one's thoughts are generally kept quite *private,* so—absent some unlikely future technological breakthrough, which would allow us to literally 'read minds'—no one can be arrested simply for their thoughts; so this freedom is unobjectionable.

To a somewhat more limited extent, one can also *express* such thoughts—verbally, or in writing, as well as in other formats—although they may or may not be publicly *acknowledged.* Books about very controversial subjects (e.g., religious nonorthodoxy) back in the 16th-19th centuries were sometimes only published after the death of the author.

Nevertheless, such 'heretical' or 'objectionable' thoughts *were* ultimately able to be expressed. (Granted, you might have had to *whisper* your request to the bookseller, who kept these books 'under the counter.')

In a similar way, people may engage in activities in private, to which others would object—if they were *aware* of them. For example, prior to fairly recent times, a number of 'intimate friendships' between two women may have actually involved them being '*more* than friends'; but, by such a relationship being kept quite discreet, they were not criticized. (And in fact, only *male* homosexuality was actually 'illegal' in countries like England.)

Similarly, Oscar Wilde's being gay was somewhat of an 'open secret' in his own time; but it caused him little problem until he (unadvisedly, to be sure) sued the father of his male lover for criminal libel—and ultimately, Wilde was sentenced to two years' hard labor, for something that we would nowadays certainly include within his own right of 'freedom.'

Of course, one certainly cannot truly feel 'free' if you are required to *hide* something that is deeply important to your sense of self-identity. The struggles of LGBTQ persons in recent decades to achieve their full civil rights has, of course, perhaps been the most obvious example of persons struggling to be able to live in whatever way they please, so long as others are not being *directly* harmed by this.

Earlier generations had similar struggles with so-called 'interracial' relationships. And persons expressing religious beliefs (or nonbeliefs) which are contrary to the prevailing orthodoxy of a nation have historically faced opposition; and, in some countries, they may still face persecution, imprisonment, and even death. (Witness the case of Christian missionaries in countries such as North Korea, Somalia, and Sudan.)

We might helpfully distinguish between being able to *live* openly in a manner that we wish, and being openly and unreservedly *accepted* in such a manner. One cannot compel the inner *feelings* of others; and, in fact, to *try* to do so would trespass upon their own 'freedom.'

Of course, many of our most contentious current debates in this country are not over the *permissibility,* but over the *reaction* of others to this new relatively 'openness' and freedom. Some conservative

Christians or Muslims in America, for example, may now be reluctantly resigned to the *legality* of same-sex relationships, as well as the growing presence of Transgender persons, etc., but nevertheless still feel strong reservations about being expected to be 'approving' (or at least 'neutral') about such persons. (And, it should be noted, *non*-religious persons—as well as some 'liberal/progressive' religious people—can equally well be guilty of being *intolerant* of 'fundamentalists,' as well.)

'Freedom' in this sense becomes an important personal, social, and even 'political' matter. Certainly, even as our private thoughts and feelings must remain free, they cannot be compelled. But the harder question is, what should or should not be allowed in the *public sphere*? Can I express reservations I might personally have about certain controversial subjects out loud, in public? Or on TV? Or in books, or on a website?

Censoring or restricting such expression would seem to violate our 1st Amendment rights to *free speech*. However, it must be acknowledged that our constitutional right of 'free speech' already has various restrictions: A typical example is a person falsely yelling "Fire!" in a crowded theater—since this might cause a panicked stampede to the exits, in which some persons were injured.

Another restriction is the 'imminent lawless action' test, under which speech is not 'protected' by the First Amendment if the speaker is trying to incite a violation of the law that is both 'imminent,' as well as 'illegal.' (A speaker addressing a large group of angry protesters cannot encourage them to break windows and set businesses on fire, for example.)

We have laws prohibiting *libel, slander,* and *defamation.* Someone cannot print up leaflets accusing a next-door neighbor of being a child molester, for example. But 'public figures' (such as politicians and celebrities) have far less protection from defamatory statements, and face a higher burden of proving 'harm,' when filing a lawsuit against the 'defamer.' But again, one cannot claim 'free speech' if one is violating the *law.* For example, while a person can stand outside the White House and scream, "The President is a *jerk!*," one cannot stand there and threaten (even if supposedly said in 'jest') to *physically harm* the President.

This area of law is constantly changing, of course; for example, can a baker refuse to make a wedding cake for a Gay couple? The U.S. Supreme Court recently ruled (in a rather 'limited' decision, admittedly) that it *could*. (To make the question even starker: what if, instead, the baker had refused to bake a cake for an African-American couple? Or an interracial couple? Or a Muslim couple? Or what if the couple wanted their cake 'topper' to depict the couple in *Nazi* uniforms?)

For most of us, the 'tradeoff' we may encounter in life is when a person expressing an 'intolerant' opinion is then subjected to a measure of *social disapproval* for appearing 'illiberal.' (And of course, similarly-minded persons may also vehemently *support* the person uttering the 'unpopular' opinion.) But those are simply the consequences one must accept, for making such an opinion known. For instance, if seemingly all of one's coworkers are enthusiastically supportive of a transgender woman's 'crossing over,' or of the marriage of two men, then a 'disapproving' person will probably just have to learn to *live with* their coworkers' dissatisfaction with them, if they decide to make their reservations 'public.' (A Christian in such a situation, however, might prefer to remember the words of Psalm 75:7; "*God* is the Judge," and choose to simply remain silent.)

Perhaps the 'better path' is for all of us to simply *accept* that others are going to be different from us in a variety of ways, and to refrain from our appearing to 'judge' them. After all, in a democratic society, we are all engaged in the process of *learning how to live together,* as harmoniously as possible.

15. Authority

The concept of 'authority' implies that there exists some power which is in a sense 'over' or 'above' you; one that is 'controlling' you in some respects. It is a power that has the ability to somehow *compel* your actions, or to otherwise restrict and confine them.

For example, if one attempts to go walking out on the public streets in the nude, one will probably be quickly reported to the police, and may well end up in a hospital under a 'psychiatric watch.' Although some people might strongly argue in favor of the nudist's 'right' to have done so, most of us would probably think this 'imposition of authority' was basically appropriate.

Does it matter if the nude individual has never specifically 'consented' to living in a country which prohibits public nudity? He or she was probably just born here: in a country which prohibits walking around nude in public; so his or her lack of *consent* really has little bearing on this matter of authority—*all* persons living in this country have the same restriction.

If public nudity does not happen to be an issue of particular interest to you, what about the fact that a country may either allow, or prohibit, the sale and use of alcoholic beverages, as well as tobacco products? One person may strongly feel that alcohol and/or tobacco have very 'harmful' effects on the general public, and argue that they be banned. (Indeed, during the era of Prohibition, 1920-1933, this country did—ultimately, quite unsuccessfully—attempt to ban alcoholic beverages.) Thus, we apparently have agreed as a nation to put up with the 'negative' consequences of alcohol (such as alcoholism; driving 'under the influence'; alcohol use increasing the likelihood of crimes; its increasing the incidence of domestic abuse, etc.).

While no general ban has ever been issued in this country on tobacco products, our own 'authorities' have clearly moved steadily in the direction of restricting and discouraging their use: for example, by imposing very stiff taxes on them, and also by restricting the places where one can use tobacco products. Thirty states now prohibit smoking in restaurants and bars, and nearly all of these states also prohibit smoking in workplaces. Smoking on airplanes is almost universally banned. And in 2019, the age at which one can legally purchase tobacco products was raised from 18 to 21, by the U.S. Food and Drug Administration.

The negative 'social' effects of alcohol, and the strongly harmful 'health' effects of smoking, constitute for most of us persuasive justification for restrictions about their use. But there are many other behaviors which may also have 'negative' effects, yet there is no clear desire among most people to ban them. No one has seriously proposed making *obesity* illegal, for instance; and the same with greed, and laziness (all three of which are among the 'Seven Deadly Sins' of

Medieval theology). To some extent, this may be because it is felt that such conditions as obesity do not *directly* harm others. But it could at least be argued that gross obesity in, say, a parent, *does* have potentially harmful effects upon the children—for instance, if the parent dies at an early age due to the obesity, leaving minor children without parental care. (One could also argue that such unhealthful conditions "drive health insurance rates up," or provide a "poor role model" for children.)

Parents may also have widely differing ideas about, say, the *spanking* of one's own children, as a punishment. While 'corporal punishment' was quite routine in schools up until a few decades ago, it is banned in about half of U.S. public schools these days—but it remains legal in *private* schools, however. (Fears of lawsuits filed by parents probably fuel most of the 'bans' in public schools.) But a more difficult and controversial issue is that of spanking by *parents*. Where is the line which, once crossed, differentiates 'just parental punishment' from 'physical abuse'? There are many cases where local authorities have controversially intervened in a parent's 'punishment' of a disobedient child, by taking away the child, or by restraining (or even imprisoning) one or both parents.

The fact is that in the country we live in, there are a multitude of different 'authorities' that we are *de facto* subject to: Governmental authorities regulate the contents of the food and drink we consume; the prescription drugs we may take; who we may choose to marry, and much more. When a particular case of such 'authoritarian' control comes to our attention with which we disagree, we may easily feel that someone's rights are being violated, and argue for a more relaxed 'libertarian' standard.

But I would observe there are also considerable *benefits* to being part of a society that has such authorities; one such benefit is that they provide for a greater *uniformity of treatment* of our citizens. For instance, one cannot develop one's own monetary system and print money; but the situation back when individual states (and even churches, such as the Mormon church under Joseph Smith) had their own currency was chaotic. There is a relative 'monopoly' in any given area on who can provide electricity, heat, and other utilities; but these services operate relatively effectively for most of us (although floods, wildfires, and hurricanes can sometimes put them 'out of service' for a time).

Although one can hire private security to protect a home or workplace, one cannot establish one's own 'police' system, nor create an independent court system. (American Muslims cannot, for example, establish a 'Sharia court' intended to apply Islamic laws to marriage, crime and punishment, etc., in this country.) There is also a wide network of health care available here (although one's access to it may be severely limited by what one can *afford*, of course). Life was certainly much more difficult for those living out on the 'frontier' in the 19th century, than it is for us.

But it is also the case that there are certain *costs* to being the recipient of such benefits. One has restrictions placed upon one's freedom, and becomes subject to various authorities. In perhaps the 'ultimate' restriction upon one's freedom, one can be arrested, and then put on trial for committing a crime. If convicted, we may lose money, and even our freedom—and in some cases, we may even have our very *life* taken from us, by such authorities. And even when 'due process' was seemingly observed during such a trial, there are certainly people who have been wrongly convicted and sentenced to death (and even executed), but who were later exonerated.

This is a deplorable, but also a nearly *inescapable* result of the fact that, since nearly all of us live in *communities,* we have to adhere to certain general rules and standards of behavior, in order for us to generally be able to get along; or at least, to not be actively 'at *war*' with each other. It is doubtful that there is anyone who agrees wholeheartedly with *every* aspect of our lives that is subject to some kind of regulatory authority. (Laws regarding recreational use of marijuana are now changing, in response to changing public sentiment, as an example of developing standards.) But hopefully, we are not so firmly opposed to most such restrictions, as to make living here 'unlivable' for us.

But it should be noted that, where we have objections to certain exercises of authority, we also have available numerous options to work to *change* such restrictions. Perhaps the best contemporary example of such change is concerning same-sex relations, and various Transgender issues. Same-sex relations have gone from being largely *illegal* (for males, at least) less than twenty years ago (prior to the Supreme Court's ruling in the 2003 *Lawrence v. Texas* case), to same-sex marriages now being recognized as entirely 'legitimate,' as well as entitled to all of the benefits (e.g., death benefits) of 'traditional' marriages. Many Transgender persons are now well-known in the media, and are popularly 'accepted' to a degree that would have been unthinkable, not that many years ago. And all of this was accomplished despite strong opposition from many powerful and influential forces (particularly from the conservative religious population).

Certainly, some imposed 'authorities' may be unethical, or even strongly immoral; segregation is an obvious example, from our past. Police misconduct is a very poignant current example, where protesters have taken to the streets in many cities across this country, and even around the world. In such cases, it may be deemed necessary by some citizens to resist such authority—even to the extent of breaking the law.

But seeking legislative, and other legal means to *change* objectionable situations (e.g., specifying comprehensive 'rules of conduct' for police officers, training them in such, and rigorously enforcing them) are perhaps the better solution, in most cases. Although difficult, it is far easier to *modify* an existing authority, than to simply 'tear it down' and attempt to 'start from scratch.'

And remember: that there is no *guarantee* that a newly-created authority would not be even *worse* than the 'current' one.

16. Law & Order

Occasionally, some social thinkers will (apparently) seriously propose that people should live in a state of *Anarchy:* that is, in a condition in which where there is *no* government, and *no* external 'authority'—and everyone simply does as they wish. Many or most anarchists propose this, because they believe that people are inherently 'good' and peaceful, and that it is the very existence of central authority and government that actually turns people 'bad.'

Of course, if *everyone* would simply refrain from imposing their will on others, such a society might conceivably work—at least, on a somewhat limited basis. But most likely, a neighboring *non*-Anarchist society would take notice of the non-organized condition of the Anarchist society, and take it over by force of arms—perhaps even enslaving its former inhabitants. (It is rather doubtful that a peaceful Anarchist country could long have existed next door to Nazi Germany, or Soviet Russia, for example.)

Over time, societies have found it helpful to enshrine codes of conduct in *written* form; the Babylonian *Code of Hammurabi* (from about 1750 BCE) is a good example. Taking the form of *Laws,* such regulations provide a relatively 'objective' standard by which to judge the conduct of members of a society. A person who violates a rule such as 'Do Not Murder' has clearly *broken the Law*; and the Law may likely specify a *penalty* for such violations. If everyone (or nearly everyone) generally obeys these laws, they strongly contribute to the 'order' that prevails in a society; everyone in the society is presumed to know what the laws are, and either follows them, or else is willing to risk paying the price for disobeying them.

An 'ordered' society has many advantages: when applied fairly, these laws serve for the protection of citizens, and facilitate their interactions with one another. When disagreements arise, the laws often provide for a means of *conflict resolution,* such as is offered by some kind of judicial system. And these laws can be added to, or amended, as questions arise, or new situations come up, which were not originally anticipated.

Of course, problems arise when these laws are *not* generally followed; some political Anarchists (not the peaceful and nonviolent ones, of course) have been blamed for events such as [1] the 1886 Haymarket Square bombing, in which seven police officers were killed, and sixty others were injured, as well as [2] the 1901 assassination of President William McKinley, by Leon Frank Czolgosz. Self-proclaimed 'Anarchists' have also been blamed for acts of vandalism occurring during the 1999 protests in Seattle against the World Trade Organization, as well as during 2020 protests against police violence in Portland. Such actions have given Anarchism a pretty 'bad name' among the general public, and often resulted in calls for *increased* police presence, in order to restore and maintain 'Law and Order.'

THINKING ABOUT IT   199

Not infrequently, such demands for 'Law and Order' are fueled by fear; and, on occasions when there has been widespread urban unrest in our country, a call by politicians for 'Law and Order' may find a ready audience among the majority. And certainly, when such protests are accompanied by random looting, the burning of businesses, and violent attacks upon police and civil authorities, this is quite understandable. But the governmental imposition of martial law, curfews, and the presence of 'military' forces on public streets, can make an already volatile situation even worse.

But it is very important to attempt to understand the *reasons* for such civil unrest. Protests may be started in response to legitimate injustices: such as instances of police brutality, or the cruel treatment of immigrants. It is difficult to wholeheartedly justify 'Order,' when the *Law* has not been upheld fairly and consistently.

Henry David Thoreau's famous essay, 'On Civil Disobedience,' was a strong influence on both Mahatma Gandhi and Rev. Martin Luther King Jr. In this essay, Thoreau suggested, "Unjust laws exist; shall we be content to obey them, or shall we endeavor to amend them, and obey them until we have succeeded, or shall we transgress them at once? ... any man more right than his neighbors, constitutes a majority of one already."

A significant difficulty of such protest situations is that, when confrontations seem inevitable (e.g., between police/guardsmen, and protesters), the already-volatile situation tends to make further unfortunate incidents more likely—which in turn only exacerbates, and adds on to the existing problems. If an undisciplined crowd confronts police, it is next to impossible to control the behavior of all members of the crowd (some of whom, from the anonymity of the crowd, may throw rocks and bottles at the police); and it is more likely that some members of the police will then be more inclined to take more *extreme* crowd control measures—with the result that the chances are exponentially increased of law-abiding bystanders being tear-gassed, struck by rubber bullets, etc., which can make an already-tragic situation even more tragic.

What happens if the majority of citizens of a nation were to conclude that a nation's system of 'Law & Order' is no longer valid? Well, the ultimate rejection of a nation's concept of 'Law & Order' comes in a **revolution**. But this very extreme measure can easily replace a 'bad' government with an even *worse* one: witness the case of Cuba, or of many emerging African nations—who have ended up under brutal totalitarian regimes.

The laws of a nation are changeable; they can be amended, and improved. Measures for citizen review of those who enforce the laws can be created, or augmented. Such steps can and should be taken, so that a majority of the citizens can have confidence in the system of 'Law & Order' under which they live.

(But in the meantime, engaging in constructive *dialogue* is a better means of proceeding, than simply screaming at each other across a barricade.)

17. Justice and "Fairness"

Children—even very young ones—quickly develop a sense of what is, and isn't, 'fair.' If a child is given a piece of cake that seems smaller than another child's, or if he or she is chastised for something that another child was seemingly *not* chastised for, the accusation will quickly and strongly be made: "That's not *fair!*" Of course, the child's perception is often imbalanced, and prejudiced in its own favor. Still, it is interesting that the notion of 'fairness' is almost close to being *instinctual* in children.

When such perceptions (by *adults,* of course) are extended beyond the individual and *personal* level, to the *societal* level, they are recognized as being a component of a much broader principle: that of *Justice.* The U.S. Constitution begins with the promise, "We the People of the United States, in Order to form a more perfect Union, **establish Justice**, insure domestic Tranquility, provide for the common defence, promote the general Welfare, and secure the Blessings of Liberty to ourselves and our Posterity, do ordain and establish this Constitution for the United States of America."

One may certainly ask to what extent our country had, in fact, originally 'established' Justice, since the treatment of slaves, women, and other minorities was certainly far from 'just' at the time the Constitution was ratified in 1787. But at least, the Constitution provided for a *system of justice,* which included a court system; and it also provided a Bill of Rights, as a guarantor of certain specific rights (which have been *added to,* over time).

Of course, disagreement comes when we try to decide with more precision what, specifically, this 'Justice' is. The Declaration of Independence states, "We hold these truths to be self-evident, that all men are created equal, that they are endowed by their Creator with certain unalienable rights, that among these are life, liberty, and the pursuit of happiness." This statement seems to assert that there are certain basic 'rights' which are basically *inherent* in our very existence. But these lofty statements encounter difficulties, when we try to make them more precise.

For example, what exactly is entailed in the 'pursuit of happiness'? Obviously, if one's individual pursuit of happiness entails the *unhappiness* of another, it may very well be objectionable. And, of course, convicted criminals may be deprived not only of their 'liberty,' but—in cases of 'capital crimes'—even of their very lives.

Perhaps the basic problem is the fact that certain types of *inequality* seem to be basically 'built into' our world. As we all know, 'Life isn't *fair*': some children may be born into poverty, while others are born into wealth and privilege. Some individuals seem to be 'gifted' with athletic ability, musical ability, and physical attractiveness. We can't do much of anything to change even something as simple and basic as our *height.* (As young men who wish they were at least six feet tall may lament.)

But achieving 'Justice' and a basic degree of 'Fairness' need not require the impossible task of trying to create *absolute equality:* we can, however, certainly seek to promote 'equality *under the law.*' We can, for instance, attempt to provide all or most citizens with the minimal requirements for living (such as food and shelter), and access to at least 'emergency' health care.

Income inequality is a much more difficult problem, because it is the product of so many different factors. There is a complex web of innate potential; the degree of individual effort; and environmental circumstances (such as family and education), that affect our economic circumstances. But when income can be largely passed on, from one family generation to another (without particular regard for such an individual's 'merit'), it becomes progressively an expression of apparent 'inequality.'

But before trying, say, to legislate through the income tax system an *end* to inherited wealth, we might note that the child who happened to be born into favorable circumstances didn't do anything 'wrong,' or personally harm anyone else; these circumstances were simply the 'luck of the draw,' so to speak.

It is probably not possible to establish standards in such difficult matters, that will be perceived as being 'fair' to all. But there are various ways in which we can attempt—through legislation, for example—to make the 'playing field' more 'level.' Greater subsidies and scholarships for students, for instance, and more affordable access to child care for working parents, are ways in which greater degrees of upward mobility can be achieved.

American history is filled with 'inspirational' stories of persons coming to this county with virtually nothing, but ultimately succeeding, through hard work and perseverance. And it should be noted that being able to move from one economic/social class to another, is a major component of what we know as 'The American Dream.'

But changing economic conditions have made this kind of 'upward mobility' more difficult for our current population, than for some earlier generations. The modern job market is less favorable to the kinds of jobs that were readily available to immigrants in the 19th and early 20th centuries, for example. Similarly, going into business for oneself is also more difficult, when one may now be competing against, not other small vendors, but against established multinational corporations (who may even have 'outsourced' most of their operations overseas, in order to cut costs).

But it is very likely not possible to establish a true 'Meritocracy': that is, a system under which the 'best' or 'most qualified' person rises to the top, in all situations. There is no certain way of predicting the success of a given student who is given a scholarship to an 'elite' college, for instance. In the same way, who can tell 'in advance' whether a given business venture will be a success or a failure?

Perhaps all we can do is to strive to create relatively 'equal treatment' of individuals by our public institutions—including the legislative, judicial, and penal institutions.

18. Progress?

The world is certainly *different* nowadays than it used to be. The technical advances that have been made in recent years (the Internet, cell phones, and personal computers are obvious examples) have clearly made the current living environment radically different from the world even of our parents—much less the environment of generations even earlier. But a more difficult question is: whether or not the world is *better* than it was, in times past? In short, have we made *progress,* in our society?

Many of us hearken back to idealized visions of an earlier, simpler time, that is imagined to have been preferable to our own time: a time when families were purported to have been closer, neighborhoods more congenial, and the country more unified. Some people will even go much further than this, and dream of a past 'Golden Age,' when mythical civilizations like Atlantis and Lemuria are supposed to have existed.

But almost no one, I think, would seriously like to return to, say, the pre-agricultural days of nomadic hunter-gatherers. (We certainly wouldn't want to give up our considerable advances in medical science and dentistry, for instance.) Similarly, this country will certainly not reverse the gains of the Civil Rights movement; nor will South Africa return to its pre-Apartheid conditions. And, of course, the younger generation would certainly be unwilling to give up its favorite electronic devices. (Not even just for a *few hours!*)

But there may be something to be said in favor of, perhaps, taking a 'step back' to slightly less complicated times. To a time when families in the evenings might jointly listen to a book being read aloud, rather than us all being completely focused upon our individual tablet computers and cell phones. To hearken back to a time that was less *instantaneous,* and more 'reflective'—a time when practically every event that happens around us was not immediately shared with others via social media, and we were not immediately evaluated on the basis of how many 'followers' and 'likes' we have. To return to a time when there was seemingly more time for seriously ***thinking about*** what was happening, *before* we felt compelled to publicly comment on it.

The pace of modern life certainly seems to be much faster than it was in times past; and 'stress' seems to be a very common complaint among our peers. It is interesting to note that many people are finding themselves working longer and longer hours, just to try and 'keep up' with their current financial lifestyle. And the economic uncertainties of recent years have shown nearly all of us just how *quickly* one can move from being relatively 'financially secure,' to being practically (or even literally) 'on the streets.'

Certainly, there can be no 'going back' in technological terms; no significant proportion of the population is voluntarily going to relinquish their automobiles, televisions, or cell phones—although the realities of coping with climate change may certainly force us to make *changes* in our use of transportation. No one wants to return to the days before we had ATM cards, and we had to make it to the bank before closing time on Friday if we needed money for the weekend.

But perhaps we can still recapture some of the desirable *values* and *practices* that characterized earlier eras: a time when families did more things together—such as sitting down together and sharing at mealtimes. A time when people belonged to actual *groups*: whether lodges, bowling leagues, bridge clubs, book study groups, prayer circles, coffee klatches, etc. We might even try to regain something of the lost art of *conversation,* by putting aside our cell phones for a half-hour or more a day.

Progress does not have to be an 'irresistible force'; it can and should be *steered* and shifted in its direction—because not everything that is *different* is necessarily 'better.'

19. Values

What is important to us? And, in a fundamental sense, what is *most* important to us? What are the ideals we hold dearest, and are the most resistant to change? These may be considered as our basic *values*. The values we hold can come about and develop in a variety of ways: our family upbringing; those principles taught to us in school, and higher education; religious teachings; political convictions, and so on.

We may be a 'family-oriented' person; or a 'good Catholic'; or someone committed to 'sustainable development'; or a Vegan who is a passionate defender of 'Animal Rights'; or a 'Civil Libertarian,' and many more possibilities. When we hold such convictions deeply, they tend to shape and inform our beliefs and actions in many areas of life: such as what we eat, who we marry, how we vote, where we work, and much more.

Most of our primary values were developed over time, and once formed, they tend to be quite resistant to change, barring an unusual occurrence: such as a religious conversion; or taking a shocking tour of a 'factory farm'; or researching a particular subject in depth.

Different values held by different people can, of course, cause conflict; and not uncommonly, they may cause very *sharp* conflict. The question of the legality of abortion is one obvious example. While various aspects of abortion can either be regulated, or not regulated, in various different ways (e.g., bans after a certain stage in pregnancy; making a requirement for minors to have parental consent; restrictions in coverage of the procedure by health plans; requirements for pregnant women to view an *ultrasound* before having an abortion, etc.), the general right of a woman to choose to terminate a pregnancy is one that does not readily lend itself to 'compromise'—which is one reason why our differences are so *sharp,* on the matter.

Many of our values are tied to our religious (or anti-religious) beliefs, or other similarly strong personal convictions; being strongly resistant to change, such values can place us into strong disagreement with others. A particular individual's opposition to something like abortion, or to killing animals for food, or to 'radical' environmentalism, is often not something that they are content to simply practice on an *individual* basis; such a person probably wouldn't say something like, "While I *personally* would not have an abortion, eat meat, or clearcut a forest, I *do* strongly oppose any prohibitions or restrictions upon *your* right to do any of these things." Quite often, these values are interpreted as having much wider, and even *national* implications—such as requiring complete *bans* of actions contrary to our own values.

Obviously, such disagreements create social and political conflict in our society; and these conflicts are nearly always, in principle, irreconcilable. Honest and committed persons may find themselves shouting at each other, as they stand on opposite sides of a protest line—with neither side really interested in finding any room for 'leeway,' or compromise.

It is possible, of course, for representatives from such opposing sides to dialogue, and seek to better understand each other's positions. In some cases, supporters from both sides of an issue may even agree on the reasonableness of certain regulations in the most 'extreme' situations. But probably more often, no agreement is possible, and both sides will remain firmly opposed to each other.

In a society like ours, such controversies are typically worked out through legislation, as this legislation is interpreted by the courts; such legislation is (at least to some extent) generally subject to the wishes of the electorate. And ultimately, it may simply come down to a 'majority vote,' that determines the nation's position on certain issues.

But the positions of most people *can* change, even on issues involving fundamental values, over time. The growing acceptance (or, at a minimum, the grudging toleration) of LGBTQ individuals and relationships is perhaps the most obvious example in recent years. The change of attitudes nationally that has taken place in, say, just the two decades between President Clinton's signing into law of the 'Defense of Marriage Act' in 1996, and the nationwide legalization of same-sex marriages in 2015 by the Supreme Court, is remarkable.

In a similar way, it is noteworthy that, although abortion generally remains legal, there are increasing restraints being placed upon it in individual states. The number of abortions performed in the United States has steadily declined since 1980—and this is *not* solely due to the additional regulations, which make it more difficult to obtain an abortion.

The evolution and development in our positions on such 'hot button' issues suggests that, even on positions that are firmly grounded in our individual values, we *can* often find ways to try and accommodate the views of others—and to peacefully *coexist*.

20. Conformity, and Individuality

Most of us like to view ourselves as firmly being 'individuals,' with our own independent values and ideals. But at the same time, we also often wish to associate ourselves with others in a *group*. We thus typically exhibit traits associated with *both* conformity, and individuality.

And these associated traits can also be mixed, and even celebrated. The Vegan who consumes honey, for example, or the hard-line political conservative who fully supports Transgender rights, may both actually be quite proud of their *differences* from the group 'herd.' This individuality supports their belief in the independence of their own thought.

But, from the perspective of the *group,* such 'individual' differences may be perceived to work against the *cohesion* of the group. Accordingly, social pressure may be applied (whether lightly, or more strongly) to such individuals, in order to try and persuade them to 'toe the line'—for the sake of maximizing the *group's* social or political influence. And, to be sure, individuals can easily choose to just remain *silent,* and not openly express their 'differences' from the group, while participating in corporate activities; or alternately, they may also choose to just passively *go along* with the group (who may be holding a protest, and chanting something like, "No Justice, No Peace!" or "Lock him up!").

Such conformity for the sake of supporting the *solidarity* in a group is quite understandable, and often prudent. (If you are *not* chanting along with the crowd, they may consider you an *enemy!*) But such conformity can also become *painful,* when it is ultimately perceived as 'repressive.' One may come to feel that "I can't truly *be myself* when I'm with this group," and begin to develop feelings of resentment against the group.

But it is also true that *some* degrees of individual difference in a group may be tolerated, and even celebrated, within the group. Such divergence may be cited by group leaders as evidence of the lack of 'groupthink' and *enforced* 'conformity' within the group's body. In political rallies, for example, it is common for advocates to point out the seeming *diversity* of support that a particular politician receives.

Individuality can, of course, be expressed in a variety of ways. Minor variations in such things as dress, and hairstyle, are easy ways to 'distinguish' oneself from the crowd, without being too 'radical.' But variations in even such presumably 'minor' matters can be expressed in a variety of ways that become increasingly extreme. Wearing one's hair in the 'spikes' made popular by Punk Rockers when one is attending a Republican convention, or wearing worn jeans and a dirty t-shirt when surrounded by others wearing business suits or formal attire, will make one's 'individuality' more distinctive (and probably offensive to the group).

And, it should be noted, there can be a certain amount of *fun* in being a 'contrarian': in being the rare individual in a group that is 'different' from the norm. Such a person may even view him/herself as being 'enlightened,' 'aware,' and 'awakened,' when compared to the others in the group.

But most members of a group voluntarily (and even enthusiastically) choose to remain firmly in the 'mainstream' of the group. They may try to dress, and act, as much like other members in the group as possible. This can create a feeling of one's personal sense of power and influence being *expanded*, as a result of membership in this larger group. But such homogeneity can also work against the goals of the group, as outsiders may dismiss the group's perceived 'herd conformity' as demonstrating its members as being incapable of independent thought and action.

Ultimately, one does not *have* to 'conform' to many or most of the standards and norms that surround us. One can remain happily outside the 'masses,' and feel quite satisfied with one's own individuality. But most of us have sufficient similarity of our ideas, that we quite willingly associate with others, and even seek to minimize our 'differences,' in non-essential areas.

So, in the end, we may even choose to express our individuality *through* a certain measure of conformity.

21. Individual Taste

There is an old Roman adage, *"De gustibus non est disputandum,"* which we typically render from Latin to English as something like, "There is no accounting for taste."

We have all had the experience of strongly liking some particular type of food; but when we try to share it with someone else, they inform us, "I don't like it." Our initial reaction is usually one of surprise (or even shock), and we may suggest slight modifications in how the food is presented, or seasoned, in hopes of enabling the other to experience the same pleasure we do from the food—but, we are usually unsuccessful.

This experience is so common, that we often simply dismiss it as unimportant. "She likes broccoli, and I don't; I like my steaks red and juicy, and she likes them *very* well-done." We quickly become accustomed to such differences among people, and it doesn't usually bother us.

But food is not the only area of life in which such differences are encountered. Tastes in music are another example. After revealing our favorite kind(s) of music to another person, we may be told, "Well, I don't like Country music"; or "Hip-Hop just doesn't appeal to me"; or "Classical music is boring." While we may not be upset if a loved one doesn't like all the same foods that we do, we may feel more strongly about our tastes in music: rejection of our favorite music can be felt almost as a personal rejection of *us*.

However, it should be noted that such tastes can be *developed*. Eating 'fine food' and drinking 'fine wine' on a regular basis can help one develop a more sophisticated palate, so that one no longer enjoys the same greasy hamburgers and too-spicy tacos one used to love.

Similarly, musical taste can be developed, through exposure and education. Appreciation of Classical music and Jazz typically requires a greater degree of background knowledge (and perhaps, age and sophistication) than appreciation of 'popular' music.

Taste in works of art such as painting is still another example. While nearly everyone can appreciate 'classical' art (e.g., Greek and Roman statues) and Renaissance art, art from the 'Modern' era (e.g., Van Gogh, Picasso), or 'Abstract Expressionism' (e.g., Salvador Dali, Jackson

Pollock, Andy Warhol), and 'Postmodern' works (such as 'Performance Art') gets a much less unified reception.

Appreciating art from cultures other than one's own background (e.g., classical African art; East Asian music) can similarly require more exposure and background, before it can be fully appreciated.

When dealing with art and music, one can come up with seemingly 'rational arguments' for why one's personal preferences are 'justified' (and perhaps even 'superior'), when compared to the preferences of others. Similarly, wine connoisseurs can find myriads of extremely subtle ways of describing a wine, of which the average wine drinker (who may only really distinguish between 'red' and 'white') is unaware.

But still, in the end, once all the rational arguments have been used, one still has little more hope of *persuading* another person to accept your views of art or music as 'superior' to theirs, if—after your having provided them with appropriate background—they still conclude, "I just don't *like* it!"

Which is fine: there is a tremendous profusion of art in the modern world: ranging from the finest art galleries, to the 'Street Art' graffiti that seemingly adorns every available surface in urban areas. Similarly, in nearly any even medium-sized American city, there are restaurants that serve Italian, Mexican, Vietnamese, Indian, French, Chinese, Japanese, Thai, Soul Food, and every other conceivable kind of cuisine.

We can and should *celebrate* such diversity, which only adds to the richness of our lives.

22. Entertainment

No one wants to "work all the time." (Or at least, very few people do.) There are all sorts of 'productive' activities we might engage in during our 'free time': we can participate in various learning activities: take classes, read serious books, research a subject online, etc. We can also develop skills, such as playing musical instruments. We can engage in healthful activities, such as walking, jogging, exercising, and team sports. We can participate in 'group' activities, such as attending religious services, or social clubs.

But such activities nevertheless require a substantial expenditure of *energy;* we are usually ready to just "sit down and *rest*," afterwards. In fact, we may wish to "just relax, and *turn my mind off,* for a while." Thus, we may seek not so much to be 'enlightened,' as to be *amused, or entertained.*

Although Americans on the average work longer hours than our peers in most European countries, we still have a reasonable amount of time available for recreational activities. We may watch TV, visit movie theaters, attend concerts, read popular novels, and devote ourselves to the Internet and social media, in such periods of rest.

Entertainment has actually become a very large *industry* in this country, and this industry is growing rapidly in other countries as well (particularly China and India). It is interesting to take note of the changes that have taken place in our tastes in popular culture over the past one or two centuries. On the 'lowbrow' side, traveling 'Freak Shows' used to be popular: where persons such as conjoined twins, or individuals with facial or bodily deformities were exhibited to the public in decidedly unsympathetic settings. Fortunately, such shows have almost entirely disappeared, being illegal in many states.

On the 'highbrow' side, as strange as it might seem to us today, *operas* in Europe used to be a form of 'popular' entertainment. Before movies existed, operas were often practically the only time that such 'large scale' public entertainment would be presented—with impressive scenery, costumes, acting, and music—to a general audience. Perhaps predictably, the 'grand opera' of composers like Meyerbeer eventually tended to give way in the general public to 'Comic Opera' or 'Opera Buffa,' which were a less 'highbrow' form of entertainment.

When full-length motion pictures were developed, there initially seemed to be a desire on the part of many movie-makers to use the new medium to present 'enlightening' and 'uplifting' films. But in the 1940s and 1950s, *Film Noir* became the rage, with its gritty portrayals of hardboiled detectives, untrustworthy 'dames,' and generally *seedy* areas of cities.

Then television came along in the 1950s, and there was originally a tendency for it to be considered as 'family entertainment,' with shows such as *I Love Lucy, Ozzie and Harriet,* and *Leave It to Beaver.*

Vast 'biblical dramas' such as *The Ten Commandments* and *Ben-Hur* were also very popular in the 1950s (although they often substituted 'cinematic drama' for biblical literalism).

But there were, in fact, considerable problems with such forms of entertainment—which were largely unnoticed by the general public at the time: In television, for example, African-Americans were largely absent (except perhaps as maids and cooks), and the gender stereotyping of women was nearly universal. And of course, LGBTQ issues would not have even been *dreamed* of by the producers.

For several decades, there were the three major TV networks—which imposed a rather severe limit on the opportunities for creative persons to 'break into' the field. But the modern development of cable TV has led to the profusion of hundreds of separate channels, and the advancements of digital technology has enabled programs and shows to be produced at a drastically reduced cost.

This reduction in costs has led to the exponential growth of so-called 'Reality TV' shows ('unscripted' is perhaps the better term), which seemingly deal with almost every conceivable topic or subgroup out there. And, in the name of 'entertainment,' they are often turned into 'games' or competitions (e.g., where chefs must complete a complex recipe very quickly).

On the 'positive' side, these tendencies enable programs to be produced that are targeted for a smaller and more specific 'niche' or subgroup, than was the case when there were only three networks. Programs (and entire channels) tailored for African-American, Latino, and LGBTQ audiences are now common, and available 24 hours a day.

But on the 'negative' side, it also seems to be the case that movie and TV producers are striving to appeal to our increasingly 'jaded' sensibilities. For example, not long ago, it was almost unheard of for women to be physically and graphically struck on camera; in addition to other motivations, such violence was quite contrary to the women's movement's strong emphasis of opposition to violence against women. But now, not only are there female boxers and MMA fighters, but in movies, brutal rapes, physical assaults, and even murders are depicted in gory detail, and in high definition (with viewers able to 'pause' the program, and replay a segment, if they wish).

It also used to be 'beyond the pale' for *children* and young people to be hurt, much less killed, in horror and drama movies. While this is still an area being explored somewhat tentatively, this is apparently no longer a 'line' that cannot be crossed by producers. And of course, sexuality is shown routinely (whether it really has anything to do with the story, or not), in graphic depictions that would have been restricted to 'X-rated' theaters, in decades past.

No one (well, hardly anyone) would seriously propose a return to the censorship of past years. (It would be impossible anyway, with the advent of the Internet.) But perhaps we can all become somewhat more conscious of how our entertainment dollars are spent—and what kind of media they are *encouraging*.

23. Civility

Unless one lives all alone in the wilderness, one will encounter other people with some frequency. One may simply wave, and quickly greet one's neighbors when heading off to work in the morning, without ever engaging in any serious conversations with them; or (less frequently), you can also choose to ignore them completely.

However, when you go to the grocery store, or perhaps even out to buy gasoline, this is more difficult; you may have to deal with clerks, attendants, and other workers. And if we go to the movie theater, or a play, or a sporting event, we will certainly encounter other people, even if we *try* to keep to ourselves. And for most of us, we *have* to encounter others at work, at school, or in any voluntary organizations we belong to (such as churches, mosques, temples or synagogues); in most of these, we typically have relatively little choice about the others who are present.

We've probably all had any number of very *unpleasant* experiences with other people, in various situations. Such experiences can lead us to want to withdraw from associating with those who are outside of our own 'select' circle of friends and family. But at the same time, we've all certainly also had numerous experiences of encountering someone casually, and then having a very agreeable exchange with them.

And certainly, it is much more *pleasant* to get along with your neighbors, your coworkers, and others who you see on a regular basis. So the question is, perhaps, how are we to best just 'get along' with others, without causing disagreeable conflicts?

It has long been said that, to avoid arguments, one should never discuss sex, politics, or religion with most people. Certainly, this is wise advice if one wishes to preclude the possibility of disagreements. These are, after all, three topics about which most people have rather passionate feelings. And we may consider our own opinions in these areas to be part of our very *essence;* and thus, a rejection of our opinions in these areas may equate to a feeling of rejection of *ourselves,* as such. Most of us, therefore, gradually establish certain 'boundaries' for our conversations with persons we encounter on a semi-regular basis (e.g., a checkout clerk at a store we shop at frequently; a waiter or waitress at a favorite restaurant), so that we are careful to not veer into areas that might create conflict.

But this is not possible with persons that we encounter for the first time. Here, we don't have the advantage of experience; and we are seemingly required to *improvise.*

Yet, actually, there is a time-honored set of practices that can guide us in such situations; and, in fact, most of us used to be *trained* by our parents or other adults in these practices, which are usually referred to as **Civility**. This is actually a rather simple concept: it simply means being pleasant and considerate toward others—even if we don't know them. It also involves treating even perfect strangers with a considerable degree of *respect,* and *courtesy.*

Pundits and social commentators these days sometimes bemoan the 'loss of civility' in the modern world. I haven't actually studied any social science research on this particular subject, so I can hardly 'quantify' any *reductions* in the 'average' degree of civility that have taken place in my own lifetime. (But I *do* recall that when I was young, persons openly uttering some mildly *racist,* and other clearly *sexist* remarks, were far from 'infrequent' in some social contexts. So I think that, in some respects, we may have made *some* progress, since then.)

But it is certainly true that incidents illustrating a *lack* of civility are becoming much more widely *known,* these days. The increasingly pervasive influence of social media, and the ubiquity of *cameras* with *video recording* capabilities, certainly allows incidents of **un**-civility to become immediately 'shared' and widely known by many thousands of people—almost as soon as they occur.

I sometimes wonder if television might not be one of the key 'influences' in this apparent decline of civility. Television shows strive to be 'entertaining'; and, for better or worse, most of us seem to be more 'entertained' by watching two people *argue,* than by seeing them speak in a friendly and respectful manner. Both 'scripted' television shows, and purported 'reality' shows, often emphasize conflicts between people. (These are always the 'teaser' segments they show just before a commercial break.) In fact, such conflicts are often the supposed 'comedic' element for many shows.

TV talk shows also frequently bring *deeply conflicting* viewpoints together (a tradition which perhaps had its origin in the FCC's 'Fairness Doctrine,' which required radio and TV broadcasters to present 'fair and balanced coverage' of controversial issues); but this deliberate juxtaposition of sharply diverging viewpoints may create near-explosive scenarios—and they can transform what could have been relatively calm *discussions,* into bitter *arguments* (sometimes even descending into physical altercations).

And it should be noted that the *anonymity* which social media allows, permits some persons to be much more *rude* (or to 'throw shade,' to use the currently popular slang term), than they would have been 'in person.' Many people do not hesitate to send someone a 'flaming' E-mail, or make a sarcastically critical Instagram/Twitter post, that they probably would never have said *directly* to the person. And the ease and *speed* with which we can now send 'nasty' or 'snarky' comments to others— often adding offensive *emojis* (including the popular 'pile of poo') or other graphics with a simple click—tends to make us willing and able to say rude things, without having first 'thought it over.' Whereas, in an earlier time, when we had to physically write a letter to someone in longhand, put it into an envelope, add a stamp, then take it to a mailbox, we had much more time to reflect, and perhaps 'cool down,' before doing something that we might later regret. (Think of how often public figures quickly delete a Twitter or Instagram post, when they see that it immediately triggers lots of negative comments.)

As with so much else in life, if we would just first ***think about it,*** before taking some action, there would be a much greater degree of courtesy and civility in our society—which would be a very good thing.

24. Discussions, Versus Arguments

Many of us don't like to get into certain types of discussions with others, because "it always ends up as an *argument!*" And certainly, all of have had situations where we end up in a very unpleasant exchange with someone: where neither of us could succeed in persuading the other person, and the discussion just seemed to go around in circles, perhaps degenerating into name-calling, or worse. (Such arguments can occur, even when you are adhering to the maxim of "Never discuss sex, politics, or religion.") You can end up in a heated argument about a football team; or a favorite singer; or what color to paint the house; or what toppings to put on the pizza, for that matter.

In some cases, such disagreements are insoluble, because they are based on inherently subjective feelings; I can probably argue/explain why *I* prefer one kind of soda to another, but I can't really argue that this particular soda is 'better' than another kind. It's largely the same with favorite sports teams, or favorite singers; we can *provide* 'rational-sounding' arguments defending our preferences; but ultimately, such choices are really are based on *feelings*, not facts—and thus, they are basically unresolvable.

So does that mean that there is no point for us to ever discuss 'serious' topics with anyone? That we should *never* discuss sex, politics, or religion? I don't think so. We can all learn some techniques to enable us to 'disagree *agreeably.*' One excellent illustration of this point can be found in the *Dialogues* of Plato; the majority of these dialogues feature Plato's teacher, Socrates, engaging in a philosophical discussion with someone on a topic such as Justice, the Soul, or Love. While Socrates' protagonists may disagree with him, both sides typically remain 'civil.'

But these *Dialogues* also illustrate an important point: Socrates was himself sentenced to death by the Athenian court on several charges, including that he encouraged the 'corruption of the youth.' (After all, teaching young people how to rationally *argue* against the viewpoints of their *elders* is certainly perceived as 'corruption' by most of us in the older generation.)

If one views the point of such a discussion as being simply to *explain/share* viewpoints, rather than trying to *persuade* the other person (or trying to 'win' an argument), this will in itself minimize potential conflicts. You and the other person may simply reach a point where you have to acknowledge, "I don't agree with you; but after our discussion, I now understand much better *what* you believe, and *why* you believe it—and I respect your point of view."

How can we keep a rational discussion from degenerating into a pointless argument? Perhaps the best way is to attempt to follow the standard rules of *rational argument:* that is, striving to simply present objective *evidence* about the question at issue, and avoiding irrelevant and irrational approaches. For example, one should strive to avoid *logical fallacies,* such as the following:

1. **Argumentum ad hominem ('against the man'):** Verbally attacking the person *presenting* an argument, rather than trying to refute the person's argument. Note that even a convicted serial *murderer* can assert that 'The Earth circles the Sun, and not vice versa'; but this person's *immorality* doesn't make that statement false.

2. **False Dilemma:** This is when something is falsely claimed to be an 'either/or' situation, with only two possible positions— when there actually are one or more *other* options. For example, some religious conservatives may assert, "Either you believe in the Bible and God, or else you believe in Evolution." But many (most?) people, in fact, see no irreconcilable conflict between believing in God, and believing in some form of Evolutionary theory.

3. **Post hoc, ergo propter hoc ("after this, therefore because of this"):** This fallacy is illustrated by the common argument, "Such-and-such person was elected President, and *this* is the

reason the economy is in its current (bad or good) condition." The President might very well be *one* of the causes of the current condition of the economy; but there could be numerous *other* causes, as well. To make this argument, you would need to attempt to establish a cause/effect relationship between the *actions* of the current President, and the economy.

4. **The Fallacy of Composition**: That is, assuming that something which is true of a *part* of a whole, must also be true of the whole. An illustration would be, "*All* of the people who were engaged in that protest downtown are responsible for the vandalism and damage done to stores, and office buildings." It could well be the case that the people doing such damage were *counter-protesters*—or, at least, persons who are not representative of the entire *group* of protesters (whose organizers may have strongly rejected, and later condemned such actions).

5. **Argumentum ad populum ("appeal to the people")**: Arguing that whatever the 'majority' believes must be so, such as stating that "*everyone* knows this is wrong!" In reality, there is probably almost *nothing* that literally 'everyone' agrees is wrong; or even anything that 100% of, say, '*all* Republicans' or '*all* people who aren't racists' agree on.

If we could avoid common fallacies such as these (and I dearly wish that some 'required' college or high school courses covered these and others, in some detail), as well as retain our sense of *civility,* our discussions would be much less likely to devolve into contentious *arguments.* We may ultimately come to a point of strong disagreement about certain *facts,* but of course, many 'factual' statements cannot be absolutely *proved* one way or another; again, this is an opportunity for us to disagree, without being *disagreeable.*

25. The Sense of History

In Abraham Lincoln's second Annual Message to Congress (given on December 1, 1862), he said, "Fellow citizens, we cannot escape history.

We, of this Congress and this administration, will be remembered in spite of ourselves. No personal significance, or insignificance, can spare one or another of us. The fiery trial through which we pass will light us down in honor or dishonor, to the latest generation."

The Civil War had begun the April of the previous year, with the firing on of Fort Sumpter by the Confederacy. This was indeed a dark time for the United States, as this war was to rage on for nearly two-and-a-half more years, resulting in more casualties (counting those from both sides) than the U.S. military suffered in World War I, World War II, the Korean War, and the Vietnam War combined.

Yet, we can now take a 'historical' perspective on the Civil War: and we see that the so-called 'verdict of history' about President Lincoln and his conduct of the war has generally been *positive*. (Those sympathetic to the Confederacy have a much different view of 'The War Between the States,' of course.) But, as freedom fighter (and later Prime Minister of India) Jawaharlal Nehru said in his book, *The Discovery of India,* "History is almost always written by the victors and conquerors and gives their view. Or, at any rate, the victors' version is given prominence and holds the field."

Is this true? If Hitler and the Nazis had triumphed during the Second World War, the accounts given in our history books would certainly be much different. So, is the statement (attributed to automobile entrepreneur Henry Ford) that "History is bunk," accurate? Is history deliberately 'slanted' one way or another, depending primarily on who is telling the story? (Historians will argue, for example, for or against the so-called 'Whig Interpretation of History,' which viewed history as the continuous *progression* towards greater degrees of liberty and democracy.)

Part of the reason for such diverse opinions is that much of 'history' does not consist simply of *factual* matters. While it may be unanimously agreed that the Confederate firing on Fort Sumpter took place on April 12–13, 1861, countless other matters about the War are still vigorously debated by historians, as well as by many other commentators. A statement such as, "Slavery was the main cause of the Civil War," is to some degree a matter of *interpretation*, and does not have an objectively 'right' or 'wrong' answer—one that *all* reasonable observers will agree upon.

But that really isn't the main point I wish to make here. I would simply observe that viewing the situations we currently find ourselves embroiled in through the 'Lens of History' can be a very useful perspective. When we are immersed in current events, we often 'lack *perspective*' on them; we perhaps see such events as being unique, and of much greater significance, than we would if we were looking back on them from, say, ten or twenty (or two hundred) years later.

The rise of social media has, I would suggest, helped to foster a climate of 'immediacy' in our country (and the world). For example, consider the now-widespread use of the term 'meme' in social media (which is quite unlike its original meaning by biologist Richard Dawkins, who coined the term in his first book, *The Selfish Gene*), where a 'meme' is a relatively transient bit of media (a photo, short video, cartoon, a brief blob of text, etc.), that spreads rapidly over the Internet.

This kind of 'instant attention' is the polar opposite of what is meant by the 'historical perspective.' An Internet 'meme' that gets several million 'views' in just hours or days may achieve this 'fame' on a very *temporary* basis—but then be completely ignored and forgotten, in just weeks (or even days); that's hardly enough time for anything to be considered 'historical.'

This difference perhaps provides us with another way of assessing the events that happen around us. As I suggested earlier, it is common for us to view current events as being of greater significance, than they are when viewed from such a 'larger' perspective. If one is discouraged about the current state of political events, for example, it can actually be somewhat reassuring to see that our present situations are not completely 'unique'; in fact, when compared to many past political situations, they may actually seem somewhat *minor* in character. (Compare the significance of issues like repealing slavery, and giving the vote to women, with some of our current political disputes.)

The Spanish-born philosopher, George Santayana, wrote in his book, *Reason in Common Sense:* "Progress, far from consisting in change, depends on retentiveness… when experience is not retained… infancy is perpetual. Those who cannot remember the past are condemned to repeat it."

Although historical situations are unique, they often have *parallels* in the past that can be quite striking. Greek and Roman law and politics can still carry many valuable lessons for us moderns. It is relatively easy for us to hastily conclude that the decision or action of some long-dead political figure was wrong; but it is much harder for us to decide whether *we* are, in fact, engaging in a similar error.

History will most likely *not* 'remember' many of the events which seem extremely important to us now. This can help us to appreciate that, with time, things will fall into a more appropriate context and significance. The passionate debates in the Roman Senate; the debates over fine points of Christological doctrine in the early Church; the debates between the Federalists and the anti-Federalists at the foundation of our country, and similar controversies, were epochal in their time— but nowadays, they are often just skimmed through, in contemporary history classes.

History is a fascinating subject, and one that we can, and *should*, learn from. Otherwise, we will likely face the result that Santayana warned us about.

26. Technology

Is the time we are living in 'unique'? Are things occurring now that have *never* happened before, in all of human history? Certainly. Caesar didn't have text messaging when he decided to cross the Rubicon; the Apostle Paul didn't have E-mail when he wrote to the Galatians; Lewis & Clark didn't have the benefit of GPS, or even drones, during their pioneering explorations.

Perhaps the most obvious illustrations of how our times are different from previous times are due to our ever-increasing use of *technology*. Just as the Industrial Revolution of the 18th and 19th centuries forever changed our working lives, and electricity and the automobile revolutionized the late 19th and early 20th centuries, so computers, television, satellite technology, and the Internet have revolutionized our own lives. And the *pace* of such change shows no signs of slowing down.

A ready and striking example was provided with the Coronavirus pandemic that began in late 2019. The world has seen pandemics before; and previous outbreaks were often even deadlier (e.g., the Black Death of the 14th century; the Spanish Flu of 1918, etc.). But one of the most remarkable things that was done in response to the COVID pandemic was the large number of people who were now instructed to 'work from home.' This is something that would have been completely unthinkable, just a few decades ago.

But now, with E-mail, Zoom, FaceTime, and countless other 'virtual' tools and software, this was actually *possible*—and close to half of all American workers were now *telecommuting,* rather than driving to work five or more days a week. Most schools, from preschool through colleges, struggled to make the transition to 'distance learning,' in lieu of in-person classroom instruction; but it nevertheless took place. Most restaurants were, during some periods, closed to in-person dining; but we were still able to place orders online or on the phone, and either pick them up, or have them delivered. Football and basketball games (including playoffs) continued—albeit often with only 'virtual' fans in the stands. Online shopping likewise often took the place of visiting the local shopping mall every weekend.

But long before the pandemic, new technology was profoundly shaping our lives. Families began to stay at home in evenings in the 1950s and '60s and watch television, rather than go to church, to a lodge meeting, to the weekly Bridge Club, or participate in the company Bowling League. Telephone conversations began to replace in-person visitations of family and friends.

There are many, many *blessings* to which we rightfully credit technology: persons with various disabilities can now receive substantial help from computer programs, using software that can be easily carried in their pockets. Vast libraries of information are now readily accessible through the Internet—often for free. Video and audio recordings of historically important events can be instantly retrieved.

But of course, there are also considerable *drawbacks* that come along with such technology. The new industrialized factories of the

19th century belched out smoke into the air, and often polluted nearby sources of water. Commuters driving cars to work created not only CO_2 emissions, but snarling traffic jams, both to and from work. And of course, our peaceful solitude at home is now frequently interrupted by literally *billions* of unsolicited 'Robocalls.'

And, while it may sometimes be convenient to have helpful 'suggestions' made to you when you log on to one of your favorite Websites to do some shopping, what happens when such online merchants *sell* information about your buying habits to other stores? Sure, you may be able to 'opt out' of such releases of information (assuming that you bothered to read, and then respond to, their annual 'Privacy Notice'), but the amount of such information that is now available about each of us on the Internet can be shocking, and even frightening. (Just 'Google yourself,' for instance.)

Certainly, if you're considering dating someone that you just met via an online 'Dating' website, it may be wise to look them up on the Internet (just to make sure that you're not potentially going out with someone who has a prison record for violent crimes, or a history of accusations of fraud, etc.). And, while most or all of us applaud when a movie or TV show depicts law enforcement authorities identifying terrorists and serial killers via CCTV, face-recognition software, drone cameras, electronic 'bugging' devices, etc., by the same token, it can also be disturbing to think of such technology being used *against* us, by a totalitarian government.

The ease with which photos and videos can now be modified, manipulated, and just plain *invented,* is daunting. The incredibly realistic 'Computer-Generated Imagery' (CGI) that we see in mainstream movies makes one begin to become somewhat suspicious of claims of someone having 'photographic evidence' of something. One shudders to think how such technology could have been misused by a nation led by a Hitler, or Stalin; and in fact, the recent appearance of 'fake political ads' on various social media platforms is just one early indication of how such technology can and will be misused.

But most of us have, by now, developed a certain degree of *trust* in companies like Facebook, Instagram, Twitter, TikTok, and such. (Of course, Facebook now *owns* Instagram.) And we are reassured by the fact that, after all, Congress is regularly summoning the heads of such companies to testify before them, right?

But such companies are now also being placed in the difficult position of trying to balance our 'Free Speech' rights, with policing against: [1] 'Fake News,' [2] the spread of *deliberate misinformation*, [3] 'hate speech,' and similar controversial postings. (As well as dealing with the 'practical' problem of trying to *make money*, when information available on the Internet is so often *free*.) And 'public figures,' naturally, have more difficulty in defending themselves against libelous statements on the Internet, because they typically must prove: 1. the party defaming them *knew* the statements were false; 2. The defaming party made them with actual malice; and/or 3. The defaming party was negligent in saying or writing them.

Certainly, we are never going to go *backwards* in time, and relinquish technology that makes our lives better, and easier. (Notwithstanding that a few people *would* love to return to an earlier era; symbolized, perhaps, by Thoreau living simply in his one-room cabin at Walden.) But we are all faced these days with difficult decisions concerning technology, and its various applications; and, as citizens, we have to try to keep ourselves somewhat 'informed' in these areas, since our political decisions are often impacted by the implications of technology.

Technology can, unfortunately, be used by white supremacists and other 'hate groups'; convincing-looking misinformation about a political figure can appear very 'genuine'; conspiracy theorists can peddle their ideas (along with selling dietary supplements and other products, in some cases) by making us feel like 'insiders,' who have been given access to 'secret' information that the 'unenlightened' average person is unaware of.

Technology is thus, in many ways, a double-edged sword; its advantages also come with a significant *cost*. But that is also the case with nearly every other aspect of modern life. We have to try and find the necessary 'balance' between the 'real' and the 'false,' the 'useful' and the 'unhelpful,' and the 'benefits' versus the 'costs,' from modern technology.

27. Nature/Ecology

Some of us find spending time 'out in nature' to be among our most enjoyable, and enriching times. To walk in an open field, to admire the majesty and beauty of a tree-filled forest, to feel a gentle rain while sitting on a bench in a park, can even be perceived as an intensely *spiritual* experience.

Of course, as with all things human, not everyone feels this same way. The novelist/philosopher Ayn Rand, for example, apparently preferred the 'beauty' of a modern skyscraper, to observing a tall redwood out in nature.

There is seemingly no particular reason why such differences *must* create disagreements among people. If one person is a 'tree-hugger,' and another a 'tech-lover,' that's fine: people have different tastes in music, food, and nearly everything else. Except, of course, for the fact that *politics* often intervenes in such matters.

There are thousands of 'protected areas' in this country, that are managed by government agencies such as the National Park Service, the United States Forest Service, the Bureau of Land Management, and so on. Currently, more than 650 million acres fall under the oversight and control of the federal government (which is about 28% of our total land area).

There have, of course, been calls (particularly in these days of rapidly increasing federal deficit spending) to either allow private, non-governmental entities to manage such areas; or to simply *sell* such lands to private companies. Environmentally-concerned persons are, however, staunchly opposed to this, arguing that private firms would simply let developers take out what natural resources these areas possess (lumber, wildlife, etc.), and then abandon them—thus depriving future generations of an irreplaceable natural resource.

Economic concerns can also factor in strongly to such issues. In an area where jobs are scarce, the interests of loggers who need to provide for their families may seem a much more important priority, than the concerns of environmental activists (such as the late Judi Bari) to preserve old-growth redwoods from destruction. Similarly, when concern about an 'endangered species,' such as the Snail Darter, can lead to stopping the construction of the (very controversial) Tellico Dam, and fears about the fate of the Northern Spotted Owl slow, or even halt tree-cutting activities, there is bound to be considerable controversy.

It is true that biologists estimate that more than 99% of the species that have ever lived on Earth are now extinct; so extinction is hardly a 'new' phenomenon. Still, *modern* extinctions quite rightly raise more concerns than do 'ancient' ones, because of the possibility (likelihood?) that we *human beings* have been the cause of them. Human poachers didn't cause the trilobite to become extinct, but human activities certainly caused the extinction of Passenger Pigeons, the Tasmanian Tiger, and the Baiji River Dolphin, among others.

Ingrid Newkirk (president of the animal rights activist organization, 'People for the Ethical Treatment of Animals' [PETA]), said in a 1989 interview for *Vogue* magazine, "Animal liberationists do not separate out the human animal... A rat is a pig is a dog is a boy. They are all mammals." This highlights a related controversy over the difference between 'animal *welfare*' (i.e., that humans should generally strive to protect animals from cruelty and suffering) and 'animal *rights*' (i.e., the view that animals have rights similar to, or the same, as humans). Animal rights advocates may view the animals we keep as pets ('animal companions') as being *enslaved,* and argue strongly against the use of animals in medical testing, the production of clothing, and for food.

Practitioners of the most radical forms of environmental protest have, in recent years, seen their most radical acts described as 'Eco-Terrorism,' and persons convicted of such crimes (which are typically nonviolent 'property crimes,' in which *humans* were intentionally not harmed) have been threatened with, or even sentenced to, very long prison sentences—potentially serving these sentences in federal 'supermax' prisons.

Regardless of one's viewpoints on such matters, all of us should be concerned about the environment. The illegal deforestation of the Amazon rainforest in Brazil has been increasing, and this has various negative consequences for the environment, such as soil erosion, the loss of biodiversity in the area, increased risk of fires, etc. Global Warming and other aspects of Climate Change are making their impacts felt in the increasingly damaging wildfires on the Western coast, as well as in the devastation caused by more-intense hurricanes and floods. Weather temperature 'records' are constantly being set worldwide, and international agreements are attempting to address such issues.

However, many or most of us in America (we are, of course, the biggest 'Carbon Polluter' in history, although China has now taken our place as the largest emitter of carbon dioxide) are hesitant to embrace stricter environmental standards that would negatively impact our perceived 'freedoms' (such as our wide use of single-person vehicles), particularly when rapidly-industrializing countries like China and India are (not surprisingly) protesting having such stricter standards imposed on them, since the United States and Europe did not have to follow such constraints when *they* were developing industrially.

Of course, we have various *alternatives* to environmentally-damaging power sources like oil, coal, and natural gas: namely, solar energy, wind power, and geothermal energy, plus hydropower and biofuels. (Admittedly, the availability of wind and solar energy are quite dependent upon the time of year, and the weather.) Most industrialized nations of the world, however, are slowly attempting to begin the difficult and costly transition from nonrenewable fossil fuels, to renewable 'Green' power sources.

But hopefully, we can ultimately succeed in such a transition, so that our children and grandchildren will have the same kind of beautiful environments that we were able to enjoy, when we were their age.

28. Aesthetic Experience

Is there such a thing as 'Beauty'? Is it something that is *objectively* present, or is it simply a *subjective* feeling? And are some philosophers (such as Immanuel Kant) correct in distinguishing 'the Beautiful' from 'the Sublime'? Good questions, all—which have propelled conversations about art for thousands of years.

But we should first notice that, in the modern world, terms such as 'beauty' are used rather loosely. Cosmetics companies seemingly convey the attitude that 'beauty' is something that can be *purchased,* and then applied/sprayed/brushed on, and 'beauty' will be the result. TV sports commentators may refer to a particular play in a football game as 'a *beautiful* pass/reception/run.' A politician's witty comeback to a sharp criticism may be referred to as a 'beautiful' response. None of those examples are even *close* to what I mean by 'beauty.'

In this essay, I will be referring to what are sometimes called the 'Fine Arts.' Classically, there are seven of these: Architecture, Dance, Literature, Music, Painting, Sculpture, and Theatre—with 'Cinema' being a recent addition (although arguably, it could be viewed as an extension of 'Theatre'). And particularly, I am referring to those types of 'Fine Arts' that have, historically, been held to be able to sometimes produce what is described as the 'aesthetic experience.'

Certainly, there are 'non-Fine' versions of these eight arts that would not even remotely profess to be dealing with 'aesthetics.' The crowd at an NBA game who is rhythmically stomping and shouting, "We will, we will, ROCK YOU!" is certainly enjoying the experience; a crowd of young people who are dancing to Hip-Hop or Electronica at a club may describe this music as 'awesome'; and a very sexually explicit movie may be described by its director as a 'tribute to the raw, primal beauty of human sexuality'; but once again, this is not what I am talking about. I am referring to something rarer, and more esoteric; something that many people have possibly never actually *experienced.*

Perhaps the biggest problem in discussions of this subject is in dealing with the charge that such 'aesthetic experience' is purely *subjective* (and perhaps even an extension of one's 'class consciousness'), rather than being an *objective* quality. If we reject this charge, we may be informed, "Well, *I* just listened to Beethoven's 9th symphony, and I thought it was *boring!* And so was that play by Shakespeare, and that painting by Van Gogh! And just who are *you* to claim that Bach's music is 'better' than 2 Live Crew?" Faced with such challenges, we may well wonder whether it is indeed true that 'Beauty is in the eye of the Beholder'? And further, whether there is no truly 'objective' component in the appreciation of Art, and no valid distinction to be made between 'Fine' art and 'Popular' art.

To be sure, there certainly is a very substantial component of the appreciation of even 'Fine Art' that is quite subjective. One lover of classical music, when introduced to another, may cheerfully greet the other with the question, "Bach or Beethoven?" because even persons with highly cultivated musical tastes probably don't like these two composers *equally,* and will most likely be prepared to vociferously defend their individual preference (but all in 'good spirits,' of course).

I would suggest that, while such preferences are indeed 'subjective,' they are not *merely* subjective. For example, if you ask nearly anyone who knows anything about Classical Music, "Which is the better symphony? Beethoven's 8th, or his 9th?" you would probably get a nearly unanimous response. While it is true that you might get a very mixed reaction if you asked a variety of Art lovers, "Who is the better painter: Leonardo da Vinci, or Picasso?" But I also suspect that if you instead asked, "Who is the better painter: Picasso, or Jackson Pollock?" I think you would again get a pretty unified reaction. The same with asking, "Who is the better writer: Fyodor Dostoyevsky, or Hunter S. Thompson?" Such a large degree of similarity tends to diminish the charge of 'subjectivity.'

Another way of evaluating Art is to see whether there has been a certain *consistency* in its appreciation, over a significant course of time. The *Mona Lisa,* Michelangelo's *David,* Van Gogh's *The Starry Night,* and Picasso's *The Dream,* have all been rather uniformly acknowledged and appreciated, for long periods. Again, this suggests that, although there *is* a subjective component to their appreciation, there must *also* be something that is more lasting, and objective.

Of course, this 'course of time' evaluation can be overused. Take the recent debates over whether the 'Western Canon' and the 'Great Books' identified by such scholars as Harold Bloom and Mortimer Adler should dominate collegiate studies, to the exclusion (or at least, to the reduction) of studying books by more recent authors, such as Toni Morrison, Richard Wright, Harper Lee, and Gabriel García Márquez. (To me, this should not be an 'Either/Or' issue; *all* types of literature should be included in a full college curriculum.)

But another problem with 'Fine' Art, is that it often takes a greater degree of *knowledge* and *experience* to be able to fully appreciate it. With regard to Classical music, a certain amount of musical *education* is most helpful in being able to develop one's tastes for it. It is similar with Jazz: while an artist such as, say, Kenny G, may sell far more *albums* today than John Coltrane, almost anyone who is intimately familiar with

Jazz would never agree that Kenny G's work is 'better' than Coltrane's. And, for many/most of us, taking a course in Non-Western Music may be nearly essential to enabling us to really understand and appreciate Indian music, or the music of Japan, or Bali.

'Popular' art, by way of contrast, is (almost by definition) immediately appealing: 'no experience required,' so to speak. A given song (take Pharrell Williams' *Happy,* for example), may be nearly ubiquitous in the media for a period of days, weeks or even months, yet not retain this degree of appeal for longer periods of time. (I personally still love Williams' song, however.) This is also illustrated by the fact that tastes in popular music change over time. The generation that liked Elvis Presley usually did not like the Beatles. Similarly, those folks who like Madonna and U2 may not care for Bruno Mars and Drake. (And certainly, the earlier generations who liked Ragtime, Swing, and Bebop are hardly even *part* of the current conversations about 'Pop' music)

My central point, however, is that 'aesthetic' experiences may be akin to what are called 'spiritual' experiences. Not everyone has them— but when one *does* have them, they assume a degree of importance in our lives that other experiences do not. They have a depth, and a significance, that surpasses most other experiences. They may even suggest the reality of something akin to a 'higher realm' to which we can aspire, during our lives.

Not all 'art' needs to attempt to reach such heights. One of Bach's cantatas is perhaps not the most 'motivational' music to play when you are cleaning the house, or driving home from work. And by the same token, 2 Live Crew's music would certainly seem out of place in a beautiful, historic cathedral.

But for those quiet, reflective times, it still *is* possible to find 'Beauty,' by an encounter with some of those works that have inspired countless others over the years. And if such feelings are indeed somewhat 'subjective,' just remember: so is *Love*.

29. The Emotions

Our emotions are the source (or at least, the *sign* that lingers) of our greatest happiness in life, as well as our deepest and most profound sorrows. We can emotionally reach the highest heights of joy, as well as plunge to the darkest depths of despair—despair to a degree that the thought of an end to our existence would almost seem like a great *blessing* to us.

Perhaps the biggest difficulty with our emotions is that, for the most part, they are not really subject to our rational and/or volitional *control*. Certainly, we may read books and attend seminars on topics like, 'Controlling Your Emotions,' or 'Developing Emotional Intelligence'; but we may nevertheless, soon after this, find ourselves utterly devastated by some tragic or unanticipated event.

Not only are our emotions not subject to our rational control, they often seem to assert themselves in ways that are quite *contrary* to our volitional desires. Friends may rightly advise us, "Why are you so upset that your lover *dumped* you? The two of you didn't really have anything in common, anyway!" or "You've been complaining about your job non-stop for the last two years, so you should be *glad* they just laid you off—now you're free to find something much better!" Our response to such truthful advice is often along the lines of, "I know, I know—but I *can't help it!*"

We probably wish that we could summon up the emotions of joy and happiness, simply by an act of will. Part of the problem, here, is that many of our deepest emotions are brought on by some external event, which is also not under our control. If one's favorite sports team wins a game, one may temporarily have feelings of the highest exultation—but then in the next game, your team might be 'shut out,' leading you to a feeling of near-depression. One may receive some well-deserved recognition at work one day, but then be overlooked and forgotten the following week.

In the modern world, our desire to achieve volitional control over our emotional states leads some people to utilize *drugs*, to artificially bring about states of emotion that we desire. The 'rush' brought on by cocaine is caused by the release of dopamine in the brain, thus setting off the brain's 'pleasure response.' Anti-depressant drugs like Prozac, Zoloft, and Xanax are widely prescribed in this country, although their (sometimes considerable) side effects are also increasingly (if reluctantly) being acknowledged. But such drugs will retain their attraction, because they provide us with a measure of the 'control' that we seek over our feelings.

But perhaps we also need to acknowledge that some emotions are very *natural* reactions to particular life events; and that some emotions—such as grief after the loss of a loved one—is very much a *process* that one must work through; and there are no true 'short cuts' in this process. (In fact, if we could lose a person whom we loved very much *without* feeling devastated, that would probably in itself be a 'problematic' symptom, that should be of psychological concern to us.)

Could there truly be a 'heavenly' state in which we were always in constant *bliss?* While it's true that Dante's *Paradisio* envisioned saints, benevolent rulers, and angels just sitting around in a circle and enjoying the Beatific Vision forever, this probably seems far less credible to a modern person, than it did during the Middle Ages in which Dante lived.

What makes our infrequent states of extreme joy, and our rare moments of exaltation, *so* surpassingly uplifting, is precisely the fact that they are very infrequent. They must be balanced out by our contrary emotions—including bouts of sadness, and the occasional sense of extreme loss.

Dealing with situations of great loss is perhaps the most difficult trial we encounter in this life. There are no 'magic solutions' for those who are grieving; and, unfortunately, some hurts that we can experience in life are so painful and difficult that they *cannot* genuinely be 'resolved,' during our earthly lives.

But, even in the midst of profound sadness, it is still possible to experience other emotions: including happiness. When attending a funeral and listening to a eulogy, it is not uncommon to smile, and even laugh, after being told some amusing story about the deceased. Seeing beloved family members (particularly young children) during a time of grieving can also bring a smile to one's face, and fill one with profound emotions of love.

In most cases, sadness will eventually recede. In the future, it may overcome us once again, and perhaps quite unexpectedly; but one can only stand up and face it with an opposing attitude—one that *is,* to a certain extent, subject to our volitional control: and that is the attitude of **courage**. One will not necessarily *feel* 'courageous' when facing up to a difficult situation; but one can nevertheless *act* without hesitation—as if one had no fears, and no qualms. (And, often, genuine courage will *follow* such actions.)

Perhaps an emotional state that we could profitably seek in many situations is that of *Equanimity;* this is an attitude that is often sought in Buddhism, for example. This emotional state implies steadiness, as well as a calm realization of the transient and impermanent nature of this life.

There are no 'magic' formulas for dealing with our emotions. But following a rational path can often help guide us through difficult times.

30. Seasons, Holidays

If some intelligent aliens unexpectedly found themselves on our planet (and, in the Northern hemisphere), they would presumably begin to note a number of things about the environment. First, they would notice the difference between 'day' and 'night,' which relate to the Sun appearing to pass overhead, and the Moon and stars being most visible at nighttime. The planet's temperature is also warmer while the Sun is visible, and cooler at nighttime. Next, they would probably observe that the Moon changes its appearance, over a nearly 30-day cycle: going from fully visible, to partially visible, to not readily visible at all, and then gradually back to a 'full' Moon. They would also notice that the portion of the Moon's face that is visible to us during this cycle changes, as well (beginning with the right side being visible, then changing over to only the left side being visible); but through all of this cycle, the side of the Moon that can be seen remains the same, and the 'dark side' of the Moon is always hidden from view.

As they became accustomed to these cycles, these visitors would also notice differences in the overall average temperature of the planet. If they arrived, say, in early Spring, they would certainly also notice that many different plants begin to grow, and leaves begin to appear on previously barren trees. They would also notice a steady overall increase of temperature, over the next five or six phases of the Moon.

They would probably also notice that the Sun (as well as the shadows it creates on the Earth) appears to shift in its overhead movement across the sky, as the days pass. During the first three moon cycles after their arrival it would appear to be gradually moving northward, after which it reverses, and begins a similarly gradual southward shifting over the next three moon cycles. The *length* of the daylight period would also appear to be increasing.

But following this, there would begin a corresponding *decrease* in the overall planetary temperature. Certain changes (such as plants wilting, and turning brown) would occur among much of the plant life, and leaves would begin to fall from many trees. Rainfall might commence occasionally. These changes would generally continue over the next six cycles of the Moon. The length of daylight would also be appearing to decrease, further lowering the average temperature—a colder temperature that sometimes manifests itself as *ice* on plants and on the ground, and even *snow* in the air.

By the time the weather began to return to the condition it was when the aliens first arrived, they would presumably understand the 'cyclic' nature of this change. Although they would probably have noticed that this entire cycle lasted about twelve moon cycles, it might take some time before they determined this annual cycle 'length' more precisely.

Now, there certainly will not be any intelligent aliens landing on our planet anytime soon. But in fact, these 'cyclical' observations were similarly noticed by ancient humans, who over time progressed in their understanding of these changes. The 4th century BCE Greek astronomer Hipparchus is credited with having determined that the length of the solar year is 365.24 days. The imaginary geographic lines known as the 'Tropic of Cancer' and 'Tropic of Capricorn' mark the extreme north and extreme south latitudes, respectively, where at one point of the year the Sun appears to be traveling directly overhead, and after which it appears to 'reverse direction' in its annual seasonal motion. (For those living on the Equator, the Spring Equinox and Autumnal Equinox are the times when the Sun seems to be moving directly overhead.)

As humans began to develop agriculture, the 'spring' time was the most common time for planting crops (at least, in the northern hemisphere), and celebrating the 'renewal' of life; mid-year was the time when the daylight (and thus the workday) lasted the longest. The fall was the time for harvesting these crops; and once the harvest was in, it was finally a time to relax, and enjoy the fruits of everyone's labors. Another important time that was noticed was the point at which the period of daylight was the shortest—which, once this time had passed, represented the hopeful sign that the days were now getting 'longer,' and the weather would start to turn warmer again.

These times of celebration were often combined with religion, and thus became 'Holy Days' or '*holi-days*.' The year was subdivided into four three-Moon cycles, representing what we now refer to as 'seasons': Spring, Summer, Fall, and Winter. The beginning of Summer, and of Winter, were known as 'Solstices' (derived from two Latin words, meaning "sun stand still"). The Winter Solstice became a time for celebration, and in the Julian Calendar (mandated in the Roman Empire by Julius Caesar in 46 BCE), and the Gregorian calendar (introduced in 1582 by Pope Gregory XIII), a date shortly after the Winter Solstice (January 1, on our calendars) was chosen to recognize and celebrate a 'new year.' The coming of a 'new Moon' was the source of the later divisions of our calendars into 'months.'

The origin of the 7-day 'week' is more obscure. (Of course, in the Western world, we have traditionally attributed its origin to the testimony of the Book of Genesis, concerning the seven days/periods of Creation. The 24-hour period from Friday evening until Saturday evening was the weekly 'Sabbath,' a biblical day of rest.) Perhaps the earliest *historical* evidence of the 'week' is from the Mesopotamian Empire, in about the 22nd century BCE. The Babylonian calendar had a seven-day week, as well, and this may have been a possible source for the biblical authors.

Of course, over time, more and more 'holidays' have been added to the Church Calendar (with far fewer holidays added to the later Islamic calendar), as well as to secular calendars. The rulers of the United Kingdom had declared various 'bank holidays,' in which such financial institutions were closed. Some religious groups (such as the Puritans, who were Calvinist Protestants) firmly rejected what they considered as 'Popish' holidays (Easter and Christmas, in particular; but also any days assigned by the Catholic Church to various 'saints'), though even the Puritans joyfully celebrated Thanksgiving, as well as 'Commencement Day' (the day they were finally allowed to enter Universities, to be educated).

Of course, supposed 'national' and even 'international' holidays have proliferated greatly in recent decades. Many of these supposed 'holidays' bear the marks of having originally been suggested for *marketing* purposes (e.g., National Margarita Day, National Miniature Golf Day, National Lipstick Day, National Cheeseburger Day, etc.), while some of the others may just make most of us smile and shake our heads (such as National Proofreading Day, National Wear Your Pajamas to Work Day, International Talk Like a Pirate Day, Saxophone Day, etc.).

In this country, New Year's Day starts off our calendar of the 'major' holidays, followed by Valentine's Day; St. Patrick's Day (for some); Easter; Mother's Day; Father's Day; the 4th of July; Labor Day; Halloween; Thanksgiving, and the biggest of them all, Christmas. Although certain restaurants may try to make 'National Pancake Day' or 'National Spaghetti Day' seem like important occasions, most mainstream stores and shopping malls save their 'big' decorating projects and marketing campaigns for those 'major' holidays listed above.

In recent years, the Thanksgiving holiday seems to be receiving less and less attention. Perhaps this is because, apart from many families getting together and having a large *meal* on this day, they otherwise don't tend to *spend* very much on this holiday: no costumes, indoor decorations, outdoor lights, or greeting cards. (Plus, although one can purchase CDs of Thanksgiving *hymns* and such, Mariah Carey and other artists have yet to put out any bestselling Thanksgiving *Pop* albums; maybe like, "All I Want for Thanksgiving Is FOOD.")

It now seems like there might be a growing desire to have another holiday to celebrate in the *summer*, sometime prior to the 4th of July. (The number of 'Christmas in July' TV schedules one sees nowadays, seems to cater to this unspoken desire.) Who knows? Perhaps someday the Summer Solstice will once again be celebrated, in the Western world.

One important function of holidays is to mark the passage of time. Individualized 'holidays' such as birthdays and anniversaries do this explicitly, while others (such as Halloween, and Christmas) may do this in a more subtle fashion—such as by us choosing to change the way we celebrate, as we get older. (For example, deciding *not* to 'dress up' on Halloween: "I'm *too old* to put on a costume!" Or skipping putting up extensive decorations in one's home, at Christmas.) And the holidays themselves change somewhat and evolve, over time; Halloween in the earlier 20th century was a somewhat raucous and rowdy holiday, rather than the children-centered day it now is becoming.

But holidays are also a very welcome time to reflect on the passage of time; to fondly remember past times; and to make (semi-solemn) vows to make changes in one's life, for the future.

Happy Holidays!

PART D
MISCELLANEOUS
WRITINGS

⸺◦◦◦⸺

(These are examples of my writing over the years that still have some "sentimental" value to me; plus a brief autobiographical essay.)

1. Beyond the "Wars" of Christmas (2012)

(This was published in a Tumblr blog on 12/12/12; an interesting and unique date—that I didn't realize, until I saw it posted. I have now added two paragraphs [about Clement of Alexandria, and about Pope Gregory's letter] to my original blog posting. Biblical quotations are from the New Revised Standard Version, or the King James Version.)

The entire end-of-the-year holiday season—encompassing Advent, Chanukah, Las Posadas, the Winter Solstice, Christmas, Kwanzaa, and New Year's, as well as Bodhi Day, Ta Chiu, and other lesser-known winter holidays—is viewed by many of us as "the most wonderful time of the year." But certainly, the most prominent among these seasonal celebrations is Christmas, which is considered a time for bridging our differences, spending time with family and loved ones, and participating in traditions that have been handed down from generation to generation.

Yet this is also often a season for contention: some shoppers lose self-control during "Black Friday" sales at retail stores, and may even participate in violence and near-riots. Municipal holiday displays featuring nativity scenes may spur protests from some members of the community, who are then accused of engaging in a "War on Christmas." Christians may argue that "Jesus is the reason for the season," and plead to "Keep Christ in Christmas," while others contend just as strongly for a purely secular civil holiday, like the 4th of July. Merchants must also decide whether to wish their shoppers a "Merry Christmas," or utilize the more general greeting of "Happy Holidays"—and they risk offending a portion of their customers with either option.

But there is yet another source of controversy at this time of year: Although about two billion Christians celebrate Christmas, there are also several million professing Christians who are opposed to the celebration of Christmas: whether on December 25th (the traditional date, according to our Gregorian calendar), or on January 6th (for Eastern Orthodox churches, under the older Julian calendar used for religious festivals). At this time of year, you may have your doorbell rung by sincere persons distributing literature that describes Christmas as a "pagan holiday," and asserts that the gospels do not identify Jesus' date of birth. Let us consider this matter further.

Our word "Christmas" comes from the Old English words, *Christes maesse*—meaning "the Mass (i.e., religious festival) of Christ." The vast majority of Christians joyfully celebrate the holiday, believing that the Christian church was certainly given authority on earth [e.g., Mt 16:19] to do such things as establish an annual festival to thankfully remember the birth of Jesus. Yet opponents of the Christmas celebration suggest that the early Christians did not recognize nor commemorate the birth of Jesus; they add that the gospels do not specifically identify the date of Jesus' birth, and argue that in any case he could not have been born in December or January.

Taking the material in the gospels as it stands, the gospel of Luke says that Jesus was born about the time of "the first registration and was taken while Quirinius was governor of Syria." [2:2] Since Jesus was six months younger than John the Baptist [1:36], establishing John's time of birth will establish that of Jesus. John's father Zechariah served in the Temple in the priestly "division" of Abijah [1:5], which was eighth in the sequence [1 Chr 24:10]; his wife Elizabeth became pregnant after his weeklong, twice-a-year service in the Temple ended [1:8 & 23-24]. Jesus would thus have been conceived six months later, and presumably born after nine months.

Since the Temple was destroyed by the Romans in 70 CE, it is difficult for us to reconstruct the Jewish priestly calendar. (According to the Mishnah, the priestly cycle begins on the first Sabbath of the month of Nisan, which usually falls in March/April on our calendars; but we don't know whether this was Zechariah's first or second period of service in the year.) We may also have historical and archaeological difficulties reconciling the census of Luke 2 with his statement that these events were "In the days of King Herod of Judea" [1:5]. But a 1st century audience of the gospels would likely not have had the same problems we do. Thus, the gospels *did* indicate the time (if not the day) of Jesus' birth to their original readers: he was born fifteen months after the conclusion of Zechariah's Temple service.

It is also worth noting that the apostle Paul in Galatians 4:4 notes that

Jesus was "born of a woman, born under the law." So the circumstances of Jesus' birth were recorded very early in the New Testament.

Many doubt the traditional December 25th date for Jesus' birth, because Luke 2:8 says that the shepherds were "living in the fields, keeping watch over their flock by night." Since the rainy season in Israel begins in October, shepherds and sheep wouldn't normally have still been staying *outside* at night in December [which is called the 'rainy season' in Ezra 10:9, 13], when nighttime temperatures can be quite chilly. Also, the travel required by the census of Luke 2:1-3 probably wouldn't have been ordered by the Romans during the rainy season.

However, Israel isn't Minnesota; grazing in Palestine may resume in December when green grass appears following the initial rains [James Kelso, *An Archaeologist Looks at the Gospels;* Paul Maier: *In the Fullness of Time: A Historian Looks at Christmas*]; Alfred Edersheim also suggests [*Life and Times of Jesus the Messiah,* Ch. VI] that these shepherds might have been watching "Temple flocks" that were kept outside year-round; and of course, it might have just been a mild winter—so who knows?

The suggestion is often made (including by some Christian historians) that December 25th was selected by the church in the mid-4th century to provide a Christian alternative to the birthday celebrations of the Persian god Mithra, the Phrygian god Attis, or the Roman celebration of the sun god Sol: *Natalis Solis Invicti* ("Birth of the Unconquered Sun"). The Winter Solstice—the shortest day of the year, in our hemisphere—and the weeklong festival of Saturnalia also occurred shortly before this date, and the new year or *Kalends* festival occurred shortly after. Thus the charge that the traditional December 25th date has "pagan origins."

This argument, however, requires the assumption that the early Christians would have been willing to try and "Christianize" a pagan festival, celebrated by a Roman empire whose pagan practices they had firmly opposed, and whose emperor Diocletian had violently persecuted Christians as recently as 303 CE.

"Evidence" produced for this claim includes a letter purportedly written by Pope Gregory to Abbott Mellitus in about 601 CE. (The letter no longer exists, but the English church historian Bede includes it in his *Ecclesiastical History of the English People.* [I.30]) Concerning pagan temples found when Christians 'convert' an area, Gregory advised, "the temples of the idols should on no account be destroyed. The idols are to be destroyed, but … if the temples are well-built, they must be purified from the worship of demons and dedicated to the service of the true God. In this way, we hope that the people, seeing that their temples are not destroyed, may abandon their error and … may come to know and adore the true God." But let us note that a letter written about England in 601 CE hardly tells us anything about what might have happened in the 3rd and 4th centuries. Moreover, this letter says nothing about reinterpreting 'pagan festivals,' or the days on which festivals are to be held, or proposes any redirecting of religious practices, and so on; it was solely about not destroying the *buildings* used for worship.

It should also be noted that the Roman *Natalis* festival wasn't established on December 25th throughout the Roman empire until Emperor Aurelian so ordered in 274—which prompts the question, did Christians observe Jesus' birth before then? It's true that Christmas wasn't included in the formal 2nd and 3rd century lists of feasts recorded by the church fathers Irenaeus and Tertullian; but since Christian worship was unlawful before Constantine's Edict of Milan in 313, Christian celebrations had to be kept secret—thus, the fact that Christmas wasn't an obligatory "feast" for the entire church doesn't mean that some individual Christians didn't remember it; in fact, there is evidence supporting that notion.

The gospels record the details of Jesus' birth, so it was certainly intended to be remembered; in fact, we are told in Matthew 2:3 that not only was King Herod disturbed by the news about Jesus, but also "all Jerusalem with him." Luke's gospel says that an angel notified the shepherds about Jesus' birth, and "suddenly there was with the angel a multitude of the heavenly host, praising God." [2:9-15] After seeing Jesus, the shepherds "made known what had been told them about this child; and all who heard it were amazed at what the shepherds told them." [2:17-18] The shepherds "returned, glorifying and praising God for all they had heard and seen, as it had been told them." [2:20] Eight days later, Jesus was celebrated in the Temple by Simeon [2:25-35], and the prophetess Anna "began to praise God and to speak about the child to all who were looking for the redemption of Jerusalem." [2:38] Thus,

Jesus' birth is portrayed as a *joyous* occasion, which many people might have known about, remembered, and passed down historical details of its time and circumstances.

In his 8th sermon on Leviticus, Origen (185-254) was critical of those who celebrated the birthday of Christ—which, ironically, shows that some Christians *were* celebrating the day. Justin Martyr [100-165] said in his *Dialogue with Trypho* that Jesus had been born in a cave near Bethlehem. [Ch. 78] Origen said in his book *Contra Celsus* [Bk. I, Ch. 51] that the cave in Bethlehem where Jesus was born was "greatly talked of in surrounding places, even among the enemies of the faith."

Clement of Alexandria (d. 215) records [*Stromata*, Bk I, Ch. 21] that some believe that Jesus was born on the twenty-fifth day of Pachon (May 20). Clement of Alexandria also says in his *Stromata* [I, xxi, 145] that from the birth of Christ to the death of Commodus was one hundred and ninety-four years, one month, and thirteen days—which marks November 18th, 3 BCE for the birth of Jesus.

A possibly spurious passage in Hippolytus of Rome's *Commentary on Daniel* [4.23.3; about 204 CE] suggests that Jesus was conceived on March 25th, and thus would have been born nine months later. In about 221, Sextus Julius Africanus suggested in his *Chronographiai* that Jesus was conceived on the Spring Equinox, and therefore would have been born on December 25th. The writing *De Pascha Computus* (written in 243) said that Jesus was born on March 28th. Also, Augustine said [sermon No. 202] that the schismatic Donatists do not celebrate Epiphany (and presumably also Christmas) "with us"; this had to occur before the schism in 311. (See Thomas J. Talley, *The Origins of the Liturgical Year;* and J. Neil Alexander, *Waiting for the Coming.*)

So some relatively early Christians were mindful of Jesus' birth, although it was not yet a mandated "festival"; and some had even suggested the traditional date of December 25th. So this also shows that there *were* relatively early traditions about the circumstances of Jesus' birth.

Christian critics of Christmas note that the Bible nowhere commands the observance of Jesus' birth. Citing prohibitions imposed on the theocratic kingdom of ancient Israel [e.g., Dt 12:30-32], as well as Jesus' rejection of "human precepts as doctrines" [Mt 15:9], in addition to

Paul's exhortation to not be enslaved by "special days, and months, and seasons, and years" [Gal 4:9-10], they may argue that any such festivals must have express biblical sanction.

In some Protestant traditions (e.g., Scottish Presbyterians), this is called the "Regulative Principle of Worship." But one should note that the Westminster Confession of Faith allows "vows, solemn fastings, and thanksgivings upon **special occasions**, which are, in their several times and seasons, to be used in an holy and religious manner." [XXI, V]

It's also true that neither does the Bible expressly *prohibit* such celebrations; nor does a Christmas celebration seem contrary to general Christian principles. [1 Cor 6:12;Col 2:20-22] Paul also advised, "do not let anyone condemn you in matters of … observing festivals, new moons, or sabbaths." [Col 2:16] He also said, "Some judge one day to be better than another, while others judge all days to be alike. Let all be fully convinced in their own minds. Those who observe the day, observe it in honor of the Lord." [Rom 14:5-6]

But even if early Christians did deliberately choose to remember Jesus' birth on a day that was also being used—for a much different purpose—by pagans, would that make it inherently wrong? There is no obvious reason why early Christians couldn't create an "alternate" celebration on December 25th, even as some modern churches have alternative celebrations on Halloween, or New Year's Eve. In fact, most Christian critics of Christmas hold their main weekly meetings on Sunday—a day with obvious pagan "sun-worship" origins—despite the fact that there is no explicit biblical command to change the day of worship from the Jewish Sabbath (on Friday/Saturday) to Sunday. And what happens when December 25th happens to fall on a Sunday (or Saturday, for Sabbath observers)? Are Christians supposed to not attend church, because of December 25th's supposed "paganism"?

To draw an analogy, early Christians were initially ordered to "abstain from what has been sacrificed to idols" [Acts 15:29 & 21:25]. Nevertheless, Paul later permitted this, acknowledging that Christians might even be seen "eating in the temple of an idol" [1 Cor 8:4-10]. (Paul calls "weak" those Christians who were offended by such practices.) If Christians could visit an idol's temple and eat meat that had literally been sacrificed and offered to pagan gods just hours before, it's difficult to see why Christians thankfully remembering Jesus' birth on December 25th should necessarily be considered objectionable.

The charge is often made by critics that many or most popular Christmas customs are not only unbiblical but also "pagan" in their origin, and therefore should be avoided by Christians. And it must be admitted that some Christmas traditions (e.g., mistletoe, the Yule log) are clearly pagan in origin. Others, such as the Christmas tree, have both pagan and Christian sources: for example, trees were used in worship ceremonies by the ancient Druids, and an evergreen tree brought indoors during the dead of winter encouraged the ancient Scandinavians during the year's harshest weather—but a later Christian origin for the Christmas tree is also attributed to both St. Boniface (8th century) and to Martin Luther, as well as medieval Germanic plays (usually staged in December) depicting the "Paradise tree" of the garden of Eden.

Although some critics claim that Jeremiah 10:2-4 prohibits Christmas trees, in context this passage is referring to a large tree that is "worked with an ax by the hands of an artisan" into an idol, which was adorned with silver and gold—not a Douglas Fir purchased at a Boy Scout lot that is decorated with garland bought from Wal-Mart. (It's also interesting to note that in Hosea 14:8, *God* states that "I am like an evergreen cypress.")

The purported connection between present-day Christmas traditions and much earlier pagan customs is often dubious, because many of the Christmas customs we now enjoy (e.g., Santa Claus; Christmas cards) only came into common usage as late as the 19th century—they were not continuously practiced from antiquity. Thus, there are few if any legitimate *historical* connections between, say, ancient Druidic or Roman traditions, and the contemporary observance of Christmas. If someone lights a candle in church in 1800, and Druids also lit candles in their ceremonies two thousand years earlier, so what? There is no historical "connection."

And of course, modern Christians celebrating Christmas strongly affirm to objectors that they are *not* worshipping Baal, Tammuz, or Mithra when they attend a Midnight Mass or Christmas Eve service—they are expressing humble thanks to God for the birth of Jesus.

It is true that the Puritans famously banned the public celebration of Christmas on several occasions in England and in America. In 1644, the English Puritans declared that Christmas was a time for fasting and repentance, not feasting, and they banned it outright in 1652 during Oliver Cromwell's Protectorate; however, Christmas celebrations were reinstated just a few years later with the 1660 "Restoration" of the monarchy under Charles II. The celebration of Christmas was also outlawed in colonial Massachusetts in 1659; but this law was repealed just 22 years later.

Such bans were often proposed because Christmas back then was sometimes a rather raucous and disorderly celebration, unlike the more family- and child-oriented holiday it is today. (Ironically, the reinstated Christmas holiday actually became *more* secular than it had been prior to the Puritan ban, since some religious observances of the season had now been forgotten.)

Some critics note that Christmas was not declared a federal holiday in this country until 1870; but remember that federal holidays were far less common in the 19th century than they are now. Our notion of a "federal holiday" derives from the English concept of "bank holidays," of which there were about forty prior to 1830; this number had been reduced to four by 1834, and Christmas was one of those retained. Even Thanksgiving did not become a national holiday in this country until 1863, and most states had recognized Christmas as a legal holiday by 1856; Oklahoma was the last to do so (in 1907).

Critics are correct, however, in stating that a number of common images we have of Christmas (in nativity scenes, for example) do not agree with the story in the gospels. The so-called "Three Kings," for example: The gospel of Matthew doesn't say there were three of them—only that they brought three gifts (Mt 2:11); thus, there might have been two, or (as Augustine thought) there might have been a dozen, perhaps leading a whole caravan of offerings. They also weren't "kings": the Greek word *Magi* meant "Wise Men" or sages; it was medieval legend that identified them as kings Gaspar, Melchior, and Balthasar.

Nativity scenes that show the Magi visiting Jesus at the same time as the shepherds likewise don't match the gospel accounts. (In fact, the traditional date on the Christian calendar for the visit of the Magi is Epiphany—January 6th—twelve days *after* Christmas.) In the gospels, the angel told the shepherds that Jesus had been born "this day" [Lk 2:11], whereas the Magi first came to Herod "after" Jesus was born in Bethlehem [Mt 2:1]. The shepherds found a "baby" [Lk 2:12 & 16], whereas the Magi saw a "child" whose parents were now living in a "house" [Mt 2:11]. The family was also in Bethlehem forty days after Jesus' birth (since "When they had finished everything required by the law of the Lord, they returned to Galilee, to their own town of Nazareth"; Lk 2:39) for Jesus' "presentation" in the Jerusalem Temple [Lk 2:22, Lev 12:2-7], and hadn't yet fled to Egypt [Mt 2:13].

Also, the offering they presented [Lk 2:24] was for those lacking financial means (see Lev 5:7, 12:8). If the Magi had just given them gold, they presumably would have offered the traditional lamb. Furthermore, Herod, "according to the time that he had learned from the wise men," gave orders to kill all boys in Bethlehem *two years old or under,*" rather than just newborn babies [Mt 2:16]. So the Magi wouldn't have seen a newborn babe, such as the shepherds saw.

The use of the Magi's offerings to Jesus [Mt 2:11] as justification for our modern gift exchanges is also flawed, because there was no *exchange* of gifts taking place; Mary and Joseph didn't give the Magi nice woolly sweaters for their return trip back east, for example, nor did Mary give Joseph a tie, or he give her a bottle of perfume.

But the biggest seasonal exaggeration is with regard to Santa Claus; although the vast majority of professing Christians celebrate Christmas, a smaller number endorse Santa Claus.

But it should first be noted that there *was* a historical "Saint Nicholas," who was a 4th century Christian bishop in Myra (in modern-day Turkey), and is reported to have attended the important Council of Nicea. As a Christian bishop, Nicholas certainly believed in, and taught others about Christian love. He is said to have anonymously provided dowries for several poor girls, for example, to save them from lives of prostitution.

The legend of Nicholas grew, until he was one of the most popular saints of the Middle Ages; he became the patron saint of children. Starting in the 17th century, Dutch immigrants to this country brought their tales of the gift-bearing "Sinterklaas" (Saint Nicholas), and this eventually became anglicized into "Santa Claus." Still, Santa wasn't widely known in this country until the early 1800s, when an anonymous story "The Children's Friend" was published in 1821, and writers John Pintard and Washington Irving began collecting and publishing Dutch stories about him.

Then in 1822, an Episcopalian seminary professor named Clement Clarke Moore wrote a poem for his children that we now know from its first line as, *'Twas the Night Before Christmas.* It's interesting to observe that Moore's poem refers to "St. Nicholas" or "Saint Nick," not "Santa"; his St. Nick was an *elf,* who was small enough to slide down a chimney, and he drove a *"miniature* sleigh" pulled by "eight *tiny* reindeer." Instead of being clad in an immaculate red and white outfit, his all-fur clothes were "tarnished with ashes and soot." It was Moore who named St. Nick's eight reindeer (although his original "Dunder and Blixem" has since become "Donner and Blitzen").

But it was the drawings by political cartoonist Thomas Nast in *Harper's Weekly* beginning in the 1860s that clad Santa primarily in red (the traditional color worn by a bishop, incidentally), and located him at the North Pole, reading children's letters and compiling his "naughty/nice" list. Finally, a popular series of ads for Coca-Cola done by artist Haddon Sundblom from 1931-1964 completed our modern image of Santa as an overweight, jolly giant.

Santa Claus—unlike his bishop predecessor Nicholas—is indeed a secular figure; still, he has much in common with the Christian ethic: Santa gives gifts, without ever asking anything in return... other than good behavior from children; this is conduct seemingly in accord with Jesus' Sermon on the Mount.

This broad secular spirit of giving is also embodied in Charles Dickens' *A Christmas Carol*—although one must also note that Dickens' first description of Scrooge describes him as an "old sinner," and Scrooge's ultimate change of heart is surely akin to a religious conversion. Scrooge's nephew says about the day, 'God bless it!' Furthermore, Tiny Tim makes his first appearance in the book after returning with his father from church, where Tim hoped the parishioners would see him and remember the healing miracles of Jesus; and of course, Tiny Tim's signature saying was, "God bless us, everyone!" It was also Dickens' book that popularized the greeting, "Merry Christmas"!

To avoid giving offense, should we now generally wish people "Happy Holidays" or "Season's Greetings," rather than "Merry Christmas," as December 25th approaches? We might first observe that federal law [5 USC 6103] does call the December 25th holiday "Christmas." While one certainly should respect the feelings of everyone, and strive not to offend those who do not celebrate the holiday, the term "Christmas" is certainly as appropriate to use for December 25th as "Thanksgiving" is for our earlier national holiday.

The 1984 Supreme Court decision in *Lynch v. Donnelly* [465 U.S. 668] ruled that a Nativity scene or crèche (French for crib, manger) placed on government property was allowable if the display also contained secular holiday symbols, such as a Christmas tree, Santa, reindeer, etc. It's entirely appropriate that modern displays attempt to be more inclusive and multicultural, by also incorporating symbols of Chanukah, Kwanzaa, and the Winter Solstice; a Christian celebration of the holiday certainly doesn't preclude other celebrations.

The fact is, the modern celebration of Christmas can mean vastly different things to different people. It can be a deeply spiritual holiday for Christians, but it can also be a completely secular holiday for atheists and freethinkers. (The famous agnostic lecturer Robert Ingersoll said in his essay "The Agnostic Christmas" that he observed December 25th with his family as the celebration of the birthday of the sun god.) Christmas is widely celebrated even in predominantly non-Christian countries like Japan and India, as well as largely Muslim countries such as Turkey and Lebanon. Christmas, in fact, has the potential to become the first nearly universal holiday.

Yet there is also a more somber undercurrent to the celebration. Some people actually find themselves more depressed during this time of year, and feel separated from the apparent happiness they perceive all around them; there's even a name for this condition: "seasonal affective disorder." (It is a myth, however, that suicide rates increase during the Christmas season; they actually *decrease* slightly.) There are also at this time of year many lonely people in jails and prisons, in hospitals or nursing homes, or living on the streets without a home. That's why Christmas is such an appropriate time to help feed the hungry; to clothe the poor; to visit the sick, and those in prison. [Mt 25:34-40]

Christmas has been observed on December 25th for perhaps 1700 years—which makes it an ancient and venerable tradition. It is a wonderful time for getting together with family and friends; for decorating your home, your workplace, and your neighborhood; for giving special gifts to those you love; and for enjoying some special music reserved for just this time of year. It is a time of forgiving others, and seeking reconciliation with those we've wronged. And above all, it is a time for being thankful for the many blessings we have, and for appreciating the special "magic" of this season—which, after all, comes only once a year.

While some retail sellers seem to push the beginning of the season earlier each year (from the traditional day after Thanksgiving, to now the day before Halloween, or even earlier) for purely commercial purposes, there is nothing wrong with celebrating Christmas for an entire *season,* rather than just a particular day or two. Historically, the Christmas celebration began with *Advent,* which began four Sundays before Christmas, and continued for the "Twelve Days of Christmas" afterward, until the feast of Epiphany on January 6th. So we can and should enjoy the entire Holiday Season!

In conclusion, let me simply wish everyone a happy holiday season… particularly including a Merry Christmas!

2. The Intellectual Love of God (2009)

(Published in the 'Sacreligious' column of the *Sacramento News & Review* on 5/14/2009; also available online at: https://www.newsreview.com/sacramento/content/the-intellectual-love-of-god/979757/)

Back in college during the mid-1970s (during the 'born again' craze), I was a belligerent atheist. You know the kind: My favorite book was Bertrand Russell's *Why I Am Not a Christian*, and my favorite play was *Inherit the Wind*. If someone professed to believe in the Bible, I was ready to attack: "In Joshua 10:12-13, he commanded the sun to stand still, so he obviously thought it was the sun that moves, not the Earth! How can you believe this Bible junk?"

I no longer think of such figures of speech as necessarily implying ignorance. In the late 1970s, motivated by curiosity about these irrational "religionists," I began visiting different local churches, about 120 in all. While I did not share their beliefs, I really liked most of the people I met there: kind, caring folks; ones you would want as co-workers, as neighbors.

Today, I think of most people who attend churches, synagogues and mosques as my spiritual brothers and sisters. Certainly, I feel more kinship with them than with someone drinking a beer and watching TV sports on Sunday morning.

Some church folk may feel that I would be eternally damned if I was to die today, but that's on them, not me. Traditionally religious people admit that "God is the judge." I can accept the judgment of a being wise enough to design the genetic code. The only problem I have is with lesser beings who attempt to carry out their own interpretation of God's judgment in this lifetime.

But the sarcasm and arrogance of the "new atheists" (Dawkins, Dennett, Harris, Hitchens), is nearly as repugnant to me as a King James-Version-thumping segregationist. One who belittles people who attend a traditional church is as intolerant as a churchgoer who thinks of unchurched folks as "infidels." Religion is not truly represented by a few deluded people burning down abortion clinics or blowing themselves (and others) up. Spirituality is our way of dealing with the numinous, the mysterious and the inexpressible ecstasy occasionally available in life.

If I had created the universe, I wouldn't have made death mandatory, age irreversible, nor debilitating illness practically inevitable. But we must deal with these realities as best we can; for most people, this involves religion. Humans can no more have a single spiritual path than there can be a single meal that will appeal equally to all palates in all countries, in all cultures and for all times.

I suspect that life is much more of an astonishing enigma than creationists, "New Atheists" or any of us in between can possibly imagine. Even if we be no more than microbes in an indifferent universe, we are at least microbes that know what it is to have thought "I am."

We may all end up at different places, at the same place or even no place at all, but the quest for meaning and purpose is a worthy goal, and philosophy, spirituality and religion are all time-honored ways of exploring the mysteries of our existence.

3. Y2K Essay (1999)

(Published in the *Neighbors* section of the *Sacramento Bee* on December 23, 1999)

Fearmongers Mislead with Y2K Stories of Mass Hysteria, Mayhem

When I was young, I used to wonder if I would like to see the year 2000 and the dawn of the new millennium. At the time, age 44 seemed like an unimaginably old age to me.

Yet that time is here, and all of us will experience the turning of the calendar on Jan. 1, 2000.

The dispute over whether the millennium begins in 2000 or 2001 cannot be definitely resolved because it is not a factual question and depends on certain assumptions, such as "Does a millennium have to contain 1,000 years?" and "How do you adjust for the fact that there was no Year Zero?" and so on.

For the majority of the Western world, because the most noticeable part of the calendar change takes place on Jan. 1, 2000, this is what most of us are waiting for.

Which brings us to the Y2K controversy.

Books, videos, newsletters, Web sites, television movies and many other sources advise people—in language often borrowed by survivalist literature or certain evangelical Christian eschatological theories—to sell their homes and move to the country, convert their investments to cash and store food, water and other supplies.

There is nothing wrong with being prepared for a contingency. Having a supply of water, batteries and foods, which you would normally use anyway, is perfectly reasonable.

Being able to cope with temporary power outages or flooding would be a wise decision for every household. And for areas that are subject to earthquakes or hurricanes, a greater degree of preparedness is even more sensible.

The problem is that much of the current Y2K information suggests that on Jan. 1 the power grid will go down, the money system will collapse, electronic devices will fail, national government will be abandoned in favor of anarchy and the leaders will be those with the most supplies or the most weapons.

Over the past few years, the increased demand caused by Y2K fears has probably been a financial bonanza for people who previously marketed such goods only to a few survivalists.

The pundits who are excited that major government agencies were not claiming to be fully Y2K compliant as of a year ago, to allow a full year to test and debug system changes, have probably never worked for the government, where waiting until the last minute is practically standard operating procedure.

I don't think that Western civilization will collapse in the year 2000. Nor do I believe the overall power grid will go down, the banking system will collapse or centralized government will be overthrown.

I do think a number of people will have an awful lot of freeze-dried foods on hand as of Jan. 2.

Why? For one thing, only computer programs with date-dependent calculations are really at risk, such as programs that compute your age or interest charges.

But even many programs that are date-driven are not driven by the year but only by the month or the day of the week. A traffic signal is not likely to be programmed to treat one year differently from another, although time-of-day and seasonal variations would be necessary.

Furthermore, for many programs that do use the year, it is purely an informational item. Your credit card may list an expiration date of 04-00, but it is unlikely that the company's purchase authorization representative will turn down your requested purchase, thinking that your card expired 99 years ago.

Moreover, almost all systems provide ways to manually override and restore themselves, even if they initially experience Y2K problems. And as a desperation stopgap measure, one could always reset the system time to a pre-2000 date, temporarily.

The Y2K problem is not a myth or mass hysteria. Companies and government agencies are spending billions of dollars and enormous amounts of staff time to minimize the problems it might cause. But to think that airplanes, automated teller machines and power plants suddenly will shut down as of Jan. 1, 2000, seems unrealistic.

If nothing else, I have faith in the self-interest and greed of bankers, utility companies and government bureaucrats that they have taken sufficient steps to ensure that their livelihoods will not disappear Jan. 1.

4. Why New Age Music Is Not "Yuppie Muzak" (1995)

As I write this, my immediate environment is filled with a number of distracting and unpleasant noises: My upstairs neighbor is playing her stereo (characterized by booming drums and bass guitar) distressingly loud. And, although it is both late and a 'school night,' her young son is running and jumping around on his living room floor (i.e., my ceiling). Outside my apartment (which is less than 100 feet from a busy intersection) there are racing engines, screeching brakes, and more booming stereos, which ebb and flow with each change of the traffic light, as well as occasional sirens and police cars. It's enough to make you lose your serenity.

Not infrequently, my response to this is to plug in my portable CD player, put on headphones, and listen to some 'New Age Music.' At least, that's what the local record stores call it; 'Yuppie Muzak,' 'Sonic Wallpaper,' and 'Audio Valium' are other terms which have been used to describe this type of music. One thing you should note about such alternate terms is that they are *not* intended as a compliment.

I would like to suggest that 'Muzak' and its synonyms are not useful terms for categorizing this kind of music. Traditional 'Muzak' (i.e., the stuff they play at shopping malls and grocery stores) is a highly commercial enterprise, closely linked to industrial psychology, and is normally intended to either make us work faster, or shop harder. Muzak is characterized by its tendency to transform even relatively good songs (e.g., by the Beatles) into something bland and inoffensive. Unfortunately, by smoothing out a song's 'rough edges,' you may make it palatable to the diverse kinds of people who come to a shopping mall, but you also destroy much of the song's individuality and character.

It is often said that 'All New Age Music sounds alike,' but this assessment is sometimes made by persons unacquainted with the genre. To the uninitiated, virtually all music in a particular category (whether Classical, Jazz, R&B, Pop, or Rap) is indistinguishable, but this only shows our relative lack of familiarity with an aesthetic and its subtleties. In the case of New Age Music, its characteristics (whether pleasing or aggravating to you) are inherent, part of the design.

I would suggest that the distinguishing characteristics of New Age Music are the following: It is **instrumental** and **improvisational**; **introspective**, yet **inclusive**; and finally, it seeks to be **inspirational**.

I am personally not wild about the term, 'New Age Music.' I would prefer to call it 'Contemporary Instrumental' or 'New Instrumental Music,' to distinguish it from other available kinds of 'instrumental' music (e.g., the neo-Postromantic stuff they play on 'Beautiful Music' radio stations). But that's beside the point: The current reality is that most record stores, music magazines, and even the Grammy Awards categorize this type of music as 'New Age,' so I retain the term here.

The first characteristic of New Age Music, which most sets it apart from mainstream or 'popular' music, is that it is almost exclusively **instrumental**; that is, without words or human voices. This is significant because our mental apparatus is such that words tend to draw our attention (e.g., when you suddenly hear 'your' name being mentioned in someone else's conversation that you were not consciously listening to). Notice how hard it is to carry on a serious conversation when vocal music or the television is on—the words are a 'distraction.' The absence of words from New Age Music leaves your mind undiverted, and able to focus on the music itself, or (frequently) on whatever else you are engaged in.

While this lack of lyrics may at first be disconcerting to new listeners of New Age, the relative significance of vocals to music is perhaps overrated; most people don't really pay attention to the words of Pop music songs anyhow. (Or when you do, you often notice that they're kind of stupid, in any literal sense.) Witness the thousands of young women who can ignore the offensive lyrics in some Rap and Hip-Hop songs, saying that "I don't listen to the words; I just like the beat." It is the overall sound and style of the genre that is important, not the conjunction of text and music; the instrumental nature of New Age Music allows it to make a deliberate understatement.

Words in music were probably important (even essential) to us when we were adolescents and teenagers; then, we relied on our idols on the radio and TV to express in words the thoughts and feelings which we were ourselves unable to articulate. However, since becoming post-teenagers, we have likely discovered that we can invent our own texts and narratives, as accompaniment to our lives. Thus, we can now say to the lyricist, "Thanks, but we won't be needing your services anymore; or at least, not as often."

(And besides, 'adult' concerns like mortgage payments, retirement plans, and purchasing bonds for your children's education tend to not lend themselves to lyricism as readily as youthful lust did; so, to a certain extent our evolution away from words is simply maturational.)

A second characteristic of New Age Music is its **improvisational** nature. New Age Music is much like jazz, in that there is not necessarily an 'established' reading or interpretation of a particular piece. (Which may explain why written scores of New Age Music were unavailable until fairly recently.) New Age Music readily accommodates (and even encourages) changes in instrumentation and orchestration, tempo and key, tone and timbre, to adapt a piece to changing environments.

While this improvisational tendency may lead music critics to describe a concert by a New Age artist as mere 'noodling' on the piano or guitar, at its best this trait represents spontaneity and freedom, and allows for the most direct possible interaction between the performer and the audience. (Granted that the 'best' is often not achieved in a live performance situation.)

A third characteristic of New Age Music is that it is admittedly **introspective**. It does not attempt to 'demand' your attention to itself, but instead quietly adapts to your situation; I think the term 'non-intrusive' is quite appropriate. By deliberately not being distracting, New Age Music thus encourages (but does not require) reflection and contemplation; it may open the door, but it does not compel you to come in.

One common criticism of New Age Music (which I have some sympathy with) is that too much of it (particularly the more 'ambient' and 'environmental' types) is 'peaceful,' 'soothing,' and 'nice'; to the point of rendering one comatose, some would say. (Thus the earlier comparison to Valium.) One would search in vain in most New Age Music for the kind of blazing emotion or tumultuous passion to be found in Beethoven or Shostakovich, for example; it is not always easy to find in New Age even the depth of feeling to be encountered in Blues or Gospel.

Fortunately, this situation is now changing somewhat, particularly as increasing influences of other types of music (such as World Beat, and Jazz) are having an impact in New Age Music circles. (I definitely feel that there is still more to be done in this area, though.)

As its fourth characteristic I would suggest that New Age Music, while not striving to be 'popular,' is **inclusive** of a broader spectrum of listeners than most other types of music, at least potentially. This is perhaps why it is increasingly being used as 'background' music in airports, movie theaters, and on television. (On this and many other points, I would highly recommend Joseph Lanza's excellent 1994 book, *Elevator Music.*)

Pop music, on the other hand, is by its very nature divisive and dualistic. Either you're 'with it,' or you're not. 'In,' or 'Out'; 'Hot,' or 'Not.' Most of us still only like the kind of Pop music we listened to when we were young, and dislike most of what has come since. (Have you noticed all of the 40- and 50-year old Pop/Rock stars who are still touring?) The generation that loved Elvis usually did not like the Beatles, whose generation typically did not care for Van Halen, whose generation can't stand Dr. Dre or Public Enemy. That fact that your parents hated your music was a definite point in its favor, for most of us. By way of contrast, relatively few people (principally music critics) 'hate' New Age Music, though many would not choose to be its patrons.

Classical music, unlike New Age, has been criticized (unfairly, I would think) as 'elitist' since it often requires a certain amount of background knowledge in order to fully appreciate it. (Which is why classes in 'Music Appreciation' are offered for classical music.) New Age typically does not; if you dislike it, taking a class is probably not going to change your opinion.

A corollary of this fourth characteristic is the fact that New Age Music is much less 'political' than, say, folk music. (I would include Rap as a type of 'folk' music, since Rap is essentially an urban folk poetry more related to literature than to music.) While a 'message' may indeed be intended by a New Age artist (e.g., an album can be dedicated to a particular social issue), the specific content of the message is left unstated, since there are no words to formalize and rigidify this intent. New Age Music may stimulate similar feelings in listeners, but this does not mean that we will all go out and vote for the same person, or walk the same picket line.

Politically active persons may find this appalling, but there are some advantages to being politically equivocal—for example, it may prevent you from being aesthetically exclusionary. If your message excludes a certain group of people, then they are not going to hear you, anyway; whereas if they hear you, there is still a chance that they will get your implied message.

The fifth and final characteristic I would identify is that New Age Music seeks to have an **inspirational** or 'spiritual' focus. (In fact, the term 'New Age Music' apparently originated as a kind of marketing term, based on the sort of metaphysical/occult bookstores and shops in which it was first available for sale.) On the other hand, any sort of 'spiritual' focus is absolutely foreign to traditional Muzak, as indeed it is to most varieties of Jazz, Rock, and Pop. New Age Music seems to harmonize very well with the 'questing' attitude of a 'seeker,' which is why it is often used in recovery programs.

Now, do not misunderstand me; I am certainly not trying to convey any false impressions of personal mysticism or religiosity, which are definitely not part of my nature. What I am thinking of is more like the title of one of Kierkegaard's books, *Purity of Heart Is to Will One Thing,* where what is being willed or sought is something essentially related to our deepest values. There may be notable exceptions, but normally when popular music asks you to 'Be Here Now,' it is talking about the 'Here and Now' of ordinary experience (e.g., "If only you could be here with me now, baby…"); it is not attempting to suggest something more transcendent. New Age Music, on the other hand, may be appreciated for its capacity to subtly remind the listener that it is at least *possible* that we are something more than just wandering lumps of protoplasm, twitching aimlessly in a malevolent universe.

Certainly, New Age Music is not unique in this capacity: Wonderfully expressive music among classical composers can be found in Bach's sonatas for solo violin; Mozart's late string quartets; the slow movements of Beethoven's piano sonatas; Chopin's *Nocturnes;* French composers like Satie and Debussy; John Cage's acoustic piano pieces from the 1940s; Messiaen's chamber music; modern composers like Gorecki and Crumb, or minimalists like Philip Glass and Gavin Bryars. And, as many people are now finding out, there is a large and very beautiful body of music in Gregorian Chant, as well as other liturgical and spiritual traditions (such as Jewish, Hindu, Buddhist, Native American, etc.).

What New Age Music can do is gently remind us that there is a different realm of experience available to us. With only a portable stereo and a set of headphones, you can temporarily refrain from centering your attention on the disharmony and ugliness around us, and again remember that this life is potentially a thing of wonder and beauty.

5. Autobiographical Reflections (2020)

(Something that the grandkids might one day be interested in, long after I'm gone...)

I was born on October 2, 1955, in Berkeley California, where my Oklahoma-born parents (in tandem with several other uncles and aunts) ran a boarding house for students at UC Berkeley. My wonderful sister is nearly three years older than me. When I was almost 5, we moved to Galt, California (then and now a small town), where my father taught 6th grade, and I started school. (I clearly remember being told by a classmate in the school's parking lot that President Kennedy had been shot.)

I was particularly attached to the comic strip 'Peanuts'; its creator, Charles M. Schulz, became my idol, and for a time I wanted to become a cartoonist. Schulz even (as was his practice) personally responded to three fan letters I sent him. My interests grew to include Marvel superhero comic books. (I am both amazed and amused to now see my favorite superheroes—such as Spider-Man and the Avengers—achieve near-cult status with the younger generations.)

In fifth grade, I joined the school band program. I wanted to play the trombone, but there weren't enough instruments to go around, so I was instead given a baritone horn. I also played basketball and joined a Little League team (though I exhibited only minimal athletic skill).

But family difficulties began the summer before I entered fifth grade. My father began drinking (later acknowledging his alcoholism), became increasingly ill-tempered, and (at least once) was physically abusive to my mother. My mother (probably sensing the necessity of soon having to support my sister and I) began substitute teaching that same year. Early in the summer, Mom packed my sister and I up and we spent the summer with our relatives in Berkeley, while she got a divorce, a job in Elk Grove (back then, a very small town; but no longer!), and found us a place to live.

(I later learned that my father paid not a penny of his court-ordered alimony/child support; a few years later, he moved back to Oklahoma.

I visited him a few times in the summer, but we never developed much of a "relationship." He passed away in 1996.)

In the fall of 1966, Mom began teaching Typing at the Junior High. We lived in a rented duplex, where the elementary school was literally just over our back fence, and the Junior High was just across the street. There was also a 'Congregational' church (United Church of Christ/ UCC) at the end of the block we lived on, and the three of us began attending Sunday services there. (I was even 'confirmed,' at age 13— with a minister who assured us during Confirmation Class that "You don't have to literally believe in the miracles recorded in the gospels, to be a Christian." I liked him, though, and he was a good minister, and a fine person.)

Divorce (in my experience, at least) was much less common then, than it is now, and I felt embarrassed and stigmatized by it. Not until high school did I ever invite any of my friends over to our home (which was, after all, just across the street from the school), fearing them discovering that my father didn't live with us.

Our mother, however, was an absolutely incredible person. Supporting us on a meager mid-'60s teacher's salary, she realized she needed more education to boost her salary, so—while teaching full-time, raising two children, and receiving no financial help from my father— she also enrolled at Sacramento State College (later CSU Sacramento/ CSUS) and earned her Master's Degree, writing her thesis on the advantages of the Dvorak typewriter keyboard versus the QWERTY arrangement. Later, she also taught Adult Education two nights a week, in addition to her 'day job.' Thanks to her amazing efforts, we never felt we were 'lacking' anything. (A lifelong smoker, she passed away in 2003—and is greatly missed.)

Surprisingly (given my 'life turmoil' during this year), in 6th grade I was the one student who received the "Bank of Alex Brown Award" (and a $50 savings bond) at the end of the year. With the assistance of I.Q. tests (my sister and I scored 139 and 140, respectively), I was invited to participate in the "Gifted" program at the Junior High. But I most enjoyed playing baritone in the Concert Band, under its excellent teacher Harlan Skar. (Who I kept in touch with throughout my college years; I even wrote two compositions for the band.)

By high school, I grew to my present 6'2" height, had come out of my self-imposed 'shell,' and began developing some very good friends—particularly in music classes. (I was described as "the world's only Jazz Baritone player" in the Stage Band.) 'Academic' classes, however—such as Geometry and Chemistry—had at this time become 'boring' to me, so I stopped taking them; a decision which I now greatly regret.

By my junior year I had stopped attending church on Sundays (professing to my disappointed mother that "I get more out of listening to *Jesus Christ, Superstar,* than from going to church"). But I was occasionally invited to a 'Youth Group Service' by some of my Evangelical friends (who worried about me, since I didn't seem to be 'saved,' and—according to Hal Lindsey and others—the *Rapture* was imminent, and I would possibly be 'left behind'). But I reassured them, "I believe in God, and Jesus, and all that stuff."

I graduated from Elk Grove High School in 1973 at age 17, and was vastly relieved that only 19-year-olds were being drafted and sent off to Vietnam. (I would not have gone to Canada to avoid the draft, but I definitely feared the prospect of being "the *last* U.S. soldier to be killed in the Vietnam conflict.")

I signed up to attend Cosumnes River Community College (CRC). Needing to select a *Major*, I reasoned that, "Since I like Music classes the best, I'll major in Music, and become a music teacher." (Unfortunately, colleges were then turning out far too many teachers for the jobs available—and yes, we were told this at the time.) Mom—always the practical one—talked me into adding a Minor in Business, however.

I happened to enroll at CRC during what later seemed to me a 'high water mark' in its music program, when Ed Avila and Dr. David Yoder were the two instructors. I felt completely 'in my element'; I played valve trombone in the school's Jazz Band, and baritone in the Concert Band. (But I was now becoming aware of the severe limitations of the baritone horn, in terms of repertoire, etc.) By contrast, when I had to take 'Beginning Piano,' I soon found that (with my newly-acquired obsession for Classical music) the piano had **loads** of music that I wanted to learn to play.

I also discovered my 'singing voice,' and participated in all three choirs that CRC offered; I even sang in a barbershop quartet with three

CRC friends. My favorite, however, was the Chamber Singers ensemble, which performed frequently in the area (particularly at Christmas time). I transferred to 'Sac State' in 1975, to get my teaching credential, but I also continued taking performing classes at CRC. In 1978/79 I was even the student director (under Dr. Yoder) of the CRC Chamber Singers (a personal highlight was my directing them in Ligeti's *Lux Aeterna* at a choral competition!), which certainly represented the apex of my 'musical' days.

A very profound change occurred in me in 1976, however, when at Christmas I had been given (by my future brother-in-law) Robert Pirsig's book, *Zen and the Art of Motorcycle Maintenance*. I was immediately attracted to both Philosophy and Eastern religions, which I started to read voraciously—making me seem quite strange to my fellow students at CSUS, who might see me in my marching band uniform (after the halftime show), sitting barefoot in the bleachers in the full lotus position, and reading the *Upanishads,* or the *Tao Te Ching*.

Before Pirsig's book, I had never really encountered traditional Western philosophy (except perhaps an occasional mention in one of Robert H. Rimmer's novels, whose influence and bibliographies had gotten me started in reading nonfiction). I devoured every Philosophy book I could afford (I was fortunate to get a part-time job in a coin laundromat, an experience which later inspired a couple of chapters in my book, *Saved By Philosophy*), regretting that it was now "too late to change my major to Philosophy." (Philosophy being, of course, another field with no better job prospects than Music had, in the late '70s.)

Convinced that "I only believe in God because that's how I was raised," I soon became an Agnostic, and then an Atheist; I entered what I now call my 'Existentialist Phase,' during which I enjoyed freaking out my Christian friends by somberly announcing, "Life is meaningless," and similarly depressing slogans.

All good things, alas, must come to an end. I left CSUS in June 1978 with my single-subject teaching credential, a minor in Business, and one year of graduate study towards a Master's (which was recommended for those of us getting teaching credentials, back then). To my surprise, graduate studies and writing research papers (particularly under Dr.

Gene Savage) really attracted me; it was, however, time to 'enter the *real* world.'

The passage of Proposition 13 (the 'People's Initiative to Limit Property Taxation') in June 1978 certainly didn't help the job prospects for music teachers. Receiving no offers of employment, and still living at home, I became a substitute teacher, which was almost uniformly a miserable experience. (I rarely subbed in Music classes, usually getting anything from Algebra to Home Economics.)

Thinking that I needed some more 'directing experience' (in the nonexistent job market for music teachers), as well as extra cash, in two successive seasons (79/80, 80/81) I even served as Choir Director at a Methodist Church in Elk Grove, then at a UCC church in South Sacramento (while ignoring the internal 'cognitive dissonance' caused by my now being an Atheist).

Following my sister's example (who was by now married, and would soon have a daughter and a son with her husband, and later two adorable granddaughters), I took several employment tests with the State of California, and was relieved in June 1979 to begin full-time employment with the Public Employees' Retirement System (CalPERS), discovering to my surprise that this was the same department in which my sister worked, as a Paralegal. I also—with the help of my mother's recommendation to the principal—took over teaching her two Adult Education night classes (Bookkeeping and Business Machines), since she no longer needed to work two jobs to support us.

I remained at CalPERS for the next 35 years. I worked with a large number of extremely capable persons there, and I remain in touch with a small number of very dear friends to this day. (I even had the chance to use some of my residual musical skills, performing each December with the CalPERS 'Holiday Chorus.') But by October 2014, I was more than ready to leave behind me the frustrations of CalPERS, and retire.

However, I shall be eternally thankful for one consequence of having worked at CalPERS. After being there three years, I transferred to a different division to accept a promotion to supervisor, and was duly introduced to all of the division staff—among whom was a beautiful young woman named Nancy. (One of our close friends, whose desk was next to hers, later claimed that she could tell it was 'love at first sight' on my part; I *will* admit that I can still clearly remember the colorful skirt Nancy was wearing when I met her.)

Over time, Nancy and I became good friends. Some mutual friends (perhaps 'matchmaking') invited both of us to join them in once a month going out to dinner, and then attending a classical concert in the nearby city of Davis. Before long, Nancy and I were driving to this outing together ("to save gas," we reasoned), and then 'hanging out' afterwards. By 1986, love had blossomed.

Nancy had three children—two daughters and a son—from her previous marriage. However, since these kids were all relatively 'grown,' and all had a good relationship with both their father and Nancy, I was relieved of the anxiety of becoming a 'step-parent.' (Given my lack of a fatherly 'role model,' I doubted my ability to fulfill such a task.). I firmly love the three of them ('like my own,' as they say) to this day.

There was, however, a very dark 'cloud' beginning to loom over the horizon: alcohol. Having seen my father's bad example, as a pre-teen I was puritanically opposed to alcohol in any form. However, in high school, I experimented with it, and discovered that I liked its effect; and so I drank alone, or with some close friends (not the Evangelicals, of course). After high school, I also smoked marijuana (which was quite illegal back then) for a little more than two years.

But then, my new love of philosophy had its first 'life effect' on me. (The title of my book, *Saved By Philosophy,* reflects this feeling of mine.) Righteously indignant after discovering that Alan Watts (one of my favorite authors) had been an alcoholic, and that Bertrand Russell (by then my favorite philosopher) reportedly drank a whole bottle of whiskey each day, I quit both alcohol and marijuana completely, feeling quite 'self-righteous' about this—particularly since many of the Christians I knew in college drank (and often smoked weed, as well).

Reading lots of books often inspires such readers to want to *write* books, as well; and I was no exception. I began jotting down notes as ideas occurred to me, for what I projected as two books: *Inquiries,* a book of my own conceptions of philosophy; and *Sacrificium Intellectus,* my proposed 'refutation' of the kind of Christian apologetics that were popular in the 1970s: Josh McDowell, John Warwick Montgomery, Walter Martin, etc. Reading such books with which I vehemently disagreed has now become a habit with me—but one that I have found enormously valuable, in 'stretching' my mind, and eliminating some prejudices of mine.

I (rather arbitrarily) told myself that I needed to finish both books before I was 25 years old, which—with one month to spare—I did, having both books in typescript.

Feeling the need to 'celebrate,' I remembered that one of my cousins (not aware of my anti-alcohol stance) had given me a bottle of wine as a Christmas present the year before—so I drank the whole thing. I enjoyed the effect of alcohol even more than I had in high school; but now—being gainfully employed—I could afford to legally *buy* it.

I don't know whether there actually exists a 'genetic predisposition' to it, but I progressively declined into full-blown alcoholism—complete with occasional *grand mal* seizures (from withdrawal, after a weekend 'bender') and one DUI. After an occasion of *Delerium Tremens*, I even spent one Christmas week in the hospital—fully expecting to die soon, as my health was rapidly deteriorating. Why Nancy was willing to put up with me through this period, I don't know—although I am forever *grateful* that she did. (I guess that's what **true love** is…)

Ultimately, my mother and sister convinced me to enter a Recovery House in downtown Sacramento for 90 days. The House was run on AA (Alcoholics Anonymous) principles; at this point, I had no hesitation in admitting, "My name is Steve, and I'm an alcoholic." (I recounted many of my own experiences from this period in my novel, *Tattered Pilgrims*.) My 'birthday' (i.e., sobriety date) is May 17th, 1991. I've remained sober from then, to this day: no 'slips' or 'lapses.' (But, following AA principles, I still cautiously just take it "One Day at a Time.")

After the first 30 days in the Recovery House, Nancy was allowed to pick me up on Friday late afternoons, take me to an AA meeting, and then we would both stay at either her home or my apartment until Sunday evening, when she would drop me back off at the House. My sobriety, inspired by my love for Nancy, allowed me to get my life back together.

Which brings me back to writing. Having written two books by age 25, I had fully expected to find fame and/or infamy (if not fortune) as a philosophical writer. As an Atheist and virulent anti-Christian, I thought for sure that my 'greatness' would be immediately recognized. Thus, in 1980 I dutifully sent off the typescript of *Inquiries* to several publishers, only to have it returned unread. (Of course, I now know of the extreme unlikelihood of manuscripts being read, much less published, by unknown authors that were sent 'over the transom' to publishers.)

I did manage, however, to get a number of 'Letters to the Editor' published in the two local newspapers. And I was excited when the 'Ombudsman' columnist for the *Sacramento Bee* devoted his September 12, 1982 column to a letter I'd written him, critiquing Astrology as an irrational pseudo-science. He agreed with my arguments, but concluded that newspapers only provide what readers like to read, and the daily Horoscope feature was quite popular. I also participated in a Humanist Association in Sacramento (HAGSA) in 1982-1983.

My hopes were quite high when, also in 1982, the American Humanist Association (AHA) announced its 'North American Essay Contest,' intended to identify young (age 30 or less) writers with Humanist leanings. I entered the contest four times, never getting more than a tie for third place. (Alcohol, however, was there to deaden the pain of rejection.) My best effort (which I have now lost) was an essay, '1984: The Affirmation of Humanism,' but it was awarded only an 'Honorable Mention' in that year's contest—a crushing blow to my hopes for Humanist literary fame. (I was interested to see, however, that a few years later, AHA developed a list of '*Affirmations* of Humanism'; so maybe someone there noticed my essay, after all.) I stopped writing, at this point, and began drinking even more (not even attending the April 1986 AHA convention in Sacramento), until I finally 'hit bottom' in 1991. (Thus ended my 'Humanist Phase.')

But after achieving sobriety, my interest in writing eventually began to revive. The *Sacramento Bee* had a section that would publish an essay from a reader once a week, and I had several short articles published by them—including one published on December 23, 1999, which predicted that the 'Y2K catastrophe' being expected by many would be 'no big deal.' I also made several unfruitful attempts to submit articles to magazines (including a 1995 essay, "Why New Age Music Is Not 'Yuppie Muzak'").

On July 10, 1997, the *Sacramento Bee* sponsored a contest to write the first page of a mystery novel set in Sacramento. I entered, and became one of the runners-up (with an entry entitled, 'Work, Death & Taxes'). Several friends of mine at work noticed this in the paper, and suggested to me, "You should write the rest of the story!" So I began writing a chapter or two every week, and handing out photocopies to half a dozen people at work, who continued encouraging me; I finished the book in typescript in 1998, but had no hopes of it ever getting published. (I did give photocopies to some friends and family.)

But in mid-1999, I saw an advertisement for a publishing company called 'iUniverse,' which specialized in 'print-on-demand' books. I revised the manuscript and sent it off to them in December 1999 (shortly before Y2K). Thus, my first novel, *Work, Death & Taxes,* was published in early 2000. Since then, I've written another two dozen books, all published by iUniverse.

A number of my books have stimulated (required?) me to do considerable background reading in preparation; although I eschew using footnotes in a *novel,* I typically include a lengthy Bibliography at the back of the book.

Having now read literally thousands of books about religion and philosophy, and (having originally felt like an anthropologist conducting research) visiting about 120 different local churches in the late 1970s-early '80s, I've long since renounced Atheism. (I call myself an 'Agnostic Deist': meaning one who definitely believes in God, but is somewhat doubtful that 'everything happens for a reason' which is *intended* by this God for our good). A short essay I wrote, 'The Intellectual Love of God,' was published in the *Sacramento News & Review* in 2009, and remains a good brief summation of my personal views.

Conceivably, I'll run out of topics I want to write about after another two or three books; if so, I might devote my spare time to developing a Website, or doing more with social media.

In 2009, I began doing book reviews on Amazon (mostly as a way of summarizing a book's most essential content for myself). I've moved up in Amazon's reviewer 'rankings' over time, so that I've now been a 'Top 500 Reviewer' (and even a 'Top 100 Reviewer') for several years. To date, I've done more than 11,000 individual book reviews; but, since

I read several books a week, I've always got a large stack of 'Books I need to review.'

In 1999, our first *grandson* was born! Another grandson was born in 2002, still another in 2004, followed by twin granddaughters in 2006, and the youngest granddaughter in 2007. So, although I've never had 'children of my *own*,' I feel that I've experienced much of the *joy*, through our grandkids. And I've particularly enjoyed chronicling our experiences with them in my four *Family Lessons* books.

So I'm now a happily retired 'independent researcher'—still loving Nancy with all my heart, treasuring our time with the kids and grandkids (and now with a *great*-granddaughter!), and feeling enormously grateful for the life we have. True, I'll never write a bestseller, never win the Templeton Prize, and never be invited to give the Gifford Lectures; but I'm a very happy, and satisfied man.

BIBLIOGRAPHY

Science, Cosmology, & Evolution:

Allmon, Warren D.; Kelley, Patricia H.; Ross, Robert M. (Eds.): *Stephen Jay Gould: Reflections on His View of Life*

Atkins, Peter: *Conjuring the Universe: The Origins of the Laws of Nature*

Atkins, Peter: *Creation Revisited*

Atkins, Peter: *The Creation*

Ayala, Francisco: *Am I a Monkey? Six Big Questions about Evolution*

Baggott, Jim: *Farewell to Reality: How Modern Physics Has Betrayed the Search for Scientific Truth*

Ball, Philip: *Beyond Weird: Why Everything You Thought You Knew About Quantum Physics is Different*

Barbour, Julian: *The End of Time: The Next Revolution In Physics*

Barrow, John; Silk, Joseph: *The Left Hand of Creation*

Behe, Michael: *Darwin Devolves (The New Science About DNA That Challenges Evolution)*

Behe, Michael: *Darwin's Black Box: The Biochemical Challenge to Evolution*

Behe, Michael: *The Edge of Evolution: The Search for the Limits of Darwinism*

Bell, J.S.: *Speakable and Unspeakable in Quantum Mechanics*

Boslough, John: *Stephen Hawking's Universe*

Bricmont, Jean: *Quantum Sense and Nonsense*

Brody, Jed: *Quantum Entanglement*

Byrne, Peter: *The Many Worlds of Hugh Everett III*

Carmeli, Moshe: Cosmological Special Relativity

Carroll, Sean B.: *The Making of the Fittest: DNA and the Ultimate Forensic Record of Evolution*

Carroll, Sean M.: *The Big Picture: On the Origins of Life, Meaning, and the Universe Itself*

Carroll, Sean M.: *Something Deeply Hidden: Quantum Worlds and the Emergence of Space-Time*

Carroll, Sean M.; Craig, William Lane: *God and Cosmology: William Lane Craig and Sean Carroll in Dialogue*

Clegg, Brian: *The God Effect: Time Travel, Teleportation, and the Ultimate Computer*

Coyne, Jerry: *Faith Vs. Fact: Why Science and Religion are Incompatible*

Coyne, Jerry: *Why Evolution is True*

Cramer, John G.: *The Quantum Handshake: Entanglement, Nonlocality and Transactions*

Davies, Paul: *The Goldilocks Enigma: Why Is the Universe Just Right for Life?*

Davies, Paul: *The Origin of Life*

Dawkins, Richard: *Climbing Mount Improbable*

Dawkins, Richard: *The Blind Watchmaker*

Dawkins, Richard: *The God Delusion*

Dawkins, Richard: *The Greatest Show on Earth*

Deutsch, David: *The Beginning of Infinity: Explanations That Transform the World*

Deutsch, David: *The Fabric of Reality*

DeWitt, Bryce S.; Graham, Neill (Eds.): *The Many-Worlds Interpretation of Quantum Mechanics*

Dick, Steven J.: *Life On Other Worlds: The 20th-Century Extraterrestrial Life Debate*

Dick, Steven J.: *The Biological Universe: The Twentieth-Century Extraterrestrial Life Debate and the Limits of Science*

Dick, Steven J.: *The Impact of Discovering Life Beyond Earth*

Drees, Willem: *Creation: From Nothing to Now*

Dyson, Freeman J.: *A Many-Colored Glass: Reflections on the Place of Life in the Universe*

Dyson, Freeman J.: *Origins of Life*

Dyson, Freeman J.: *Disturbing the Universe*

Dyson, Freeman J.: *Infinite In All Directions*

Fanchini, Felipe Fernandes; Pinto, Diogo de Oliviera Spares (Eds.): *Lectures on General Quantum Correlations*

Fine, Arthur: *The Shaky Game: Einstein, Realism and the Quantum Theory*

Fodor, Jerry: *What Darwin Got Wrong*

Futuyama, Douglas J.: *Science on Trial: The Case for Evolution*

Futuyama, Douglas J.: *Evolutionary Biology*

Gilder, Louisa: *The Age of Entanglement: When Quantum Physics Was Reborn*

Gisin, Nicolas: *Quantum Chance: Nonlocality, Teleportation and other Quantum Marvels*

Gould, Stephen Jay: *Life's Grandeur: The Spread of Excellence from Plato to Darwin*

Gould, Stephen Jay: *Punctuated Equilibrium*

Gould, Stephen Jay: *The Structure of Evolutionary Theory*

Grassé, Pierre-P.: *Evolution of Living Organisms*

Green, M.B.; Schwartz, J.H.; Witten, E.: *Superstring Theory, Volume I – Introduction*

Greene, Brian: *The Elegant Universe*

Greene, Brian: *The Fabric of the Universe*

Greene, Brian: *The Hidden Reality*

Greenstein, George: *The Symbiotic Universe*

Gribbin, John: *In Search of the Multiverse*

Gribbin, John: *Six Impossible Things: The Mystery of the Quantum World*

Grimbol, William R.; Astrachan, Jeffrey R.: *Life's Big Questions*

Guth, Alan: *The Inflationary Universe*

Halpern, Paul: *The Quantum Labyrinth: How Richard Feynman and John Wheeler Revolutionized Time and Reality*

Hawking, Stephen, Mlodinow, Leonard: *The Grand Design*

Hawking, Stephen: *The Theory of Everything*

Heisenberg, Werner: *Philosophical Problems of Quantum Physics*

Kirschner, Mark W.; Gerhart, John C.: *The Plausibility of Life: Resolving Darwin's Dilemma*

Kitcher, Philip: *Living with Darwin: Evolution, Design, and the Future of Faith*

Krauss, Lawrence: *A Universe from Nothing*

Krauss, Lawrence: *Hiding in the Mirror: The Mysterious Allure of Extra Dimensions, from Plato to String Theory*

Kumar, Manjit: Quantum: *Einstein, Bohr, and the Great Debate about the Nature of Reality*

Leslie, John: *Modern Cosmology & Philosophy*

Lewis, Geraint F.; Barnes, Luke A.: *A Fortunate Universe: Life in a Finely Tuned Cosmos*

Losos, Jonathan B.: *Improbable Destinies: Fate, Chance, and the Future of Evolution*

Lurquin, Paul F.: *The Origins of Life and the Universe*

Marcella, Thomas V.: *Quantum Entanglement and the Loss of Reality*

Maudlin, Tim: *Quantum Non-Locality and Relativity*

Miller, Kenneth R.: *Finding Darwin's God: A Scientist's Search for Common Ground Between God and Evolution*

Miller, Kenneth R.: *Only a Theory: Evolution and the Battle for America's Soul*

Morris, Simon Conway (Ed.): *The Deep Structure of Biology: Is Convergence Sufficiently Ubiquitous to Give a Directional Signal?*

Morris, Simon Conway: *The Runes of Evolution: How the Universe became Self-Aware*

Morris, Simon Conway: *Life's Solution: Inevitable Humans in a Lonely Universe*

Musser, George: *Spooky Action at a Distance*

Nagel, Thomas: *Mind & Cosmos*

Pigliucci, Massimo; Müller, Gerd B. (Eds.): *Evolution: The Extended Synthesis*

Prothero, Donald: *Evolution: What the Fossils Say and Why It Matters*

Randall, Lisa: *Knocking on Heaven's Door: How Physics and Scientific Thinking Illuminate the Universe and the World*

Randall, Lisa: *Warped Passages: Unraveling the Mysteries of the Universe's Hidden Dimensions*

Redhead, Michael: *Incompleteness, Nonlocality and Realism: A Prolegomenon to Philosophy of Quantum Mechanics*

Rees, Martin: *Before the Beginning: Our Universe and Others*

Rees, Martin: *Just Six Numbers: The Deep Forces that Shape the Universe*

Rodrigo, Enrico: *The Physics of Stargates: Parallel Universes, Time Travel and the Enigma of Wormhole Physics*

Rose, Steven; McGarr, Paul (Eds.): *The Richness of Life: The Essential Stephen Jay Gould*

Sagan, Carl: *Contact*

Sagan, Carl: *The Cosmic Connection*

Sagan, Carl; Page, Thornton (Eds.): *UFO's: A Scientific Debate*

Sagan, Carl; Shklovskii, I.S.: *Intelligent Life in the Universe*

Shapiro, James A.: *Evolution: A View from the 21st Century*

Smolin, Lee: *Einstein's Unfinished Revolution: The Search for What Lies Beyond the Quantum*

Smolin, Lee: *Life of the Cosmos*

Smolin, Lee: *The Trouble with Physics: The Rise of String Theory, the Fall of a Science, and What Comes Next*

Smoot, George: *Wrinkles in Time: Witness to the Birth of the Universe*

Sober, Elliott: *Evidence and Evolution*

Somit, Albert; Peterson, Steven A. (Eds.): *The Dynamics of Evolution: The Punctuated Equilibrium Debate*

Stenger, Victor J.: *The Unconscious Quantum*

Stenger, Victor J.: *God and the Multiverse*

Stenger, Victor J.: *God: The Failed Hypothesis*

Stenger, Victor J.: *The Fallacy of Fine-Tuning*

Stenger, Victor J.: *Not By Design*

Stringer, Chris: *Lone Survivors: How We Came to Be the Only Humans On Earth*

Tallis, Raymond: *Aping Mankind: Neuromania, Darwinitis and the Misrepresentation of Humanity*

Teerikorpi, Pekka; Valtonen, Mauri, et al.: *The Evolving Universe and the Origin of Life: The Search for Our Cosmic Roots*

Thaxton, Charles B., et al.: *The Mystery of Life's Origin: Reassessing Current Theories*

Thorne, Kip S.: *Black Holes & Time Warps: Einstein's Outrageous Legacy*

Unzicker, Alexander; Jones, Sheilla: *Bankrupting Physics: How Today's Top Scientists are Gambling Away Their Credibility*

Vilenkin, Alex: *Many Worlds in One: The Search for Other Universes*

Wagner, Andreas: *Arrival of the Fittest: Solving Evolution's Greatest Puzzle*

Wallace, David: *The Emergent Multiverse: Quantum Theory According to the Everett Interpretation*

Wallace, David: *Hidden Worlds* (audio, 12/15/2014) (available at: http://podcasts. ox.ac.uk/people/david-wallace)

Wallace, David: *The Plurality of Worlds* (audio, 1/6/2015)

Wallace, David; Anirban, Ankita: *Parallel World* (audio, 7/30/2012)

Ward, Peter D.; Brownlee, Donald: *Rare Earth: Why Complex Life is Uncommon in the Universe*

Wheeler, John Archibald: *Geons, Black Holes & Quantum Foam*

Wills, Christopher; Bada, Jeffrey: *The Spark Of Life: Darwin And The Primeval Soup*

Woit, Peter: *Not Even Wrong: The Failure of String Theory*

Wolf, Fred Alan: *The Yoga of Time Travel: How the Mind Can Defeat Time*

Zwiebach, Barton: *A First Course in String Theory*

God, Religion and Science:

Ayala, Francisco J.: *Darwin's Gift to Science and Religion*

Barbour, Ian: *Religion in an Age of Science*

Barbour, Ian: *When Science Meets Religion*

Broom, Neil: *How Blind is the Watchmaker?*

Bussey, Peter: *Signposts to God: How Modern Physics & Astronomy Point the Way to Belief*

Collins, Francis S.: *The Language of God: A Scientist Presents Evidence for Belief*

Collins, Francis S.: *The Language of Life: DNA and the Revolution in Personalized Medicine*

Davies, Paul: *The Goldilocks Enigma: Why Is the Universe Just Right for Life?*

Davies, Paul: *The 5th Miracle: The Search for the Origin and Meaning of Life*

Davies, Paul: *The Cosmic Blueprint: New Discoveries in Nature's Creative Ability to Order the Universe*

Davies, Paul: *The Mind of God: The Scientific Basis for a Rational World*

Davis, Christopher S.: *Designed to Evolve: Discovering God Through Modern Science*

Davis, Jimmy; Poe, Harry: *Designer Universe*

Ecklund, Elaine Howard: *Science Vs. Religion: What Scientists Really Think*

Ferguson, Kitty: *The Fire in the Equations*

Gingerich, Owen: *God's Universe*

Hoyle, Fred: *The Intelligent Universe*

Hoyle, Fred; Wickramasinghe, Chandra: *Evolution from Space*

Huyssteen, J. Wentzel Van: *Alone In the World? Human Uniqueness in Science and Theology*

Lennox, John C.: *Can Science Explain Everything?*

Lennox, John C.: *God and Stephen Hawking*

Lennox, John C.: *God's Undertaker: Has Science Buried God?*

Livio, Mario: *Is God a Mathematician?*

Macalister, Todd: *Einstein's God: A Way of Being Spiritual Without the Supernatural*

Marshall, Perry: *Evolution 2.0: Breaking the Deadlock Between Darwin and Design*

McGrath, Alister: *A Fine-Tuned Universe: The Quest for God in Science and Theology*

McGrath, Alister: *Dawkins' God: Genes, Memes, and the Meaning of Life*

McGrath, Alister: *Glimpsing the Face of God: The Search for Meaning in the Universe*

McGrath, Alister: *Why God Won't Go Away: Is the New Atheism Running On Empty?*

Murphy, Nancey: *A Philosophy of the Christian Religion for the Twenty-First Century*

Murphy, Nancey: *Bodies and Souls, or Spirited Bodies?*

Murphy, Nancey: *Religion and Science: God, Evolution and the Soul*

Murphy, Nancey: *Theology In the Age of Scientific Reasoning*

Murphy, Nancey; Russell, Robert John (Eds.): *Physics and Cosmology: Scientific Perspectives on the Problem of Evil*

Nelson, Kevin: *The Spiritual Doorway in the Brain: A Neurologist's Search for the God Experience*

Newberg Andrew: *Neurotheology: How Science Can Enlighten Us About Spirituality*

O'Connell, Michael: *Finding God in Science: Extraordinary Evidence for the Soul and Christianity*

O'Leary, Denyse: *By Design or by Chance?*

Peacocke, Arthur: *Paths from Science Towards God*

Peacocke, Arthur: *Theology for a Scientific Age*

Polkinghorne, John: *Belief in God in an Age of Science*

Polkinghorne, John: *Serious Talk: Science and Religion in Dialogue*

Rolston, Holmes: *Science and Religion: A Critical Survey*

Sagan, Carl (Ann Druyan, Ed.): *The Varieties of Scientific Experience: A Personal View of the Search for God*

Selbie, Joseph: *The Physics of God: Unifying Quantum Physics, Consciousness, M-Theory, Heaven, Neuroscience*

Stannard, Russell (Ed.): *God for the 21st Century*

Stannard, Russell: *The Divine Imprint: Finding God in the Human Mind*

Stannard, Russell: *The God Experiment: Can Science Prove the Existence of God?*

Teilhard de Chardin, Pierre: *The Phenomenon of Man*

Templeton, John Marks; Giniger, Kenneth Seeman (Eds.): *Spiritual Evolution: Scientists Discuss Their Beliefs*

Tippett, Krista: *Einstein's God: Conversations About Science and the Human Spirit*

Ward, Keith: *God, Chance and Necessity*

Ward, Keith: *Is Religion Irrational?*

Ward, Keith: *More than Matter? Is There More to Life than Molecules?*

Witham, Larry: *By Design: Science and the Search for God*

Artificial Intelligence; Mind/Brain, Consciousness

Chella, Antonio; Manzotti, Riccardo (Eds.): *Artificial Consciousness*

Copeland, B. Jack (Ed.): *The Essential Turing: The Ideas that Gave Birth to the Computer Age*

Elvidge, Jim: *Digital Consciousness: A Transformative Vision*

Garreau, Joel: *Radical Evolution: Promise and Peril of Enhancing Our Minds, Our Bodies ...*

Hameroff, Stuart R.; Kaszniak, Alfred W. (Eds.): *Toward a Science of Consciousness: The First Tucson Discussions and Debates*

Hameroff, Stuart R.; Kaszniak, Alfred W. (Eds.): *Toward a Science of Consciousness II: The Second Tucson Discussions*

Hameroff, Stuart R.; Kaszniak, Alfred W. (Eds.): *Toward a Science of Consciousness III: The Third Tucson Discussions and Debates*

Harel, David: *Computers LTD: What They REALLY Can't Do*

Hofstadter, Douglas: *I Am a Strange Loop*

Kaku, Michio: *The Future of the Mind: The Scientific Quest to Understand, Enhance, and Empower the Mind*

Kelly, Edward F.; Kelly, Emily Williams, et al. (Eds.): *Irreducible Mind: Toward a Psychology for the 21st Century*

Kelly, Kevin: *What Technology Wants*

Koch; Christof: *The Feeling of Life Itself: Why Consciousness Is Widespread But Can't Be Computed*

Kosko, Bart: *The Fuzzy Future: From Society and Science to Heaven in a Chip*

Kurzweil, Ray: *How To Create a Mind: The Secret of Human Thought Revealed*

Kurzweil, Ray: *The Age of Spiritual Machines: When Computers Exceed Human Intelligence*

Kurzweil, Ray: *The Singularity Is Near: When Humans Transcend Biology*

Lanier, Jaron: *Dawn of the New Everything: Encounters With Virtual Reality*

Lanier, Jaron: *You Are Not a Gadget: a Manifesto*

Lennox, John C.: *2084: Artificial Intelligence and the Future of Humanity*

Lovelock, James: *Novacene: The Coming Age of Hyperintelligence*

Minsky, Marvin: *The Emotion Machine: Commonsense Thinking, Artificial Intelligence, and the Future of the Mind*

Minsky, Marvin: *The Society of Mind*

Noë, Alva: *Out of Our Heads: Why You Are Not Your Brain, and Other Lessons from the Biology of Consciousness*

Seung, Sebastian: *Connectome: How the Brain's Wiring Makes Us Who We Are*

Stock, Gregory: *Metaman: The Merging of Humans and Machines Into a Global Superorganism*

Tallis, Raymond: *Why the Mind is Not a Computer*

Life After Death; Near-Death Experiences

(Books)

Abanes, Richard: *Embraced By the Light and the Bible*

Abanes, Richard: *Journey Into the Light*

Alexander, Eben: *Proof of Heaven: A Neurosurgeon's Journey Into the Afterlife*

Alexander, Eben: *The Map of Heaven: How Science, Religion, and Ordinary People are Proving the Afterlife*

Alexander, Eben: *Living In a Mindful Universe: A Neurosurgeon's Journey Into the Heart of Consciousness*

Alger, William Rounseville: *The Doctrine of a Future Life*

Almeder, Robert: *Death & Personal Survival*

Atwater, P.M.H.: *Beyond the Light*

Atwater, P.M.H.: *Children of the New Millennium*

Atwater, P.M.H.: *Coming Back to Life*

Augros, Michael: *Who Designed the Designer? A Rediscovered Path to God's Existence*

Berman, Phillip L.: *The Journey Home*

Besteman, Marvin J.: *My Journey to Heaven: What I Saw and How It Changed My Life*

Blackmore, Susan J.: *Dying to Live*

Blackmore, Susan J.: *Seeing Myself: The New Science of Out-of-Body Experiences*

Blum, Deborah: *Ghost Hunters: William James and the Search for Scientific Proof of Life After Death*

Braude, Stephen F.: *Immortal Remains: The Evidence for Life After Death*

Braxton, Dean: *In Heaven! Experiencing the Throne of God*

Brinkley, Dannion: *Saved By the Light*

Brinkley, Dannion: *At Peace in the Light*

Brooke, Tal: *The Other Side of Death*

Brubaker, Don: *Absent From the Body*

Burke, John: *Imagine Heaven: Near-Death Experiences, God's Promises, and the Exhilarating Future That Awaits You*

Burpo, Todd: *Heaven Is for Real: A Little Boy's Astounding Story of His Trip to Heaven and Back*

Darling, David: *Soul Search*

Delacour, Jean-Baptiste: *Glimpses of the Beyond*

Ditchfield, David: *Shine On: The Remarkable Story of How I Fell Under a Speeding Train, Journeyed to the Afterlife*

Ducasse, C.J.: *A Critical Examination of the Belief In a Life After Death*

Eadie, Betty: *Embraced By the Light*

Eadie, Betty: *The Awakening Heart*

Ebon, Martin: *The Evidence for Life After Death*

Eddy, Sherwood: *You Will Survive After Death*

Edwards, Paul (Ed.): *Immortality*

Fenimore, Angie: *Beyond the Darkness*

Fenwick, Peter & Elizabeth: *The Truth in the Light*

Fiore, Charles; Landsberg, Alan: *Death Encounters*

Flew, Antony: *Merely Mortal?*

Flynn, Charles P.: *After the Beyond: Human Transformation and the Near-Death Experience*

Fortune, Dion: *Through the Gates of Death*

Fox, Mark: *Religion, Spirituality and the Near-Death Experience*

Geis, Robert J.: *Personal Existence After Death*

Gibson, Arvin: *Echoes from Eternity*

Gonzälez-Whippler, Migene: *What Happens After Death*

Green, Joel B.; Palmer, Stuart L. (Eds.): *In Search of the Soul: Four Views of the Mind-Body Problem*

Greene, H. Leon: *If I Should Wake Before I Die: The Biblical and Medical Truth About Near-Death Experiences*

Grey, Margot: *Return From Death*

Greyson, Bruce; Flynn, Charles P.(Eds.): *The Near-Death Experience*

Grof, Stanislav & Christina: *Beyond Death*

Groothuis, Doug: *Deceived By the Light*

Grosso, Michael: *Soulmaker*

Guggenheim, Bill & Judy: *Hello From Heaven! A New Field of Research—After-Death Communication*

Habermas, Gary; Moreland, J.P.: *Immortality: The Other Side of Death*

Habermas, Gary; Moreland, J.P.: *Beyond Death: Exploring the Evidence for Immortality*

Harpur, Tom: *There Is Life After Death*

Harris, Barbara: *Full Circle*

Hick, John C.: *Death and Eternal Life*

Iverson, Jeffrey: *In Search of the Dead: A Scientific investigation of Evidence for Life After Death*

Kason, Yvonne: *A Farther Shore: How Near-Death and Other Extraordinary Experiences Can Change Ordinary Lives*

Kastenbaum, Robert: *Is There Life After Death?*

Kellehear, Allan: *Experiences Near Death*

Kircher, Pamela M.: *Love Is the Link*

Kübler-Ross, Elizabeth: *Life After Death*

Lamont, Corliss: *The Illusion of Immortality*

Leslie, John: *Immortality Defended*

Lommel, Pim van: *Consciousness Beyond Life: The Science of the Near-Death Experience*

Long, Jeffrey; Perry, Paul: *Evidence of the Afterlife*

Long, Jeffrey; Perry, Paul: *God and the Afterlife*

Luck, Coleman: *Proof of Heaven? A Mental Illusionist Examines the Afterlife Experience of Eben Alexander*

Lund, David H.: *Death and Consciousness*

Lundahl, Craig R.: *A Collection of Near-Death Readings*

Lundahl, Craig R.; Widdison, Harold A.: *The Eternal Journey*

Malarkey, Kevin: *The Boy Who Came Back from Heaven*

Malz, Betty: *My Glimpse of Eternity*

Marsh, Michael: *A Matter of Personal Survival*

McAdams, Elizabeth E.; Bayless, Raymond: *The Case for Life After Death*

Miller, Sukie: *After Death*

Moody, Raymond A.: *Coming Back*

Moody, Raymond A.: *Life After Life*

Moody, Raymond A.: *Paranormal: My Life in Pursuit of the Afterlife*

Moody, Raymond A.: *Reflections On Life After Life*

Moody, Raymond A.: *Reunions*

Moody, Raymond A.: *The Last Laugh*

Moody, Raymond A.: *The Light Beyond*

Morse, Melvin: *Closer to the Light*

Morse, Melvin: *Parting Visions*

Morse, Melvin: *Transformed by the Light*

Morse, Melvin: *Where God Lives*

Neal, Mary C.: *To Heaven and Back: A Doctor's Extraordinary Account of Her Death, Heaven, Angels, & Life Again*

Nieman, Carol; Goldman, Emily: *AfterLife*

Orr, Leonard: *Physical Immortality*

Osis, Karlis; Haraldsson, Erlendur: *At the Hour of Death*

Peck, M. Scott: *In Heaven As On Earth*

Pillow, William: *Near-Death Experiences are Real—But Only for Survivors!*

Piper, Don: *90 Minutes in Heaven*

Rawlings, Maurice: *Beyond Death's Door*

Rawlings, Maurice: *To Hell and Back*

Reyes, Benito F.: *Scientific Evidence of the Existence of the Soul*

Ring, Kenneth: *The Omega Project*

Ring, Kenneth: *Heading Toward Omega*

Ring, Kenneth: *Life at Death*

Ring, Kenneth: *Lessons from the Light: What We Can Learn from the Near-Death Experience*

Ritchie, George: *Return From Tomorrow*

Rogo, D. Scott: *Man Does Survive Death*

Rogo, D. Scott: *The Return from Silence*

Sabom, Michael: *Light & Death*

Sabom, Michael: *Recollections of Death*

Schwartz, Gary E.: *The Afterlife Experiments: Breakthrough Scientific Evidence of Life After Death*

Sharp, Kimberly Clark: *After the Light*

Sigmund, Richard: *My Time In Heaven: A True Story of Dying... and Coming Back*

Smith, Alson J.: *Immortality: The Scientific Evidence*

Smith, Joyce: *Breakthrough: The Miraculous True Story of a Mother's Faith and Her Child's Resurrection*

Solomon, Grant & Jane: *The Scole Experiment: Scientific Evidence for Life After Death*

Spraggett, Allen: *The Case for Immortality*

Stearn, Jess: *Immortality: Startling Evidence*

Steiger, Brad: *One With the Light*

Storm, Howard: *My Descent Into Death: A Second Chance at Life*

Sutherland, Cherie: *Reborn In the Light*

Sweetie Bee: *Heaven Is for Real—Is Todd Burpo?*

Swihart, Phillip J.: *The Edge of Death*

Tipler, Frank J.: *The Physics of Immortality*

Valarino, Evelyn Elsaesser: *On the Other Side of Life: Exploring the Phenomenon of the Near-Death Experience*

Viney, Geoff: *Surviving Death*
Ward, Keith: *In Defence of the Soul*
Weber, Stephen; Plant, Katherine: *The Place Between Here and There: A True Story*
Weiss, Jess E.: *The Vestibule*
Weldon, John; Levitt, Zola: *Is There Life after Death?*
Wheeler, David R.: *Journey to the Other Side*
Wiese, Bill: *23 Minutes in Hell*
Wilkerson, Ralph: *Beyond and Back*
Wilson, Colin: *After Life: Survival of the Soul*
Wilson, Ian: *The After-Death Experience*
Woodford, Jim: *Heaven: An Unexpected Journey: One Man's Experience with Heaven, Angels, & the Afterlife*
Zaleski, Carol: *Otherworld Journeys*
Zaleski, Carol: *The Life of the World to Come*

See also: Debate: *Is Death Final?* May 14, 20141:54 PM ET Eben Alexander, Raymond Moody, Sean Carroll, Steven Novella (available at: https://www.npr.org/2014/05/14/310719887/debate-is-death-final https://www.intelligencesquaredus.org/debates/death-not-final)

(Films)
90 Minutes In Heaven
Flatliners (1990)
Flatliners (2017)
Heaven Is for Real
Saved by the Light

(DVD/VHS Documentaries)
Eadie, Betty J.: *Embraced By the Light: An Evening with Betty J. Eadie* (VHS)
Habermas, Gary: *Is There Scientific Evidence for Life After Death?* (on the John Ankerberg show)(DVD)
Harpur, Tom: *Life After Death: The Investigative Journey of Tom Harpur* (DVD)
Moody, Raymond A.: *Life After Life* (VHS)
Robertson. Pat: *Life Beyond the Grave Part I* (DVD)
Robertson. Pat; Robertson, Gordon: *Life Beyond the Grave Part II* (DVD)
Afterlife (with Paul Perry, etc.) (DVD)
Beyond Death (Into the Light & Through the Tunnel and Beyond) (DVD)
Infinity: The Ultimate Trip. Journey Beyond Death (DVD)
Mysterious Forces Beyond: Death & Paranormal (DVD)
Round Trip: The Near-Death Experience (DVD)

The Evidence for Heaven (DVD)
The Near-Death Experience: Transcending the Limits (VHS)
The Search for Heaven (DVD)
There and Back: Interviewers with Near-Death Experiencers (VHS)

Psychic Phenomena:

Abell, George O.; Singer, Barry (Eds.): *Science and the Paranormal: Probing the Existence of the Supernatural*

Blackmore, Susan: *The Adventures of a Parapsychologist*

Brandon, Ruth: *The Spiritualists: The Passion for the Occult in the Nineteenth and Twentieth Centuries*

Davenport, Reuben Briggs: *The Death Blow to Spiritualism, Being the True Story of the Fox Sisters*

Ebert, Jerome W.: *Are Souls Real?*

Finucane, R.C.: *Ghosts: Appearances of the Dead & Cultural Transformation*

Gardner, Martin: *Did Adam and Eve Have Navels? Discourses on Reflexology ... and Other Dubious Subjects*

Gardner, Martin: *How Not to Test a Psychic: Ten Years of Remarkable Experiments with Pavel Stepanek*

Gordon, Henry: *ExtraSensory Deception: ESP, Psychics, Shirley MacLaine, Ghosts, UFOS...*

Hall, Trevor H.: *The Enigma of Daniel Home*

Hall, Trevor H.: *The Medium and the Scientist: The Story of Florence Cook and William Crookes*

Hansel, C.E.M.: *ESP: A Scientific Evaluation*

Houdini, Harry: *A Magician Among the Spirits*

Keene, R. Lamar: *The Psychic Mafia*

Kurtz, Paul (Ed.): *A Skeptic's Handbook of Parapsychology*

Nickell, Joe; Fischer, John F.: *Secrets of the Supernatural*

Polidoro, Massimo: *Final Séance: The Strange Friendship Between Houdini and Conan Doyle*

Radin, Dean: *The Conscious Universe: The Scientific Truth of Psychic Phenomena*

Randi, James: *An Encyclopedia of Claims, Frauds, and s of the Occult and Supernatural*

Randi, James: *Flim-Flam! Psychics, ESP, Unicorns, and other Delusions*

Sagan, Carl: *The Demon-Haunted World: Science as a Candle in the Dark*

Shermer, Michael: *Why People Believe Weird Things: Pseudoscience, Superstition, and Other Confusions of Our Time*

Stein, Gordon: *The Sorcerer of Kings: The Case of Daniel Dunglas Home and William Crookes*

Tanner, Amy: *Studies in Spiritism*

Taylor, John: *Science and the Supernatural*

Wiseman, Richard; Morris, Robert L.: *Guidelines for Testing Psychic Claimants*

Printed in the United States
By Bookmasters